Counting Down
A Scarecrow Press Music Series

Counting Down is a unique series of titles designed to select the best songs or musical works from major performance artists and composers in an age of design-your-own playlists. Contributors offer readers the reasons why some works stand out from others. It is the ideal companion for music lovers.

Titles in the Series

Counting Down Bob Dylan: His 100 Finest Songs, by Jim Beviglia, 2013

COUNTING DOWN BOB DYLAN

His 100 Finest Songs

Jim Beviglia

THE SCARECROW PRESS, INC.
Lanham • Toronto • Plymouth, UK
2012

Published by Scarecrow Press, Inc.
A wholly owned subsidiary of The Rowman & Littlefield Publishing Group, Inc.
4501 Forbes Boulevard, Suite 200, Lanham, Maryland 20706
www.rowman.com

10 Thornbury Road, Plymouth PL6 7PP, United Kingdom

British Library Cataloguing in Publication Information Available

Library of Congress Cataloging-in-Publication Data

Beviglia, Jim.
Counting down Bob Dylan : his 100 finest songs / by Jim Beviglia.
pages cm. -- (Counting down)
Includes bibliographical references and index.
ISBN 978-0-8108-8823-4 (cloth : alk. paper) -- ISBN 978-0-8108-8824-1 (electronic)
1. Dylan, Bob, 1941---Criticism and interpretation. 2. Dylan, Bob, 1941- Songs. 3. Popular music--History and criticism. I. Title.
ML420.D98B45 2013
782.42164092--dc23
2013016471

Printed in the United States of America

For Marie,
*Without your love I'd be nowhere at all
I'd be lost if not for you*

CONTENTS

ACKNOWLEDGMENTS

Although this endeavor may seem like the work of one Bob Dylan fan with a bevy of opinions and way too much time on his hands, it is, in truth, the product of many, many people who have, directly and indirectly, helped make this happen.

Bennett Graff, my editor at Scarecrow Press, was not only the person who was willing to take a chance on a first-time author but also was patient enough with my reluctance to change the book from its initial form as a very personal, first-person account of one fan's love of Bob Dylan into something that might resonate far beyond that. His advice and support throughout this process have likely spoiled me for all other editors should I ever chance to do this again. In conjunction with that, the good folks at Scarecrow Press have been an integral part of this process and are responsible for putting this book in the hands of readers everywhere.

I'm very grateful as well to Evan Schlansky, my editor at *American Songwriter* magazine, who gave me a job based on nothing more than the long-winded bloviating on my blog. His faith allowed me to believe that my writing could be a vocation and not just a hobby. Even further back than that, Douglas Newman, who hired me for my first online music-writing gig several years ago, provided me with the impetus to get to this point.

Anybody who writes about Bob Dylan has some pretty impressive predecessors in that department, and many of those books formed the basis of my knowledge of Dylan history, which appears in these writings. Many of their works appear in the bibliography and the endnotes. But I'd like to thank, in particular, Greil Marcus, Howard Sounes, Oliver Trager, and Christopher Ricks for helping me to understand, through their own writings, what Dylan analysis is all about, even as they set imposing standards for me to try to meet.

Speaking of rock writers, Dave Marsh, whose books on Bruce Springsteen, the Who, and so many others are among the best in the genre, was nice enough to comment on my blog, have me on his radio show, and serve as a valuable source of information on the book-writing process, often going out of his way to do these things. In addition, I'd like to thank Karl Erik Andersen and the folks at Expectingrain.com, the ultimate Dylan website, for promoting the blog series, which served as the starting point for this book. My blog readers also deserve mention since their comments about Dylan's music have been unfailingly insightful.

I have a wonderful group of family and friends who have supported me in my writing endeavors. Chief among these: my mom; my brothers, Bob and Rich; my sisters-in-law; my nieces; my daughter, Daniele; and my girlfriend, Marie. None of these people are big Bob Dylan fans, but they have endured my endless monologues about his music, so I feel like this book belongs to them as much as it does to me.

Finally, I'd like to thank Bob Dylan himself. I know he's probably skeptical about this project, if he's even aware of it at all. Yet if he is reading this, I'd just like to say thank you, Bob, for bringing me and so many of your fans so much wonderful music. This book is my humble attempt to repay that debt.

INTRODUCTION

Degree in Dylanology Not Required

They have a name for fans of Bob Dylan who really like to delve into his work: Dylanologists. It implies that these people study his work like an anthropologist studies other cultures or a psychologist studies the human mind. It also implies a cerebral, almost clinical, approach to his songs.

While I don't doubt that this kind of in-depth study can be rewarding, and I've indulged in it myself over the years, the Dylan that I know and love engages the heart as much as, if not more than, the mind. I don't think you need to have a doctorate in folk music or a firm grasp of this particular songwriter's biography to appreciate his music. You just need to be open to it and let it work its magic.

I know a lot of people who say they don't "get" Dylan. My belief is that a lot of those people fall for the stereotype of the man with the whiny voice and the impenetrably wordy lyrics. They don't ever give his music a fighting chance, and as a result, they miss out on some of the most moving, impactful music that has ever been recorded. I wrote this book as much for these uninitiated folks as I did for the Dylanologists out there.

This project might seem, like some others, to be just another song list generated to grab attention and stir controversy. That has never been my intent, although I won't turn down a spirited debate on the matter. Ultimately, this book is intended to celebrate Bob Dylan's music, serving as a tribute not only to the brilliance of specific songs but also to the sheer number of great ones he has given us. I only went up to 100 here; I could easily have gone another 150 deep and still not run into a song I dislike.

Music can never be judged objectively, so personal feelings definitely factor into these rankings. I tried to separate the songs from any personal relevance they might have had, and I also considered certain intangibles, like the cultural impact a particular song might have had or its staying power over time. I considered chart success far less since Dylan is not a radio artist, and some of his biggest hits were almost accidental in nature and lack the beguiling depth of his finest work.

There were some rules that I put in place to make things fair and keep me sane. First of all, only official recordings were considered. While Dylan bootlegs could comprise a list of its own, my view is that he would have released the song officially if he felt it was fit for public consumption. Even though some of those outtakes and cutting-room floor numbers have tremendous merit, I don't think it fair to measure them against the rest.

In addition, I looked at songs, save for a couple of exceptions, from official recordings on their original albums. Dylan has released a lot of "official" live material, and, in many cases, the live versions of the songs eclipse the studio versions. Same goes for the alternate takes released on many *Bootleg Series* incarnations. Ultimately, it was daunting enough parsing through all the different songs. Trying to pick through four or five different versions of a certain song would have driven me over the edge. So, while I often note the extraordinary different takes and live versions in the essays that accompany each song, the rankings are, for the most part, based on the studio originals.

Now that you know the rules, it's time to get started. I sincerely hope that Dylanologists might get a few insights into these songs that they hadn't previously considered. And maybe a few casual fans of, or newcomers to, Dylan's work who read this will hopefully realize that his music is more than a code that needs cracking.

As you read these humble musings on all things Bob Dylan, I encourage you to think about his music all you want. Just don't think so much that you neglect to feel it.

THE COUNTDOWN

100. "Roll on John" (from *Tempest*, 2012)

In the wake of John Lennon's assassination in 1980, seemingly everyone in possession of a guitar or piano quickly recorded some kind of tribute to the founding Beatle. Some were quite fine, like the ones laid down by ex-bandmates Paul McCartney and George Harrison or old buddies Elton John and Paul Simon. Many more weren't so good, but it was the thought that counted during that sad time.

Bob Dylan sat all of that out. In typically counterintuitive Dylan fashion, it took him thirty-two years to get around to doing his own tribute, but when he did, it was worth the wait. Closing out *Tempest*, "Roll on John" doesn't skimp on the gruesome details of Lennon's murder ("They shot him in the back and down he went"), yet it still displays a sweetness not often associated with the man who wrote it.

Maybe it's fitting that the song is a mixture of the darkness and light because the two music titans had a somewhat complicated relationship throughout the years. Dylan was impressed by the Beatles (as the Beatles were with him) before the two men met, and it was Dylan who introduced the Fab Four to marijuana. (This was ironic, too, inasmuch as the Beatles came to be known for their foray into drug-induced creativity while Bob's music seemingly shied away from psychedelics.)

Each man sniped at the other through his music. Dylan's "Fourth Time Around" on *Blonde on Blonde* was widely viewed as a ribbing play on Lennon's folk composition "Norwegian Wood (This Bird Has Flown)." Shortly before his death, John recorded—although it wasn't released 'til years later as an outtake—a pretty savage parody of Bob's "Gotta Serve Somebody" entitled "Serve Yourself," which viewed Dylan's religious music with extreme skepticism.

A lot of this can be written off as a healthy sense of competition between two preeminent artists in their time. "Roll on John" makes it clear that no grudges were held; if anything, Dylan seems to project many of his own frustrations with fame and stardom through Lennon's experience.

Notice, for example, how the song uses the pronoun "they" throughout when referring to Lennon's antagonists, even when speaking of the murder, which was perpetrated by one man. By doing this, Dylan intimates that Lennon's ultimate demise was not just the result of a senseless act. It instead was the culmination of a series of subtle persecutions, rendered in the song much more forcefully as ambushes and violent imprisonings.

Yet a songwriter always has the power to rewrite even the saddest of histories in a benevolent way, and Dylan takes that opportunity here. By addressing Lennon directly and advising him to keep moving to stay ahead of his would-be captors, it restores Lennon to us in a way. It also allows listeners to participate in the lovely vision of Lennon sailing and shining on, cleverly evading even his most ardent of pursuers.

Throughout the song, Dylan uses bits and pieces of Beatles songs as vehicles for speaking to his old buddy. "A Day in the Life," "Come Together," "The Ballad of John and Yoko," and "Slow Down" are among the classics referenced. There is also a generous sprinkling of Beatles history spread throughout, as well as a winking nod to Lennon's famous publicity stunts for peace, which come when he tells John to "Put on your bags."

In the final verse, Dylan turns to his poetic forebear, William Blake, and the words of his poem "The Tyger" to describe Lennon's force-of-nature personality. (Lennon would have probably preferred something from Lewis Carroll, but it's Dylan's show here, after all.) The final plea to everyone to "let him sleep" intimates how now is the time to appreciate Lennon's legacy without picking it apart, something Dylan wouldn't mind applied to his own.

With "Roll on John," John Lennon joins a rogue's gallery of Dylan tribute subjects that includes the likes of gangster Joey Gallo and controversial comic Lenny Bruce. It's likely that Lennon, wherever he might be rolling right now, feels right at home alongside those anti-heroes.

"Roll on John," among its many other accomplishments, also sets the relationship between Lennon and Dylan right for eternity. Better to remember them, both high as a kite (literally and figuratively), the world at their feet, joshing each other and everything around them in a long limo ride (as seen in D. A. Pennebaker's unreleased documentary *Eat the Document*).

In many ways, Dylan's still riding in that limo. With "Roll on John," he just happens to bring his buddy along for one last ride.

99. "Love Sick" (from *Time Out of Mind*, 1997)

As so often happens with songs, perhaps more with Dylan songs than others, "Love Sick" has pretty interesting ephemera attached to it. It will forever be associated with "Soy Bomb," the bizarre message on the T-shirt a stage crasher wore during Bob's performance of it at the 1998 Grammy Awards. Perhaps more bizarre than that, it was the song used in a Victoria's Secret ad that featured the singer with lingerie model Adriana Lima, who prances around while Dylan stares ominously.

None of this craziness can obscure the fact that "Love Sick" is not just a fantastic song, but also the perfect song for its time and place. It was the first song on *Time Out of Mind*, the album that reintroduced a wary public to Dylan as a songwriter. It's important to recall that, at the time, he was some seven years removed from his previous album of original material, 1990's *Under the Red Sky*, which hadn't exactly set the world on fire.

It was also the first song that people would hear from Dylan following the serious fungal infection in the spring of 1997 that nearly claimed his life. As such, the song, and the album that contained it, would be heard by many fans as the musings of a man staring down the great abyss of death, even though the truth was that Bob was healthy when the album was written and recorded.

Daniel Lanois's production unintentionally played into this errone-ous interpretation, although he shouldn't be blamed for the misinfor-mation of others. He should, however, get serious credit for his work on "Love Sick," when he somehow humanized Dylan's pain by disembody-ing him.

Dylan seems to have had a tumultuous relationship with Lanois in the two albums they made together (*Oh Mercy* and *Time Out of Mind*). For as often as Bob has praised the producer's contributions, there seem to be just as many instances of disagreements and clashes. Yet there can be no denying the two came together in harmony on "Love Sick," an example of subject matter and production style melding together until they are inseparable.

"I'm walkin' through streets that are dead," was the way that Dylan reintroduced himself to the world as a songwriter after seven years away. Only it wasn't Dylan singing it, more like an apparition of Dylan, his voice beaming in from some radio station in purgatory with mediocre reception, all courtesy of Lanois's studio cleverness.

Augie Meyers's staccato organ stabs are like the soundtrack to some macabre carnival, while Jim Dickinson's electric piano burbles to the surface occasionally to cry for help. The verses crawl along at a somber pace before an electric guitar clears the air for Dylan's chorus: "I'm sick of love but I'm in the thick of it / This kind of love I'm so sick of it." It is a declaration of independence and a cry for help all in the same breath.

The scene that Dylan depicts alternates between an unforgiving landscape (dead streets and weeping clouds) and idyllic images (lovers in meadows and silhouettes in windows) that he can spy but not touch ("they leave me hangin' on / To a shadow").

The "shadow" to which he is referring is the object of his obsession, the girl the narrator addresses in the song. It's clear that this communication with her is one-sided, like a letter that she won't ever deign to read. Even after she shatters whatever innocence he has left ("I spoke to you like a child / You destroyed me with a smile"), he can't help but hope for some sort of turnabout in her behavior ("Could you ever be true? I think of you / And I wonder").

In the final verse, his voice giving way to the helpless sorrow that engulfs him, the narrator admits how completely screwed he is: "Just don't know what to do / I'd give anything to be with you." When you reach the point that you want the thing that is causing you the most pain, the loneliness can't even be properly measured.

"Love Sick" has become a lot of different things in the time since it was recorded, none of which it really has any right being. It's not the soundtrack for some clown dancing spastically on a stage he has no right inhabiting, nor is it the proper music for cavorting in a lace bra.

Most importantly, it isn't the last gasp of a man about to die. If anything, considering the dire straits of the character inside "Love Sick," death might be a welcome change.

98. "I Dreamed I Saw St. Augustine" (from *John Wesley Harding*, 1967)

Whenever someone tries to analyze the lyrics of Bob Dylan, one of the first things he or she has to decide is how much to trust the allusions. Does Dylan want his listeners to track down the source material or historical figures that he references and use the meanings gleaned from them for an enhanced understanding of the song, or does he mean to send us on a wild-goose chase?

The answer is probably a little of both, depending on the song. Dylan has talked about a kind of unconsciousness into which he slips when he writes his material, so the allusions likely come up in his songs without much forethought into their placement.

Yet there's no doubt that, sometimes, he knows exactly what he's doing when he references something else. Other times, it could be as simple as him liking how a certain name or phrase sounds, even if it's put into an entirely different context. It's a tricky little conundrum for fans of Bob's music more than for fans of any other artist, and a prime example of this phenomenon is the haunting "I Dreamed I Saw St. Augustine."

The two key names that come into play here are St. Augustine and Joe Hill. St. Augustine of Hippo was a religious philosopher of the fourth and fifth century AD whose teaching and writings framed the way Christianity would come to be viewed throughout the Middle Ages. Joe Hill was an early union activist who used fiery songs as his main weapon against those who would try to exploit labor. He was executed in 1915 after being charged with a murder that many of his friends and followers said he didn't commit.

Do you need to know any of that to love the song? Not necessarily. Dylan creates his own version of St. Augustine for the song's purposes anyway, which makes sense because the guy comes to him in a fever dream. It's not exactly historical fiction.

As for Joe Hill, the reference comes into play because of the song "I Dreamed I Saw Joe Hill Last Night," a tribute written in 1930 that has been covered by many folk artists. (Joan Baez sang it at Woodstock.) The first two lines of Dylan's song are identical to that tribute to Hill, with the names being the only difference.

Joe Hill was essentially martyred in the sense that his commitment to activism led to his conviction and death. St. Augustine was not killed for his beliefs, but both men certainly put a cause at the forefront of their lives, so there is that similarity to ponder. Yet Dylan likely favored the phrasing of that opening line more than he needed Hill's story to resonate with listeners.

Ultimately, the dream about which Dylan sings is a creation separate from any facts. In this reverie, St. Augustine roves wildly in search of those souls who have already been damned in an effort to let them know that theirs is not a lost cause. It is a fascinating act of empathy, especially considering that the people in these "quarters" are certainly not returning the favor ("Go on your way accordingly," he tells them).

One of the interesting facts about St. Augustine was that he spent years as a sinner before Christianity entered his life. Knowing this might help to make sense of why Dylan chose him as his muse here. Who better than Augustine to show forgiveness for these wayward folks?

In the final verse, Dylan's narrator is overwhelmed with shame for being among those responsible for the demise of this strange apparition. This character is representative of anyone who gets wrapped up in his or her own concerns, indirectly damning the rest of the world to a lonely death in the process. It's not necessarily a philosophy unique to Christianity; it's a simple plea to think of others at least as much as you think of yourself.

All of this is presented in the company of an unshowy yet lovely melody, with Bob adding an impassioned harmonica solo. The great thing about Dylan's music is that it will keep opening up new doors to you the more you explore, yet it will also grab you at first listen with its surface beauty and emotion. "I Dreamed I Saw St. Augustine" works on enough levels that you don't need to know Christian or labor history to appreciate it, although it wouldn't hurt if you did.

97. "Rainy Day Women #12 & 35" (from *Blonde on Blonde*, 1966)

It was, by all accounts, the result of one of the most chaotic recording sessions in rock history, one that rivals the Beach Boys' "Barbara Ann" in terms of whooping and hollering caught on tape. The song came from a take that the musicians assumed would be a demo, yet one Bob Dylan chose to release as a single that went to number two, despite the incendiary chorus of "Everybody must get stoned." And it's the opening track on *Blonde on Blonde*, one of the finest albums of rock music there will ever be.

Yet determining Dylan's motivation behind the song has always been a bit of a head-scratcher. There are two camps here: Those who see Dylan as advocating the use of drugs as a way to solve problems, and those who detect a streak of dark sarcasm in his use of the double meaning of the word "stoned" to throw listeners off track.

The songwriter himself has given mixed messages on the subject. He has vehemently denied in interviews that this or any of his other compositions were intended to be about drugs, nor has he ever advocated the use of drugs as a way of enhancing the listening experience. Yet, by all accounts, he insisted that he would have nobody playing on the session for the song who wasn't stoned, which can account in part for the woozy yet wondrous recording.

Dylan didn't even give us a title that made any sense. Many hardcore Dylanologists have had a field day with it and the numbers in the title, including adding, dividing, and doing all kinds of equations with them to come up with some significance, when chances are Bob probably made it up on the spur of the moment.

Taking the nonsense title in conjunction with the rim-shot-worthy lyrics, it seems safe to assume that Dylan was having a laugh with everybody. Considering that when the song was recorded in '66 for *Blonde on Blonde*, he was in the middle of a surreal ride full of concerts, recording sessions, press conferences, and the like, the hapless, put-upon nature of the song must have appealed to him immensely.

If you choose to read it as a drug song, the evidence is there for you to go wild with it. In a world where everybody wants to bring you down, the song seems to say, the only sane reaction is to soar above it all through chemical enhancement. What else can you do when people are so two-faced that "They'll stone ya and then say, 'Good luck'"?

Yet Dylan was also writing from the perspective of someone who had naysayers all around him, as he was still dealing with the backlash of his conversion to electric music from acoustic folk. In that case, maybe he was just asking for a little company. If he had to endure so much of this criticism, why did he have to be alone in it? This reading makes Dylan seem paranoid, but anybody who's ever seen the craziness surrounding him in footage from that era should realize that his paranoia might have been well earned.

As for the title, it seems to be just another playful jibe at the lifestyle he was experiencing, the one that most normal people would envy until they witnessed what it entailed. The song's already got the drugs and the rock and roll; the title adds the sex, implying that the singer has enough spare women lying around that he has to number them and that number goes at least as high as thirty-five.

Getting too deep into a heavy argument about the intent of "Rainy Day Women #12 & 35" ultimately is a counterproductive exercise since the song just wants listeners to enjoy themselves for the duration of it. Dylan's lyrics are as simple as he has ever written, and his stumbling, fumbling vocal is accentuated perfectly by the tipsy horns of Charlie McCoy and Wayne Shorter.

It's amusing to think of this subversive song soaring so close to the top of the pop charts, but this was the '60s, a decade that claimed Dylan as its spokesperson even as he rebelled against that notion every chance he had. Had he fully accepted such a role, then "Rainy Day Women #12 & 35" could be taken at face value as an ode to drug-induced oblivion. Yet how can you expect Bob to fully inhale with his tongue so firmly planted in his cheek?

96. "Most Likely You Go Your Way (and I'll Go Mine)" (from *Blonde on Blonde*, 1966)

There are two versions of this song lodged deep in the hearts of most Dylan fans, each taking the song in their own direction. The version on *Blonde on Blonde* is laconic and bemused, with Bob sounding defeated and resigned to the fact that some love affairs just weren't meant to be. This version plays up the black humor in the lyrics, with Kenny Buttrey whacking out a jaunty marching beat and the main riff doubled by Charlie McCoy on trumpet and Dylan on harmonica, a juxtaposition of instruments that sounds as insane as you might expect.

On *Before the Flood*, the tour document of Dylan's 1974 trek with The Band, the song is serious business. It becomes a blistering testament to independence and defiance. That playful main riff gets transformed into an abrasive sound akin to gears grinding, and Dylan screams the words as if the severing of this relationship is a triumph.

Maybe "Most Likely You Go Your Way (and I'll Go Mine)" is just too unassumingly profound to be limited to one definitive version. The lyrical dexterity on display here is easy and breezy, nothing too hard to follow, yet thrillingly nimble. Note that the rhymes are never forced to fit the storyline or vice versa; it seems like something you should be able to take for granted with rock songs, but it's a rare accomplishment indeed.

The title may equivocate some, but there is no "most likely" to be found when Dylan sings the song; the separation is a fait accompli. All that's left is to tally up the score at the end: "Then time will tell who has fell and who's been left behind." If those are the two alternatives, both sides seem to be on the losing end.

In the first verse, Dylan pokes a hole in everything the girl says to him, all her promises of fidelity and love laid bare as the deceptions that they are. The image that she presents is contrary to the unflattering portrait presented by the narrator: She lies, she's weak, and she's wrong about everything she says.

In the midst of these subtle accusations, the narrator takes time to reflect on the situation: "Sometimes it gets so hard to care / It just can't be this way everywhere." That line speaks volumes about a relationship on its last legs, where everything is a hassle and nothing comes easy anymore. The weary frustration in Dylan's voice when he sings this line on the original album version punctures his trademark cool.

The last verse is a clever turn of the tables. This is the only time that he agrees with her, and it's only because he's confirming what he already knows: She's been unfaithful, and she can't be trusted. With trust severed so completely, this affair needs to be put out of its misery before any more damage can be done.

Dylan saves one more zinger as a kind of parting shot before the closing refrain, a bit of feistiness poking its head above the despair:

"You say my kisses are not like his / But this time I'm not gonna tell you why that is." Could it be because he checked out of this dead-end relationship long ago? Most likely, indeed.

By seemingly joking his way through the song, the narrator is attempting to soften the blow for his own good. Listening to the way he glides through it in a seemingly unaffected dissection of everything that went wrong, you get the sense that this guy is putting up a good front to keep from losing it completely. The bouncy music accentuates that laugh-to-keep-from-crying ethos.

When he switched the tone in '74, Dylan transformed this song from an arm's-length look at a spent relationship to an in-your-face wail of exasperation. The Band responds in kind, seemingly jolted by Bob's powerful vocal. It's a thrilling performance that takes the song, to paraphrase concert patter used during the electric transformation in the mid-'60s, from one that once went like that into one that goes like this.

What version is preferable probably depends on the personality of the listener and the current state of his or her own romantic entanglements. If you're over an ex and are still standing in spite of the scars, you're probably chuckling along with the original.

If, by contrast, you're still in the thick of the misery, you're probably howling right along with Dylan on the live version. Either way, "Most Likely You Go Your Way (and I'll Go Mine)" really comes in handy.

95. "Hurricane" (from *Desire*, 1976)

As this is the first song from *Desire* to make the countdown, it's a good time to bring up the contributions of Jacques Levy. Levy was credited as the co-writer for the majority of the songs on the album, including "Hurricane," and, until Grateful Dead lyricist Robert Hunter co-wrote most of *Together Through Life*, he was the only person really to ever have worked with Dylan in this manner.

This is also the first time that we bump up against a song in which Dylan tells a story based on real-life events. Typically in these songs, Bob fudges the facts a little bit, and "Hurricane" is no different. In the case of this song, he left out crucial elements of Rubin Carter's backstory and toyed with the events in the investigation of the murder of which Carter was famously accused and convicted before eventually winning his freedom after many years in prison.

With this song, and other true-life tales that will appear in the subsequent pages, that discussion is ultimately irrelevant. Bob Dylan is not a documentarian, and as such, is not beholden to the facts of the story. (For that matter, nor were the makers of the film *Hurricane*, for which Denzel Washington was nominated for an Academy Award.) All Dylan and Levy had to worry about was the effectiveness of the song that they were creating, and they came through well enough to warrant this lofty spot in Bob's catalog.

It's important to remember how far out on a limb Dylan was with "Hurricane," more so in a lot of ways than he had ever been with any of his '60s protest material. Rubin Carter was eventually released from prison, and so Bob was ultimately on the verdict's side, although it took a while for that verdict to get there. There is no doubt, however, that there are some people who will always wince when they hear the song and think that Bob Dylan made a stand for a murderer.

Levy helped Dylan to build the story, framing it almost as if the lyrics were stage directions ("Pistol shots ring out in the barroom night / Enter Patty Valentine from the upper hall"). From the murder scene, the listener is carried along by the sway of Scarlet Rivera's violin through the murky world of double-dealing criminals and cops with shady motivations before eventually winding up in Carter's jail cell.

Dylan certainly could have been a lawyer based on the meticulousness with which he lays out his case. He also embellishes his position, like any grandstanding attorney would do, with colorful flourishes. Consider the way he mimics a ring announcer when he contrasts Carter's fate with what could have been his ultimate destination: "Put in a prison cell, but one time he could-a been / The champion of the world." He also knows how to play to the jury's emotions concerning the culprits who escape justice every day: "Now all the criminals in their coats and their ties / Are free to drink martinis and watch the sun rise."

The songwriters also don't shy away from the racial elements that hung over the case. Whether or not the police actually went so far as to intimidate a witness by saying, "Don't forget that you are white" isn't the point. Dylan had a different measuring stick when writing this song than with others in his catalog. Whereas he wouldn't be so blunt in most other songs, he realized that subtleties had no place here. He was, after all, attempting to sway public opinion to Carter's side. As a result, it was all about the impact that he and Levy could create, and there is no doubting that "Hurricane" is impactful.

And yet it never fails at being an enjoyable song. Until the movie created such a high profile for the case, it's likely that there were many listeners who didn't have a clue about who Carter was or who even might not have realized that it was a true story, so "Hurricane" had to enthrall listeners who didn't know the backstory.

Ultimately, there may not be a lot of people who can listen to this song unburdened by any connection with or opinion about the people depicted in it. For those who can, "Hurricane" is a persuasive tale told by someone stating his case without any cross-examination. Dylan's guts in presenting this argument to his audience are noteworthy, as he risked the alienation of potentially thousands in that audience on behalf of a single man in whose innocence he believed.

94. "Tight Connection to My Heart (Has Anyone Seen My Love)" (from *Empire Burlesque*, 1985)

Time magazine had the idea to celebrate Bob Dylan's seventieth birthday a few years back by doing a bunch of Dylan-related lists on their website. One of those was the ten worst Dylan songs.[1] (That seems like a rather cruel way of sending birthday wishes, but, as they say, it's the thought that counts.)

Listed along some of the usual punching bags like "They Killed Him," "Wiggle Wiggle," and "All the Tired Horses" was "Tight Connection to My Heart (Has Anybody Seen My Love"). (They also had "Forever Young" in there. Jeepers, hate kids much, *Time* magazine?)

If *Time* were judging the song on its video, a hilariously bad clip where Bob gets caught up in a love triangle and international espionage even as he busts out some dance moves with his backup singers, that harsh ranking might be understandable. It's awful in the fantastic way that *Masked and Anonymous* is awful, so Dylan fans likely have a soft spot in their hearts for it anyway.

Most likely, it's that old '80s bias rearing its ugly head. There is a stigma attached to the music of that decade, a long-standing critical view that the whole MTV-influenced output of that era was trivial at best, embarrassing at worst. That's hogwash, of course, but there is no doubting that "Tight Connection to My Heart" has the glossy production associated with the '80s, so bright and watery that you can practically see the song when you listen. That alone is a damning characteristic that some people can't overlook.

There is also the old Dylan-sucked-in-the-'80s critique that colors the song as well. That's also a misguided notion that doesn't quite hold up to close scrutiny. While it's true that Bob floundered a bit coming out of his religious period while trying to find a sound that suited him, his songwriting was as interesting as ever. There were a couple albums that had filler (although *Empire Burlesque* was a consistent affair), and there were many cases when he left out songs that he should have kept in when choosing the material for his records. Yet many songwriters would give anything to have in their repertoire one quarter of the killer songs that Dylan wrote in the '80s.

It's a shame that '80s bashers would dismiss this song, falling for the false notion that something that's a lot of fun to listen to is somehow unworthy of critical respect. You can actually follow "Tight Connection to My Heart" down some lyrical alleys as labyrinthine as any Dylan has conjured. What's more, you'll be unconsciously bobbing your head to its subtle groove the whole time.

Dylan first took a crack at the song in the sessions for *Infidels*, when it was known as "Someone's Got a Hold on My Heart." That early version can be found on *The Bootleg Series, Vol. 1–3*, containing some of the same lyrics and a similar groove. Yet Dylan's vocal on that previous take was a bit blah, something that can't be said of the eventual take of the song that made it to *Empire Burlesque*.

Bob soulfulness, a vastly underrated part of his vocal prowess, shines through in his performance. Let's face it, for all of the lyrical dexterity on display in the verses, this song ultimately comes down to the simplicity of the "Has anybody seen my love?" chorus, with Bob coming up with a great neo-Motown hook as the backup singers coo and purr all around him.

That chorus helps to simplify one of those great, twisting Dylan narratives in which you're never sure whether the "you" he's addressing is the same from verse-to-verse or, more critically, if the "you" is the love he's so frantically seeking. He adds some neat little tough-guy lines to further obfuscate the situation, but the feeling of longing that pervades his noirish journey is never far from the surface.

He wraps things up with an all-time great couplet ("I never did learn to drink that blood and call it wine / I never did learn to hold you, love and call you mine") before wringing every last bit of anguish from the extended refrain. Dismiss this song at your own peril, '80s skeptics. There's a lot of treasure available for lyric divers, and everyone else can just groove along to the master giving one of the most heartfelt performances of his career.

93. "Abandoned Love" (from *Biograph*, 1985)

"Abandoned Love," a stunning heartbreaker of a song, was recorded in 1975 but deemed by Bob Dylan not suitable for *Desire*, his album released in '76. That decision is a head-scratcher, of course, but it wouldn't be Bob if he didn't have beauties lying around unreleased, now would it? Many feel that it was a mistake to choose "Joey" for inclusion instead of "Abandoned Love," but "Joey," flaws and all, has an ambitiousness to it that's hard to resist.

If you want to nitpick, "Abandoned Love" is definitely a better song than "Mozambique," but the latter works on the album as a respite from all of the heavier stuff around it. The bottom line is that the subject matter of "Abandoned Love" is more akin to what was found on Dylan's previous album, *Blood on the Tracks*, so there's a good argument to be made for leaving it off. Why it didn't make it to subsequent releases is another matter entirely.

Anyway, songs like "Abandoned Love" tend to grow in legend over the years, especially when they aren't performed live. Dylan's lone performance of this song came when he was called onto the stage at a Ramblin' Jack Elliott concert in 1975 and performed a stunning acoustic version. He gave it a go for *Desire*, with the violin of Scarlet Rivera providing the exotic touch that could be found on so many of the songs on that album. Yet, for whatever reason, Bob didn't like the result, and, well, abandoned it.

When it showed up on *Biograph*, it immediately took its place among the other "lost" classics in the Dylan canon. Such songs really are an important part of his mystique. Other artists leave lots of stuff unrecorded for the bootleggers to fetishize until they eventually see the light of day. (Think the Beatles' *Anthology* or Bruce Springsteen's *Tracks* for two obvious examples out of many.)

Yet none can match Bob in terms of the sheer quantity and, most importantly, quality of these songs, and a few more are scheduled to make appearances on this list before it's over. While it's fun to try to get inside Dylan's head and speculate why these songs were left on the cutting-room floor, most of the best have reached consumers now through *Biograph* and the various *Bootleg Series* compilations, so they're out there for anyone to enjoy and appreciate. They're not really lost anymore.

"Abandoned Love" is all about the eternal battle between head and heart, but Dylan goes beyond the clichés to reveal that this struggle rarely produces a true winner. The protagonist can see all of the deceptions clearly now, both those perpetrated by this woman's charms and those instigated by his own foolishness ("the clown inside of me").

There is nothing on which he can rely to help him make his decision; even his "patron saint" has deserted him in his time of need. Everyone in the whole world is lying to each other and to themselves ("Everybody's wearing a disguise / To hide what they've got left behind their eyes"). Dylan recently returned to that rhyme in the excellent slow-burner "Long and Wasted Years" from *Tempest*, singing, "I wear dark glasses to cover my eyes / There's secrets in 'em that I can't disguise." The lines are slightly different, but the gist is the same: Everybody is covering up instead of revealing themselves to each other, a continuous pattern of futile behavior.

In the midst of this artifice, the narrator gains a modicum of clarity ("The pot of gold is only make-believe"), but the price he pays is the impending loss of a love he still deeply feels. So he asks for just one more look, one more smile, one more moment of passion before he brings the curtain down. Of course, the possibility exists that this experience will confuse him anew, thus beginning the whole hopeless cycle once again. It's never easy to walk away when it's real.

Dylan fans all tread their own separate paths in their allegiance. Some love the minutiae and the trivia of it all. It's certainly easy to get swept up in that from time to time, especially when it comes to the master's decision-making process and song selection. Yet that can be detrimental if it colors one's appreciation for the songs themselves.

"Abandoned Love" is a wondrous creation, no matter where it ended up. Best to just enjoy it, and let the lore take care of itself.

92. "All Along the Watchtower" (from *John Wesley Harding*, 1967)

One of the great unanswered questions in the Bob Dylan story is just what would have become of "All Along the Watchtower" had Jimi Hendrix not turned the song into the classic rock standard it is today. Would it be anywhere near as well-known as it is now? Would all of his followers still be wading through the allegorical stew of the lyrics trying to figure out what is going on and why? Or would it be just another album cut for Dylan obsessives to ponder and the rest of the world to ignore?

This list was compiled based on the original renderings of the song or, in some cases, the Dylan versions that have become definitive. So it's the version of "All Along the Watchtower" on *John Wesley Harding* that must be considered here.

It's fair to say that the song is more propulsive than the other songs on that album, which is a little bit like saying a turtle is more propulsive than a sloth. Those songs were muted by design, so for one to break out of the pack, it needed to be something special melodically or lyrically.

Melodically, the song is OK, although it's safe to say that very few people go around humming "All Along the Watchtower." Lyrically, its main calling card is its beguiling impenetrability. Basically, you've got a discussion between the joker and the thief, followed by the last verse's threatening vision of an impending battle, capped by the thrilling final line: "Two riders were approaching, the wind began to howl."

That's all that happens, really, and yet there is the sense that everything is at stake. Dylan creates a stifling air of portent and tension with his three succinct verses. That tension can be found in the agitation of the joker, who seems anything but humorous in his interactions with the thief. The series of indignities that he's forced to suffer has him on the edge, ready to strike.

The thief, on the other hand, is cool and collected, suggesting with a measured practicality to the joker that they stop dallying and get down to business. Although their motivations and demeanors contrast in just about every way, both characters are somewhat reminiscent of the outlaw ready to flip the tables and have at his enemies in "Senor (Tales of Yankee Power)" from *Street Legal*.

Whatever may be brewing in the hearts and minds of these two cats, it's clear that their resolve sets the events in motion that will bring about the final verse. Or is it? It's impossible to even be sure that the two riders approaching the watchtower are the same joker and thief from the first two verses.

Dylan flagrantly toys with narrative expectations, skipping over the important stuff and fudging with the time frame. All that can be ascertained for sure is that nothing will be the same once they arrive, the reactions of the wildcat and the wind heralding the oncoming hurt.

There may be some people who would argue that Dylan's version is better than Hendrix's because of its subtlety; it insinuates slyly while Hendrix pounds the ominous atmosphere into our brains with his furious riffs. This contrarian view doesn't hold up to much scrutiny, however; there's a reason why Bob performs Jimi's arrangement of it in concert.

Speaking of performances, "All Along the Watchtower" has been performed by Bob more than any other song. Again, it's hard to picture that happening had not Hendrix put such a definitive stamp on it. Bob left a hole in the center of the song that kept it at arm's length; Jimi came in with his searing squalls of guitar notes and unruly vocals and gave the song a raging id that seems to embody the oncoming apocalypse that Bob and his biblical allusions skirt around.

Dylan's original version is perfect in this spot. It's not an epic, but it is far deeper than what most songwriters can hope to accomplish. Bob once said a thunderstorm inspired the song's creation, and, all other interpretations aside, that might be the best way to think about his version: As a mysterious, sudden storm that disappears almost as quickly as it arrives. Hendrix's version is more like a tornado inside a hurricane in the middle of a meteor shower.

Reasonable minds may disagree about which is better, but it's impossible to deny that Jimi Hendrix deserves a great deal of the credit when we consider the durability and reputation of "All Along the Watchtower."

91. "Up to Me" (from *Biograph*, 1985)

During the making of *Blood on the Tracks*, this song lost out to the similar-sounding "Shelter from the Storm" when Bob chose the pecking order. The album turned out OK: It's generally regarded as one of Dylan's finest, which, by definition, puts it among the finest albums in rock-era music history.

In both songs, Dylan strums his acoustic guitar while bass player Tony McCoy thumps along. His bass playing is far enough up in the mixes that it becomes almost a countermelody to Dylan's main tune, a neat little effect that Bob clearly fancied. After all, he kept "Shelter from the Storm," which was one of the songs from the New York sessions of *Blood on the Tracks*, as it was, rather than re-recording it in Minnesota as he did with five other songs on the album. It can be inferred from this that he would have done the same with "Up to Me" had that stayed in the final mix.

The tunes of the two songs are also similar; so is the way that Dylan phrases the lyrics in each line. The basic song structure, a series of four-line stanzas, every one of which ends up with the refrain, is repeated in both. Even the subject matter is pretty much the same in both songs: Each ruminates on a spent love affair, the narrator's pain barely hidden behind his placid demeanor.

If there is a difference, it's in the way that Dylan frames his reflections. In "Shelter from the Storm," he spends the first half of the song talking about the good times, then changes course and spends the second half detailing how it all fell apart. "Up to Me" is more of an unruly mix, victories and defeats scrambled together, and somehow it feels just a tad truer for that messiness.

Comparing the two, "Up to Me" digs just a little deeper and comes across with a few more memorable lines. It's a song about the responsibility that both parties must take on to sustain a relationship and the subsequent fallout when those responsibilities are abandoned. Dylan's narrator is defending himself, the battles he fought and the lines he crossed, in an ultimately futile effort to keep things alive.

This guy owns up to the fact that his own notion of how life must be lived probably presented some problems, but that was the only way he knew. "If I'd lived my life by what others were thinkin', the heart inside me would've died / I was just too stubborn to ever be governed by enforced insanity," he sings. Those lines likely ring true with iconoclasts everywhere.

From there, he looks back upon the various incarnations these two souls have taken, rearranging their faces and giving them other names, so to speak, all as a way of recounting the little injuries and perceived slights that have taken the toll on their love. Later on, the narrator admits to seeking out new companions as a way of dealing with the pain of her absence, but it's all in vain.

The final verse is one of the finest closing scenes Dylan has ever yielded, as the narrator, hopeless now of her returning, asks if she will at least yield him some nostalgia. He begins, "And if we never meet again, baby, remember me / How my lone guitar played sweet for you that old-time melody." You can imagine the tears welling up in both their eyes as he continues, "And the harmonica around my neck, I blew it for you, free / No one else could play that tune, you know it was up to me."

Considering that the song was recorded in the midst of the sessions for one of rock's all-time breakup albums, it's tempting as a listener to immediately to read autobiography into these final lines. Yet it's also conceivable that the guitar and harmonica could be equivalent to any gesture made by someone in the thrall of a passionate relationship, before its purity is stained by pettiness and frailty.

It's hard to believe that *Blood on the Tracks* could have been better than it actually turned out to be, but inserting this gem in the place of "Shelter from the Storm," which is great but not quite as fantastic, would have turned the trick. With "Up to Me," Bob Dylan performed a stunning balancing act by capturing both the wonder of love and the anguish of its unraveling.

90. "Forever Young" (from *Planet Waves*, 1974)

People might have been a bit confused about Bob Dylan's assertion in the liner notes to *Biograph* that he didn't want "Forever Young," a song for his own children, to be sentimental.[2] After all, if you can't be sentimental about your kids, then who or what can you be sentimental about?

"Forever Young" stands as one of Dylan's most popular songs, likely because of the subject matter and the accessible lyrics. As is often the case with Bob's catalog, there are a few different versions of the song from which to choose. He took two different cracks at it with The Band and included them both on *Planet Waves*, 1974's quasi reunion album by Bob and the boys, going so far as to end the first side of the album with one version and start the second side with the other.

The off-kilter country rock version (later used as the theme song to the NBC drama *Parenthood*) that starts the album's second side is a bit of a non-starter, considering it drowns the loveliness of the melody. There is a sweet demo of the song found on *Biograph*, which is noteworthy if only because of the charming vulnerability of the performance. But it is the first appearance of the song on *Planet Waves* that still garners plenty of airplay today and is, without a doubt, the definitive version.

This is the version where the alchemy created by Dylan and The Band is most evident on *Planet Waves*. That intangible relationship between singer and band had transformed somewhat from what it was on *The Basement Tapes*. Back in the late '60s in Woodstock, it was a ramshackle, improvisational magic that arose, almost mystically, from those sessions. By '74, it was more polished and professional, but, at least on this track, the soul was intact.

The Band could cajole more emotion out of Dylan's lyrics than anybody else could. The instrumental passage that closes out the song, marked by Levon Helm's fluttering mandolin, Garth Hudson's watery organ, and Bob's impassioned harmonica is one of the most moving in the entire Dylan oeuvre.

All of which leads back to the lyrics and Dylan's hard stance on sentimentality. It can be argued that the worst thing about having kids is the fear about the parts of their lives that a parent simply cannot control. All a dad or mom has within his or her power is the opportunity to prepare the child for the hardness of the world. Ultimately, the child has to experience it on his or her own.

That's where Dylan's anti-sentiment stance emanates from. He's not so much making pie-in-the-sky wishes as he is giving sober and prudent advice on how an innocent child can navigate the obstacles that the future is almost certain to contain.

Not only must children have respect for the truth ("May you grow up to be righteous / May you grow up to be true"), but they also have to have the good sense to recognize it (May you always know the truth / And see the lights surrounding you"). Not only must they persist against life's many indignities ("May you always be courageous / Stand upright and be strong"), but they must make sure to never give those indignities the satisfaction of claiming their happiness ("May your heart always be joyful").

The simplicity of the wording mirrors a parent's valiant attempt to keep a child's life in a simple place where such difficulties might never arise. When Dylan sings the chorus, there is desperation in the way he howls, evidence of a father's helplessness coming to the surface. The sadness inherent in the realization that bad things will likely befall children at some point and time is palpable.

Knowing all of this, all parents can do is plead to a higher power ("May God bless and keep you always") and hope those entreaties are heard. This song understands that parents need as much courage as their kids. It may not be sentimental, but it ultimately might be the most honest lullaby ever recorded.

Like all great lullabies, it has the ability to lull a child into a comfortable slumber, safe in the beautiful wishes that Dylan intended for his own kids. At that point, watching their kids' eyes slowly close as they slide off into dreamland, parents should also take the time to appreciate the hard truths of "Forever Young," even if the sentimentalist in them wants to lie and tell their children everything will always be all right.

89. "John Brown" (from *MTV Unplugged*, 1994)

Bob Dylan playing on MTV's *Unplugged* series back in 1994 was the height of irony. After all, Dylan was partly responsible for rendering the acoustic scene irrelevant when he plugged in his guitar in the mid-'60s and left the folk protest movement behind. His appearance on the show, playing older hits at a time when he was deemed by most to be in an irreversible artistic free fall, also fueled the cynical notion that he had nothing new to say.

History has thankfully proven that notion to be hogwash, and viewed through hindsight, *Unplugged* now can be judged simply as one of the better live performances in Bob's recorded catalog. The story goes that Dylan, being Dylan, apparently had the idea of playing all old folk songs at the taping. Horrified network executives quickly put the kibosh on that and insisted that he play more of a greatest hits-type package.

Yet the one song that really stood out the most from that show was the least-known song that he played, an old folk song of his own called "John Brown." It was copyrighted by Bob back in 1963, and there are live performances of it that can be found dated a year earlier than that, but he never released it on an album of his own in the years following its creation. His early demos and live performances of it did find their way onto some obscure folk music compilations, with Dylan given an alias like Blind Boy Grunt in the credits because of contractual necessities.

Given a furious bluegrass rendering that evening, "John Brown" alone justifies the existence of the *MTV Unplugged* disc. Whether or not he was trying to get a message through to the young MTV audience by including this pointed anti-war song, well, only Bob can say for sure.

Anyone looking for some kind of connection to John Brown, the abolitionist of Harpers Ferry fame, is probably barking up the wrong tree; the name choice seems to be coincidental. Instead, Dylan borrowed the basic story from the Irish ballad "Mrs. McGrath," which portrays a similar scenario of a boy being severely injured in a war and then returning home to a horrified mother.

"John Brown" adds the bitterness of the returning soldier to the equation, a prophetic bit of writing by Bob that would anticipate the attitudes of many Vietnam vets on their return home. The chilling scene in the final lines of the soldier disgustedly dropping his medals into his mother's hand says more than most anti-war rhetoric ever could.

It's interesting to consider the mother character in "John Brown," especially when comparing it to the corresponding character from "Mrs. McGrath." In the old folk song, the story begins with one verse in which the captain comes to get the boy and make him a soldier, then shifts seven years in time to the boy's sad return. There is no real prelude, and, a result, the first real glimpse of Mrs. McGrath in the song comes when she is mourning the damage done to her son.

She is, therefore, much more sympathetic than Mrs. Brown, who is seen cheering on her son before he goes off to war, seemingly oblivious to the fact that some harm can come to him. By adding the prelude, it also makes Mrs. Brown seem callous when she practically shuns her disfigured son on his return. In this way, Dylan amps up the generational divide.

One thing that Dylan does not update in his song is the thing that causes the damage, since both Mrs. McGrath's son and John Brown are felled by a cannonball. The use of the antiquated weaponry is telling. It's Dylan's way of slyly saying that, while technology has made for more efficient methods of killing enemies, it hasn't provided an answer for the paradox of warfare: That those who make the decision to go to war aren't actually the ones who have to suffer or die for that decision.

Echoing authors like Stephen Crane and Dalton Trumbo, Dylan takes us inside the mind of this soldier, showing us the toll that is taken on his heart and soul when he is asked to take the life of an enemy whose "face looked just like mine." "John Brown" is a paradox in that it is a tale told brutally and without restraint, yet in so doing it ultimately displays the empathetic qualities of its creator.

The performance may have been "unplugged," but Bob Dylan has rarely seemed so wired with insight.

88. "Mr. Tambourine Man" (from *Bringing It All Back Home*, 1965)

Has there ever been a Bob Dylan song that projects such good feeling into the world? The joy that "Mr. Tambourine Man" elicits is not gained from sarcasm or irony; it is pure, earned through the uplift of the melody and the wondrousness of the words, which are Exhibit A to disprove any doubter who tries to say that the song lyrics of rock artists are inconsequential.

That overarching sense of joy gets lost a bit in the Byrds' famous rendering of the song, which was a number one smash on both sides of the pond in 1965, the same year Bob's version appeared on *Bringing It All Back Home*. Roger McGuinn and company essentially took the bones of Dylan's playful reading and turned it something entirely different, creating a guitar hook of their own and coming up with something a tad more sober and earnest. Then again, their pristine harmonies could have made "Mary Had a Little Lamb" sound like it contained the mysteries of the universe.

There are merits and drawbacks to both approaches. As amazing as Dylan's creation is, he almost takes it too lightly. The respectful seriousness of the Byrds' version is probably the reason it has become definitive. Even if that same seriousness obscures the meaning of the song, there can be no doubt about the respect paid to the lyrics.

It's also interesting to note that the Byrds' take on the song was one of the first major hits from the burgeoning folk-rock movement. Those who use that term to describe Dylan's own foray into electric music are way off base, however. His electric work was, for the most part, much more disheveled and ragged, and all the better for it. For all of their technical perfection, even the finest folk-rock songs sound somewhat bloodless next to Dylan's incendiary recordings in '65 and '66.

One wonders what might have happened had Dylan let some of that wildness into his own recording of "Mr. Tambourine Man." Instead, guitarist Bruce Langhorne's skipping, tripping electric lead, which truly does have a Pied Piper aura to it, drove the bus. (Langhorne allegedly was the inspiration for the title character, since he had in his possession a tambourine approximately the size of a Buick.)

Dylan's voice is unusually open and trusting in his lyrics, each word belted out without any fear or reservation, indeed "ready to go anywhere." For a bit of sharp contrast, compare the album version with the acoustic rendering on *The Bootleg Series, Vol. 4: Bob Dylan Live 1966*. Bob's precise, clipped diction on the latter version gives the song quite a different feel, as if this magical world the lyrics espouse is shutting down before his eyes and ears. The singer, wearied by his constant touring and obligations, seemed to be subconsciously implying that this muse might have been leading him astray.

Regardless of how it is performed, "Mr. Tambourine Man" is a towering set of lyrics. Dylan tells a tale of how the mundane world is bounding the narrator in ("the ancient empty street's too dead for dreamin'"). As a result, this "ragged clown" is willing to trail behind the fantastical title character and borrow some of his creative juice, spitting out some "tripping reels of rhyme" in the process.

In the final verse, Dylan cuts loose all of his poetic powers in a jaw-dropping display. Once they're in thrall to the sound of Bob's words, listeners can't help but be pulled along on the journey with the song's characters. It's at this point in the song when the narrator asks that this reverie last long enough for him to leave the tangible world behind and indulge in the glow of the "diamond sky." He dances gleefully to keep his reality at bay until it can be held back no more: "Let me forget about today until tomorrow."

Still, the laissez-faire feel of the recording makes it a bit of an effort to spot the song's brilliance. In the end, this may simply be a song that's too impressive for any performer to truly match. No matter what kind of rendition of the lyrics is attempted, it is bound to fall a tad short of the potential impact of those words.

As such, "Mr. Tambourine Man" will always be more awe-inspiring than affecting. Leave it to Bob Dylan to find a way to write a song that's too perfect to properly record.

87. "One Too Many Mornings" (from *The Times They Are A-Changin'*, 1964)

As anyone who has ever been on the crossroads of their own doorstep can tell you, it's a lonely place to be. It's a place where memories can't help but morph into regrets, where a person transcends loneliness and reaches an even darker frontier, where nothing will ever be quite the same again no matter which direction is eventually chosen.

"One Too Many Mornings" knows that place well, and benefits from having a writer who can expertly transform all of the sights and sounds he encounters into that nagging feeling in the pit of your stomach that won't go away. Without ever recounting any details about the situation that has led him to this point, the narrator wearily describes a netherworld of barking dogs and street signs that simply exists as a shell to cover the tormented region he actually inhabits.

It's sometimes easy to overlook with all the time that has passed and all of the brilliant songs that Dylan has recorded, but songs like these simply weren't commonplace in 1964. Contemporaries like the Beatles and other pop groups were tentatively trying out their first love songs at about the same time. While the results may have been catchy and heartfelt, they simply couldn't match Dylan's songs in terms of profundity.

One of the things that Bob was doing then that tends to be taken for granted now is that he was suggesting far more than he was overtly saying. He had faith at this early point in his career in his audience's ability to find their way to the meaning of the songs, even as he led them down side roads they might not initially recognize.

Another important weapon that Dylan was able to deploy was his interpretive ability as a singer. It would have been easy for him to over-emote the lyrics to hammer home the emotion he was trying to convey. Yet that wouldn't have been a realistic depiction of the character that he had created. The guy in "One Too Many Mornings" is not somebody who would be rending garments and shouting his woes to the rooftops.

He would sound dejected and emotionally spent, which is exactly how Bob sounds when singing the song.

There is a refreshing efficiency with which the songwriter delivers the goods in this song. Of course, Bob would use much longer songs in the future to brilliant effect, and he would also throw out all the old Tin Pan Alley rules of syllables and meter by stuffing his lines to the hilt in dazzling displays of verbosity. Such tactics became the stereotype of a Bob Dylan song, but they were far from the only weapons he had in his songwriting holster.

In "One Too Many Mornings," he gets the job done with three short verses of four lines each, with the refrain closing out each section. There are no polysyllabic, Scrabble-worthy words, no endless lines that read like tongue-twisting run-on sentences. Dylan still manages to create evocative phrases that don't call any attention to themselves and yet bring the melancholy feelings of the narrator into almost painful focus.

In the first two verses of the song, there is only one indication of the cause of his struggle, which comes when he talks about looking at "the room / Where my love and I have laid." Again, these things don't need to be spelled out because the plaintive melody and Bob's wobbly voice let us know with impeccable clarity just how brokenhearted this guy is.

The final verse finally addresses the lost love in a more direct fashion. "You're right from your side / And I'm right from mine," he sings, a too-little, too-late acknowledgment of the futility of their arguments. As for the refrain of "one too many mornings / And a thousand miles behind," it's a killer phrase that highlights the way that a relationship that barely misses is essentially as damaging as one that misses by a ton.

These kinds of mature songs weren't even being attempted by anybody else in 1964, let alone executed in such mesmerizing fashion, which meant that this twenty-three-year-old kid was acting as the trailblazer for all other serious songwriters to follow. Dylan famously sings at the end of "One Too Many Mornings," "When ev'rything I'm a -sayin' / You can say it just as good." That might just be the biggest lie that he ever tried to pass off on his adoring faithful.

86. "This Dream of You" (from *Together Through Life*, 2009)

Sometimes it takes a while for an album to reveal its true character. It was understandable that when *Together Through Life* was released back in 2009, the critical hosannas for it came fast and furious. Most of the major music magazines responded with five-star reviews, which seemed only fitting for a new album of Bob Dylan material, especially considering the hot streak he had cultivated in previous years.

When music historians look back decades from now on Dylan's output from the early part of the twenty-first century, it's likely that they won't have the same kind of praise for that particular release. It's a pleasant ramble of an album, but not nearly as substantial as the three albums (*Time Out of Mind*, *"Love & Theft,"* and *Modern Times*) that preceded it or the one (*Tempest*) that followed. It's fine musically, but the lyrics, on the whole, don't have quite the same heft that Bob usually produces.

That said, he did reach down and produce one undeniable classic in "This Dream of You." It is the only song on *Together Through Life* that Dylan wrote without any help from Grateful Dead lyricist Robert Hunter. Whether or not that fact and the fact that the song easily beats anything else on the album are coincidental occurrences certainly is fodder for debate. What can't be denied is that the song lingers long after many of the other songs on the disc are forgotten.

In an interview given on the heels of the release of *Together Through Life*, Bill Flanagan of British magazine *The Telegraph* told Bob that he heard echoes of both Brill Building songs and Phil Spector's ornate productions in "This Dream of You." Bob countered that, while he respected those songs, he really would have considered it a compliment if the comparison had been made to a Doc Pomus song.[3]

That seems to be a hint as to what Dylan was attempting here, since the elegance of Pomus creations like "This Magic Moment" and "Save the Last Dance for Me" is coursing through "This Dream of You" as well. The accordion of David Hidalgo not only brings the Tex-Mex flavor to make the song sound like it could have been a hit for Freddy Fender in the '70s, but it also plays up the exquisite misery of the lyrics.

The protagonist of "This Dream of You" is stranded, literally in a "nowhere cafe," figuratively in his head, where he can see nothing but the paralyzing vision that incessantly haunts him. It's easy to get swept up in the romantic nature of the music and read the song as a lament for lost love, but a closer listen suggests that it might be a little murkier than that.

For one, note that Dylan never mentions that the dream is a memory of any kind. Certainly, it could be perceived as one, that perhaps this guy is simply lost in looking back. Perhaps it could even be a dream of something he hasn't actually yet encountered. Whatever it is, it torments him to the point that he has missed his chance for redemption, as suggested by these heartbreaking lines: "There's a moment when all old things become new again / But that moment has come and gone."

Yet the dream also acts as a lifeline, so much so that he defiantly battles on its behalf: "I'll defend this place to my dying breath." Indeed, the dream is the only thing that keeps him "livin' on." Considering the song in this light, romance seems to give way to obsession, and the dream is more nightmarish in its effect than this guy might care to let on. Nor does the life that he's enduring seem to provide any kind of respite from his pain.

The way that this fellow seems completely ineffectual to the tangible world around him and the references to shadows and disappearing acts calls to mind the haunting aspects of "Red River Shore," another late-period Dylan standout featuring a tormented protagonist. Having these elements play against the lilting quality of the music only makes the depth of this guy's predicament seem even graver.

There are certain songs that seem to contain a lifetime's worth of anguish within them, and "This Dream of You" fits that category. The album from which it emanates may not be in the upper echelon of Bob's catalog, but this dusky gem of a song does far more than hold its own.

85. "Is Your Love in Vain?" (from *Street Legal*, 1978)

"Is Your Love in Vain?" is underrated, but that's no surprise, because the album that contains it, *Street Legal*, is probably the most underrated Dylan release. It was savaged by critics upon its release in large part because of its muddy sound. Whatever deficiency might have existed has long since been corrected by improved technology on CD.

That leaves the discussion about the songs alone, and there are far more direct hits than missteps on the album. "Is Your Love in Vain?"

certainly belongs in the former category, yet it's been either ignored by most Dylan scholars or, in some cases, denigrated. It's a mistaken view, perhaps exacerbated by some extenuating factors surrounding the song.

First of all, the sound of "Is Your Love in Vain?" is as close to mainstream rock as Dylan would get in the '70s. What with the silky horns and the chirping organ, it wasn't that far off from the kind of chart-ready stuff being peddled by Bruce Springsteen or Bob Seger around that time.

Why Bob was seen as capitulating in some way to an accessible sound when the others were given a pass on hits such as "Prove It All Night" or "Fire Lake" is a mystery for another time. The bottom line is that this song shows Dylan paying attention to production, and the result is a song that is smooth and soulful in all the right places.

There were also silly complaints labeling Dylan a sexist, a misogynist, or worse for the lyrics. (Let's face it, if someone is labeled something with the letters "ist" on the end, nine times out of ten it's a bad thing.) Bob had dealt with similar criticism of his depiction of women as far back as "Just Like a Woman." Those people like to hone in on certain lines and flash them as evidence, such as "Can you cook and sew, make flowers grow."

First of all, even if his intent was to be sexist, there's nothing wrong with that, since the character in the song is not necessarily a direct stand-in for Bob Dylan. Guys like Randy Newman have made a career out of portraying unsavory characters in song, so it really shouldn't even be an issue.

Second, in the context of the song, the line doesn't necessarily have to be construed as being sexist. This guy is a wounded soul, and he just wants to know what he's in for. The line that follows ("Do you understand my pain?") is far more important to the gist of the song, since it displays the vulnerability that this character cannot hide.

All of those criticisms tend to distract from all of the good stuff that this song has going for it. Dylan frames the lyrics as a series of questions, a technique used by many songs, perhaps most memorably Elvis's "Are You Lonesome Tonight?" By doing it this way, the aforementioned vulnerability is made even plainer, since there is no guarantee he'll get the answers he wants to hear.

Right off the bat, the narrator wants to know just what this girl's motives are: "Do you love me or are you just extending goodwill? / Do you need me half as bad as you say, or are you just feeling guilt?" Later on, he admits that his insular nature might not be the best fit for a relationship, perhaps even hinting at depression with the line, "When I am in the darkness, why do you intrude?"

In the middle eight, he takes a break from the questions to lay down some facts, basically saying that he doesn't want any kind of special attention because it doesn't really float his boat anyway: "I have dined with kings, I've been offered wings / And I've never been too impressed." Sounds like a man who has everything except the one thing he truly needs.

He promises to take the leap in the last verse, wondering if she'll do the same, asking her, movingly, "Are you willing to risk it all / Or is your love in vain?" This guy is out on the line, his fears about a bad outcome outweighed by his low tolerance for loneliness. "Is Your Love in Vain?" certainly comes in a gleaming package, but it contains the fragments of a broken heart yearning to be healed.

84. "The Groom's Still Waiting at the Altar" (from *Shot of Love*, 1980)

"The Groom's Still Waiting at the Altar" took a rather circuitous route to being included on *Shot of Love*. Even though it was recorded during the sessions for the album, the song was unwisely chosen to be nothing more than a B-side to the vastly inferior "Heart of Mine." It was included on the cassette release, which still meant something in 1980, but not on the album.

Dylan or someone in his camp must have sensed the error of this sizzling track being relegated to also-ran status (even though many other Bob classics have suffered the same fate) and amended the error by inserting the track when the album was released on CD in 1985. Thus, the song joins exalted company such as "Yesterday" by the Beatles and "Train in Vain" by the Clash as tracks that eventually fought their way onto albums.

This behemoth of a blues track would have been a force to reckon with no matter where it landed. "The Groom's Still Waiting at the Altar" is a fascinating mixture of the sacred and the profane, with Dylan singing with a vigor that seems to indicate he was having fun again getting deep in some Chicago-style blues after the piety of the previous few years. He had a band full of ringers at his disposal for the song, especially the unassailable rhythm section of Duck Dunn on bass and Jim Keltner on drums.

Even with the lurching, lascivious rhythm in places suggesting more lurid concerns, there is still plenty of religious content evident on this song; it's just that it's mixed up almost evenly with grittier stuff to make for quite the tasty stew. Don't forget that *Shot of Love* was one of the transitional albums at the turn of the decade that found Dylan subtly segueing into the secular from the religious. "The Groom's Still Waiting at the Altar" seems to be caught between those two poles, not so much safely treading the middle ground, but wildly and thrillingly careening from one side to the other.

The very title suggests a promise that's unfulfilled, and the lines leading up to it indicate that even if the age of enlightenment arises, personal concerns may always keep us grounded: "I see the turnin' of the page / Seen the risin' of a new age / See the groom still waitin' at the altar." It's interesting to note that the lyrics as printed on BobDylan.com read "the burnin' of the page," even though that's not what he sings on the track;[4] if he had, it would certainly have put a totally different spin on those lines. "The turnin' of the page" suggests a natural progression; "the burnin' of the page" suggests a forceful changing of the guard.

The narrator of the song finds himself occasionally looking at the big picture, seeing the "massacre of the innocent," "cities on fire," and other horrors. Yet he keeps coming back to the indignities he suffers in his own life. He's misperceived by those around him, and he struggles to keep Claudette, the hard-to-handle woman who keeps turning up in the song, from consuming him whole ("She was walking down the hallway when the walls deteriorated").

As always with Dylan, it's fun to play armchair psychiatrist and speculate that his gradual slide away from the born-again years is the impetus for a song such as this one. It's impossible to say for sure, of course, because Bob has never revealed enough of himself to the public to either corroborate or douse such speculation. That's one of the main ironies about Dylan study: By attempting to keep everyone at bay, he has unintentionally invited all kinds of theories.

Whether it was a conscious decision or not, this song is one of the first indications that Bob was returning to the super-wordy, ultra-dynamic style of the old days. In the last verse, the dying nuns and soldiers on the battlefield get his attention momentarily, but Claudette is the subject of the last word in a hilariously ribald couplet: "What can I say about Claudette? Ain't seen her since January / She could be respectably married or running a whorehouse in Buenos Aires."

Dylan, spitting out torrents of words as if he's running out of time to get them all in, suggests on "The Groom's Still Waiting at the Altar" that we all walk a path that could easily spin off into such extremes.

83. "Lay, Lady, Lay" (from *Nashville Skyline*, 1969)

Is "Lay, Lady, Lay" the sexiest Bob Dylan song ever? Without a doubt, it has to be a prime candidate. It certainly casts a sensual glow, thanks in large part to the almost hypnotic combination of lush music and Bob's creamy, country-inflected voice.

The seemingly out-of-nowhere vocal transformation that Dylan underwent for 1969's *Nashville Skyline* often overwhelms all discussion about the album. It actually wasn't that sudden; Bob had changed his vocal styling somewhat for 1967's *John Wesley Harding*, contrasting the hipster sneer of the electric albums in 1965–1966 by taking a much more muted tone. Granted, the earlier change was much subtler than the one that awaited listeners in '69, but, viewed in that context, this new croon that was heard on "Lay, Lady, Lay" is a little bit less of a shocker and more of a gradual progression.

There are also a few great "What If?" hypotheticals that surround this song. For example, what if Dylan had completed the song in time for the *Midnight Cowboy* soundtrack, which is where it was initially intended? It didn't hurt "Lay, Lady, Lay" any, since it was still a huge hit, reaching number seven in the United States. But it might have bumped off Harry Nilsson's sublime "Everybody's Talkin'" from that classic flick, perhaps depriving the world of one of the great songs of that era.

It's also interesting to wonder what might have happened to the reputation of *Nashville Skyline* had "Lay, Lady, Lay" not been chosen as a single, which was largely the doing of Columbia exec and musical *Zelig* Clive Davis. He persuaded a reluctant Dylan to allow the song's release, and it gave the album the popular anchor it might not have had.

There are other great tracks on the LP, but none that screams "hit single" like this one.

Its popularity can be in part attributed to its aforementioned sexiness. While there are other sultry numbers in the catalog that can make an equally fine case as sexiest Dylan track, it's pretty safe to say that it is the most overtly sexual song in his catalog. There are no innuendos or double entendres; the narrator is as straightforward about his intentions as he could be.

There can be no doubting what this guy has up his sleeve with his persistent entreaties, especially when he sings, "Stay with your man awhile," the twinkle in his eye almost audible. He can certainly be persuasive, poetically tapping into the girl's desires: "Whatever colors you have in your mind / I'll show them to you and you'll see them shine." That's cosmically sexy.

In the bridge, he does his best used-car salesman pitch, essentially saying that she should act now while this offer lasts: "Why wait any longer for the one you love / When he's standing in front of you." Dylan would later overplay his ardor on live versions; the shouted come-ons found on *Before the Flood*, his document of the 1974 tour with The Band, would likely scare off any prospective paramour. The relaxed tone on the studio version is far more persuasive.

None of these come-ons would be effective, however, if it weren't for the musical setting in which they were delivered, courtesy of one of those bolt-of-luck occurrences that sometimes takes place in a recording studio. It turns out that drummer Kenny Buttrey didn't know what exactly to play and got conflicting orders from Dylan and producer Bob Johnston. One told him to play the cowbell, the other told him to play the bongos.

Buttrey, frustrated by the whole deal, decided to play them both to show the pair how inane their instructions were, only to find a magical little rhythm emanating. None of it should have worked, but Buttrey's unorthodox, hiccupping beat, set behind the lyrical steel guitar of Pete Drake, is irresistible. It has a way of lulling listeners into a feeling of comfort, bringing all defenses down, the perfect accompaniment for the narrator's goal.

"Lay, Lady, Lay" turned out to be Bob's biggest-selling single, which isn't too bad for one that he didn't even want to release. The listening audience back in 1969, and ever since, clearly heard what Clive Davis heard. For over forty years, people have been putting it on whenever they retire to their resting place of choice, maybe even a big, brass bed, with their significant other. It's the perfect soundtrack for what comes next.

82. "Tempest" (from *Tempest*, 2012)

"It was sad when that great ship went down." So goes the refrain of "The Great Titanic," a folk song that arose in the aftermath of the Titanic disaster and outlived several competing songs to become the definitive musical take on the subject. That is, until Bob Dylan came along in 2012 with "Tempest," his own gargantuan rendering of the tale.

The line above is the simple way to look at the sinking of the ship that has captivated so many so long. Maybe it was just an awful tragedy, something sad that happened for no other reason than dumb, very bad luck. Yet there are many who choose to view the disaster as some kind of referendum on man's reliance on technology in the face of natural wonders like the mighty waters that claimed the ship. This view often has a religious element to it, the idea that the hubris of humans is no match for the deliverance of fate by some kind of higher power.

The wonder of Dylan's song is that it can be applied in both ways. You can read the song as Bob's subtle commentary on man's oblivious-ness at impending disaster all around, as embodied in "Tempest" by the sleeping watchman. Or you can just read the song as an extremely well-told sea chantey, a distant cousin in that respect to Gordon Lightfoot's "Wreck of the Edmund Fitzgerald."

The ship's actual sinking in 1912 took about three hours, so Bob can be forgiven for needing fourteen minutes in order to convey the full breadth of suffering on that fateful journey. To do this, Dylan takes the basic facts of the how the ship went down and lets his fruitful imagina-tion wreak havoc on the details.

As a result, Dylan includes a "Leo" who uses a sketch book, clearly referencing Leonardo DiCaprio's character in James Cameron's *Titanic* rather than an actual passenger. He also imagines passengers slaughter-ing each other in a survival-of-the-fittest competition to get to the limit-ed lifeboats. All of this is pure fiction, and yet it never rings false in the momentum of Bob's rendering.

Propped up by David Hidalgo's mournful violin, the music of "Tempest" bravely accompanies the doomed ship's inhabitants right to their watery end. This is a story where we go in knowing how it all plays out, so Dylan uses that to his advantage, as the actions of every character are tinged with foreshadowing of the inevitable conclusion.

Back on *Desire*, the song "Black Diamond Bay" featured a bunch of people on a doomed island, and "Tempest" is a quasi descendant of that underrated track. Dylan uses the backdrop of the sinking ship to show how this mass of humanity reacts in the darkest hour imaginable. Some respond bravely, such as the man who gives his lifeboat seat up to a crippled child. Others are not so noble, such as those who rise up against fellow passengers to add to the already-formidable carnage.

In the midst of it all is the fascinating character of the watchman, asleep at his post. This is another area where Dylan changes the facts; the actual watchman on the Titanic was alert and ready at his post and spotted, albeit too late, the iceberg that did the tragic damage, hampered as he was by the moonless sky and his lack of binoculars. Yet Bob's depiction of him, dreaming of the ship's demise instead of actually witnessing it, makes for a better story, adding an almost mystical element to the proceedings.

There is an unfussy beauty to Bob's lyrics here. Note the formality of his words, as if anything more colloquial somehow wouldn't do justice to the story he was telling. The aching poignancy of the characters who resign themselves to their fate once they understand the magnitude of the situation is one of the most moving elements of the song. Their unspoken dignity in their final hours does more than tug at the heartstrings; it practically yanks them asunder.

"Love had lost its fires / All things had run their course," is the ultimate result of Dylan's saga. He claimed in interviews around the album's release that the motivation behind "Tempest" came from the idea the Titanic was a topic that all songwriters must attempt at some point. To say that he rose to the occasion would be a vast understatement. Whether you view the great ship going down as simply sad or emblematic of something far worse, Dylan, as always, has you covered.

81. "Farewell, Angelina" (from *The Bootleg Series, Vol. 1–3: Rare & Unreleased 1961–1991*, 1991)

"Everything's still the same," Dylan sings at one point during "Farewell, Angelina," but nothing could have been further from the truth. He was rewriting the rules of songwriting with head-swirling compositions like this one, daring his audience to dive into these surreal worlds he was creating, getting them to enjoy the view even if they could never possibly comprehend their surroundings in full.

Dylan wrote the song back in 1964, briefly considered it for inclusion on both *Another Side of Bob Dylan* and *Bringing It Back Home*, and eventually allowed Joan Baez to have it. She used it as the title track of a 1965 album with several Dylan covers, but her own truncated take, and all the others since, fails to match the placid and mysterious beauty of Bob's solo version on acoustic guitar, which first surfaced when *The Bootleg Series* bonanza was released in 1991.

As with many songs from this era in Bob's career, the meaning of "Farewell, Angelina" is somewhat elusive. Yet a picture emerges when you take Dylan's impressionistic lyrics in conjunction with his somber delivery. What emanates from "Farewell, Angelina" is a sense of a door being violently slammed shut on a world that may never be witnessed again. Dylan's narrator is not about to be on the wrong side of the divide, hence his haste to move on, even if it means leaving behind the titular girl.

The songwriter is at the top of his game in terms of vivid descriptions and boundless imagination. For just one example, take the verse about the kings, queens, ace, deuce, and fifty-two gypsies. One can imagine Dylan spotting a deck of cards near his typewriter while he was writing the song and letting his mind go off.

It's kind of like Kevin Spacey's character Verbal Kint spinning a web of lies simply by riffing on all the objects he sees in the police precinct in *The Usual Suspects*. The mental gymnastics are of the same order, only Bob is not a fictional character (well, not most of the time anyway).

There is a sense that anarchy is about to reign in the song, as many of the verses depict, in fantastical imagery, an overthrow of the old order. The staid is being replaced with the chaotic, but Dylan's dispassionate narrator never judges which side is wrong or right. He is simply called by either his destiny or his survival instinct and has no choice but to follow; note the common use of the phrase of "I must" when he tells Angelina of his future plans.

It's important to consider the way that Bob sings the song when analyzing this material. He does a masterful job of juxtaposing the unrest that he describes with a vocal that is restrained to the point of sedate. Had he belted out the vocals in wild fashion, it likely would have been a case of sensory overload on his listeners. His measured reading seems to give the words even more impact, and it brings an element of sadness into the song that makes the narrator more sympathetic than he might otherwise be.

As such, the song provides a pretty good example of why Dylan's lyrics should not be analyzed in a vacuum. On the page, "Farewell, Angelina" is an opaque bit of mystical poetry. When Bob sings it, he breathes life into it. The loneliness of Angelina and the heartfelt regret of the narrator come into brilliant focus. It's a nifty sleight of hand that he pulls off in so many of his songs that it's usually taken for granted. It shouldn't be.

As the sky unfolds, burns, erupts, and floods over, there is no indication whether Angelina will be spared the fate that the narrator so wishes to avoid. What is impossible to deny is the sorrow of the parting, evident in that heartbreaking little chord change each time when Dylan sings the refrain. He doesn't want it to be this way, but it's the way it has to be.

It's never clear what worlds are colliding here. Maybe it's the old, square world falling in favor of the new, unkempt one. Maybe it's those who are resistant to change ceding to those who demand it. One thing is for sure, based on songs like "Farewell, Angelina": The sky over the world of popular song was certainly on fire, and Bob Dylan was the one holding the torch.

80. "Isis" (from *Desire*, 1976)

It is always tempting when analyzing rock music to spend so much time trying to hang autobiographical baggage on songs that the fact that songwriters do use their fertile imaginations on occasion is often forgotten. Suggesting that every song is somehow about the writers' personal lives is limiting the scope of their talents. When this type of narrow-minded analysis is applied to Bob Dylan, it can be downright foolhardy.

In that spirit, "Isis," one of the elusive story songs from 1976's *Desire*, might be about marriage, as Dylan introduced it in concert during his famed Rolling Thunder Revue shows in 1975 and 1976, but it doesn't necessarily have to be about Bob Dylan's marriage. If it is, that means Bob apparently moonlighted as a tomb raider in between tours and albums.

This is simply Dylan telling a roundabout story to emphasize the impossibility of love, how it is pushed to its breaking point by the recklessness and selfishness of human nature even as the hearts of lovers desperately try to protect and sustain it. Those themes may or may not have been played out in Bob's own marriage. What's important is that they resonate with listeners going through their own impossible quests for love, and, on that level, the song is hard to deny.

If there is a single key line in the song, it would be when the narrator opines toward the end, "What drives me to you is what drives me insane." As the song makes clear, he is just as much a part of this dysfunction as she is. The same part of him that craves jewelry and precious metals (maybe to give to her, but still "reckless," as she says) desires her beauty; the same part of him that is drawn to her untamable spirit is drawn to a dangerous quest with a shady, doomed stranger in the middle of nowhere.

Hanging the name *Isis* on this mysterious woman is interesting since this is the name of an Egyptian goddess who was worshipped as the ideal wife and mother. It seems that the protagonist in the song clearly feels she is ideal, but maybe not in the traditional sense of being caring and nurturing. It is her wildness and mystical nature that draw him in, the very things that may always push them apart in the end.

Dylan seems hung up on dates within the song, from the wedding on Cinco de Mayo to the narrator's pleasure that he and his companion will return by "the fourth." Doing some analytical tomb raiding for references to the significance of these dates can lead down a rabbit hole that takes a listener far from the essence of the song. Better to get caught up in the fascinating trek that the guy takes with the nefarious stranger.

The search for the tomb reads like a bizarro Western. Even though his better instincts warn him against trusting his cohort, the protagonist presses on as if he has no other choice. Whatever he is trying to prove to Isis or find in himself to make him worthy of her love can only be found at the end of his journey. It turns out that he finds not treasure, but death. Still, he "felt satisfied," perhaps learning a lesson.

Scarlet Rivera's violin acts as the tour guide for this fascinating saga, while Howie Wyeth's drums crash with portent at all the right moments. The song's thick atmosphere of dread and desire is perfectly echoed in the music.

When the man returns to Isis, all it takes is one glimpse of her to know that even his harrowing experience will not solve all their problems: "I cursed her one time then I rode on ahead." Their conversation, all small talk and brief utterances, is a testament to how these two restless souls have a bond that needs no heartfelt elocution. Yet there is a tinge of tension in the guy's snappy retorts, hinting at the combustible nature of this pair that can never quite find resolution.

It's amusing to think that co-writer Jacques Levy is often credited with bringing a theatrical sense of structure to Bob's songs, since "Isis" is thrillingly unhinged, containing two separate stories that seem to be connected only by the narrator's involvement in both. Somehow, in a twisted way, it all makes sense, since the song suggests that sustaining a marriage and raiding pyramids are parallel activities: They each offer infinite rewards if you can just make it out alive.

79. "My Back Pages" (from *Another Side of Bob Dylan*, 1964)

The phrase "old soul" is something that could certainly have been applied to Bob Dylan circa 1963. He was just a kid, really, but he sang like a grizzled prospector, insightfully elucidating topics of great complexity like race and poverty. Even now, some fifty years later, it seems impossible that someone so young could have acquired wisdom that seemed so hard earned.

At this point in his career, more than a half century since he first enraptured the world with his voice and guitar, Dylan sings with the verve and feistiness of a young buck. Even with his voice ravaged beyond all hope of repair, it's impossible to miss the youthful spark and mischievous glow emanating from every line he sings. It's almost as if the aging process has somehow reversed itself for Bob.

If you're looking for a point of demarcation between the young yet old Dylan and the older yet young Dylan, it's clearly "My Back Pages" from 1964's brilliant change-of-pace album *Another Side of Bob Dylan*.

The optimistic point of view is that, at some point in everyone's life, a realization can be reached similar to the one that Bob reached at age twenty-three, as expressed so completely in that song. It may take some folks a bit longer, and it may be more of a gradual thing, but hopefully, a less righteously rigid perspective on the world should emerge.

As with most of the songs on *Another Side*, it's just Dylan and the acoustic guitar, much like his previous three albums. The subject matter is far different, however, what with Bob taking on topics where it isn't quite so easy to draw a line in the sand. His version of "My Back Pages" is sung confidently, even as the lyrics speak of how it's OK to be doubtful.

The Byrds, perhaps the most successful longtime interpreters of Dylan's work, recorded an excellent version of "My Back Pages" in 1967, finding unabashed joy in the abandonment of ideals. The song also took on extra resonance when Bob was joined by old buddies Roger McGuinn, George Harrison, Tom Petty, Neil Young, and Eric Clapton for a spirited rendition at his thirtieth anniversary concert in 1992 at Madison Square Garden. With the aging rockers sounding so freewheelin', the song's spirit came alive all over again.

While many read "My Back Pages" as Dylan's overt denial of his protest-song past, that reading is probably too narrow by half. The song is much more of a universal plaint to which everyone can relate. Bob posits that it's not enough to know that there are two sides to every story; it's also crucial to understand both sides. He also intimates that growing up means accepting being wrong sometimes, or, at the very least, accepting that you're not always 100 percent right.

Whatever message you get from "My Back Pages," the stunning way in which Dylan manipulates the language should be evident to everyone. His willingness to stuff words into lines that you might not think would fit results in some stirringly evocative creations. "Half-wracked prejudice," "corpse evangelists," "self-ordained professor's tongue," "confusion boats"; if someone tried to use such phrases as those in normal conversation, he or she would probably get a lot of funny looks. From Bob, it all seems as natural as "See spot run."

He also messes with the syntax ("Lies that life is black and white / Spoke from my skull") and turns nouns into verbs ("foundationed"), the flouting of language's conventions emphasizing his point that everybody should just lighten up. It's also important to note the way his halting digressions within lines ("Good and bad, I define these terms / Quite clear, no doubt, somehow"), sounding almost like stammering, give the impression of someone trying too hard to prove his point, which, the song suggests, is yet another folly of righteous youth.

That memorable refrain ("I was so much older then / I'm younger than that now") gets quoted so often that its brilliance can be taken for granted. Dylan's ultimate point here is not that you should want to grow younger every day. That's impossible anyway, at least in terms of physiology. Still, if you can avoid your own personal confusion boats, you might just be able to grow younger in outlook. May we all get there at least half as fast as Dylan did and stay there for as long as he has.

78. "Going, Going, Gone" (from *Planet Waves*, 1974)

Diehard baseball fans can recite their favorite home run calls. Some folks likely favor the spontaneous ones that accompany homers in clutch, end-of-game situations or in crucial moments in the postseason that capture the moment perfectly. It's also understandable that many sportscasters develop a trademark call when they see a home run, especially since many of them have to announce hundreds of them per season. ESPN and other sports networks have turned these trademark calls into something of an amateur comedy hour, with each new up-and-comer fresh from broadcasting school trying to outdo the other in terms of cleverness.

Those new calls never match the classics though, do they? And no call is more classic than the late Mel Allen's "Going, going, gone!" Delivered with that honeyed voice rising in pitch with each word, it perfectly captures the anticipation of the fans as they watch the ball arc toward the seats, culminating in the explosion of cheers that erupts when it lands beyond the outfield wall.

It is a pretty safe assumption to say Bob Dylan is a baseball fan. The evidence to support this claim is plentiful: He devoted an entire episode of his satellite radio show, *Theme Time Radio*, to the subject, and he also immortalized then-Oakland Athletics pitcher Jim Hunter with the *Desire*-era outtake "Catfish," co-written with Jacques Levy.

Considering all of this, it's reasonable to think Bob might have had Mel Allen's home run call in mind when he delivered this powerful track, performed with The Band on *Planet Waves*. After all, the chorus delivers that same kind of anticipation, although, given the tone of the song, maybe dread is the better word. When Bob sings the word "gone" followed by a stab of Robbie Robertson's guitar, the dread is cathartically released once we know that the narrator has reached his destination, wherever that may be.

It is tempting, when listening to this song for the first time, to be swayed by the downbeat music into thinking that it is a breakup song. Closer inspection reveals that it's a bit less conventional than that. While the narrator may have been pushed to this difficult point in his life by romantic tribulations (although it's hard to say for sure), the person he is ultimately at war with is himself. As a result, he reaches a dark crossroads, which is not so much a path to escape as it is a means to eradicating all traces of the person that he has become.

It's probably going too far to say that this guy is contemplating suicide. After all, he sings, "Now, I've just got to go / Before I get to the ledge." It's more about the narrator breaking out of the prison of who he was, or maybe just who everyone expected him to be.

Taking that view, his ability to get clear of the debris of his past life can be seen as a triumph. The only thing mitigating that victory is that it's impossible to say whether this newfound freedom from himself will bring him any more comfort than his previous situation, or if it will just lead him to be bound by different chains.

That sense of the unknown hangs heavy in the air thanks to an exquisite performance by The Band. The loose-limbed rhythm sections of bassist Rick Danko and drummer Levon Helm are never where they're supposed to be and yet always just right. In addition, guitarist Robbie Robertson proves on the track why he is one of the most underrated guitarists in rock. There may be a lot of guys more technically proficient, but few can deliver the emotion that Robertson generates, particularly on "Going, Going, Gone."

Considering all the possibilities, it's fun to speculate what the song might have sounded like had Dylan chosen a different home run call as his inspiration. Somehow "It's Outta Here" or "That Dog Will Hunt" just doesn't quite cut it though. Bob ultimately made the right choice on this track, one that is generally unheralded when considering the Dylan canon, even though it shouldn't be.

Like a baseball cracked by a power hitter, the protagonist of "Going, Going, Gone" has clearly suffered quite a blow to create the momentum that gets him going. As Dylan's tender vocal implies, he can only hope he finds a soft place to land in the bleachers once he clears the fence and is gone.

77. "Ballad in Plain D" (from *Another Side of Bob Dylan*, 1964)

It is very easy, considering the cloak of secrecy that has always shrouded Bob Dylan's personal life, to get carried away with speculation about who or what directly inspired his songs. That kind of conjecture leads down the slippery slope into thinking that the songs are always intended to be veiled representations of his personal life.

With "Ballad in Plain D," the modestly titled yet epic representation of the ugly end to a passionate love affair, there is no avoiding such speculation. It's not even speculation, really, since practically all sources agree (and Dylan has effectively admitted) that the song is pretty much a blow-by-blow account of his breakup with Suze Rotolo, with her sister Carla getting pulled into the middle of it as referee.

It is surprising to note that much of the critical reaction to the song is negative. Many writers who are expert chroniclers of the Dylan catalog think that "Ballad in Plain D" fails. The general consensus is that Bob delivers the facts but doesn't do much more than that, that he comes off as self-pitying, and that he unfairly maligns Carla Rotolo for her actions on that fateful day.

The counterintuitive thing about it is that such critical negativity is leveled at such an openly autobiographical song. Many reviewers frantically search for details of Dylan's life in his songs, even when there aren't any to be found. In this song, the details were there for everyone to see, yet not too many people seemed too happy with it.

Truthfully, the song is moving, no matter what the particulars are. Some of the criticism may be valid, but the power of "Ballad in Plain D" overwhelms all of it. Was he unfair to Carla in the song? Yes. Does he feel sorry for himself at times? Definitely. Is that the honest reaction of someone coming off a bad breakup? It sure sounds like it. Besides, who could possibly have crystal clear perspective after a nightmarish scene like the one that apparently went down that night?

Any regret Dylan might have felt about writing the song was likely his conscience catching up with him and not necessarily any condemnation of the song's quality. He so expertly and fearlessly takes us into that momentous night, with all of its raw emotion, that it's painful and harrowing yet compelling nonetheless. And, while he certainly takes his potshots at Carla and Suze in the song, he doesn't spare himself either, fessing up to the mistakes he made that led them all to this point.

All that's left after the terrible fight scene are the last two verses, which serve as a touching and restrained epilogue to this blistering one-act play. In the first of these verses, his story finally told, the narrator reflects on the aftermath. "The words to say I'm sorry I haven't found yet," he sings, and then he offers her a kind parting thought, the futile gesture of a man out of chances: "I think of her often and hope whoever she's met / Is fully aware of how precious she is."

In the final verse, Bob does add a bit of the old misdirection to the equation, implying that he has "friends from the prison" who want to know how his freedom feels. He answers their question with a question, one that you first have to understand to realize that no answer will ever be satisfactory: "Are birds free from the chains of the skyway?"

Suze Rotolo, whose relationship with Dylan seems also to have inspired some of his more difficult to pin down love-gone-wrong songs from the '60s, passed away in February 2011 at the age of sixty-seven. She could have begrudged Bob the right to write "Ballad in Plain D," but she didn't, quite the gesture from someone who could have been embittered by the fact that her personal life was laid bare for the world to see. Clearly, she must have meant an awful lot to Dylan, considering he was so destroyed by their estrangement that he consequently had to put it all down without any of the masking wordplay or concealed identities found in just about all his other work.

"Ballad in Plain D" turns out to be one of the few times that Bob Dylan has ever given his audience a clear glimpse into his personal life in his songs. It's an outlier in his catalog in terms of its method, but the brilliant execution is standard Dylan.

76. "You're Gonna Make Me Lonesome When You Go" (from *Blood on the Tracks*, 1975)

One of the things that make *Blood on the Tracks* the definitive post-breakup album to so many music fans is its balance. It would have been possible for Dylan to make the album one long diatribe like "Idiot Wind" (although even that song has its subtle shadings), and that certainly might have been impressive, but it also would have failed to capture the full spectrum of emotions that are evident at such times of relationship turmoil.

Inserted humbly in the middle of all the *sturm und drang* of *Blood on the Tracks*, "You're Gonna Make Me Lonesome When You Go" is a perfect example of this balance, taking an almost amiable look at the dissolution of a relationship. Any song that rhymes Honolulu (or "Honolula," as Bob pronounces it) with Ashtabula clearly isn't taking itself too seriously.

When you also factor in the folksiness of the music, with Bob strumming old school and blowing some hyperventilating harmonica riffs against Tony Brown's nimble bass, the lightness is evident. So the song is perfectly pitched on the album as a diversion from all the more tormented stuff going down around it. Yet the song is too good to be considered just a palate cleanser; it soars no matter the context.

This does not seem to be a long-term relationship that Dylan is referencing here. It seems more like a fling that nonetheless means a lot to the narrator. He is clearly enjoying this time with this girl, and her effect on him is such that he can't help but notice the wonders all around him as if they were there for the first time. Yet his idyll is constantly interrupted by the nagging knowledge of her inevitable departure.

Indeed, biographers like Howard Sounes have noted that Dylan was not referencing Sara Dylan with this song, but rather a 1974 fling with Ellen Bernstein, a young executive at Columbia Records, Bob's record company.[5] (The mention of Ashtabula is apparently a reference to Bernstein's hometown in Ohio.) That fact seems to fly in the face of the prevailing view of *Blood on the Tracks* as a divorce album, but the album was always more complex than that simplified view anyway.

It seems to be the simplicity and carefree nature of the relationship that appeals to the narrator in the first place. Leave it to Dylan to include a reference to the tortured love affair between the French poets Arthur Rimbaud (a huge influence on Bob) and Paul Verlaine, whose wild carousing scandalized Europe and eventually ended in gunplay, in such a seemingly benign song. Comparing his previous affairs to this explosive combination highlights the lovely contrast the narrator has found with this new girl, which makes it all the more painful when they have to part.

Bob's lyrics elsewhere in the song are effortless, a mellifluous flow that plays perfectly with the breezy music. Throughout the song, there are sweet descriptions of the nature that surrounds the couple, from the "dragon clouds" to the "crickets talkin' back and forth in rhyme." These beautiful sights and sounds are perfectly in tune with the wondrous beauty of his paramour: "Purple clover, Queen Anne's Lace / Crimson hair across your face."

For all of this unfussy breeziness, the narrator's feelings are genuine, if a little bit qualified. She seems to be impactful on him not so much for the good qualities that she possesses, but rather the bad ones that she does not. He mentions his previous loves in the first few verses as being difficult and careless, more damaging than nurturing. The girl in the song is a respite from his past, providing the kind of uncomplicated pleasure that he desperately needs.

As such, it's also clear that their affair can never be anything more than temporary, since the foundation on which it's been built is some-what flimsy. Still, that doesn't mean that it's trivial to the narrator. There seems to be undeniable warmth shining through when he deliv-ers his memorable parting words: "But I'll see you in the sky above / In the tall grass, in the ones I love."

Wouldn't it be nice if all goodbyes were so heartfelt and eloquent? It's one of the great moments in "You're Gonna Make Me Lonesome When You Go," a song that proves that lightness can still make a pretty heavy impact.

75. "Goin' to Acapulco" (from *The Basement Tapes*, 1975)

There's a fascinating contrast going on between the lyrics of "Goin' to Acapulco" and how they are performed. If you just concentrate only on the words, the song seems to be an enjoyable little trifle filled with bizarre innuendo and playful non sequiturs. Yet, as sung by Bob Dylan and as played by The Band, the song becomes something more mysteri-ous and profound, to be taken with the utmost seriousness.

Such is the inhuman power of *The Basement Tapes*. *Great White Wonder* was the title given to the famous bootleg of Dylan's 1967 ses-sions with The Band that circulated for years before the official album release, and it's a name that is truly on the nose. There was indeed something wondrous at play going on in Big Pink, the home in upstate

New York where those recordings were made. Whatever was in the air, it transformed what were supposed to be trivial, hassle-free ditties into songs that revealed so much more.

"Goin' to Acapulco" is the epitome of this strange phenomenon. It is impossible to say for sure, based on the lyrics alone, that the narrator is singing about a running sex date with Rose Marie, the owner of an establishment in Acapulco with unknown business purposes, although that's the best guess. If he isn't, he really has a strange relationship with food, and it's probably best to not even speculate what he means by "blow my plum."

Since many of the lyrics that Dylan was laying down in those informal sessions were strictly improvisatory in nature, it didn't matter if one verse connected to another or if any sense could be made of it when everything was taken together. It's safe to say that he never expected these things to be heard anyway, although one wonders if the performers themselves were aware at the time how special their homemade recordings were.

Yet Dylan sings this apparent silliness as if it's a hymn, with the deepest respect and sonority. It's a monumental vocal performance, a lonely howl that makes Rose Marie's sound like not so much a place he can get his rocks off but rather the location where his wounded soul may be redeemed.

That respect for lyrics that seemingly don't deserve it is also fed by the performance of The Band, who plays the song as if it's in suspended animation. We know that it moves forward because the words keep changing, but the pace isn't so much slow as it is frozen, hanging in abeyance until it just drops out of existence after a quick fade.

Credit that in part to Garth Hudson's organ, which blankets the proceedings in a dreamlike swirl, abating only to allow Robbie Robertson's Curtis Mayfield-inspired licks to punch in and out. Note also that Richard Manuel is on drums, since Levon Helm hadn't yet arrived on the scene when the song was recorded. Manuel's staggering beat also plays an important role in setting the mood.

So who wins in the battle between lyrics and music to convey the true feeling of "Goin' to Acapulco?" The music does, by a pretty good margin. The amazing thing is that the lyrics don't so much fade into the background; that would be impossible considering the power of Dylan's vocal. Instead, the words seem to take on a different meaning, as if the vocabulary has been altered by the mystic force of the sounds being created by the instruments. Suddenly, "Goin' down to see fat gut," sounds like nothing less than the answer to all life's mysteries.

Filmmaker Todd Haynes was onto something when he placed the song in *I'm Not There*, his quasi biopic of Dylan, in the midst of a surreal funeral. It's the perfect setting for it, sadness and silliness intertwined. Jim James of My Morning Jacket does the singing honors in the film, imbuing the song with an ethereal beauty that honors its strange power.

The nature of the song is truly difficult to describe short of saying that you have to hear it to believe it. Give it a listen and bear indirect witness that something truly amazing went down in Woodstock all those years ago, something somehow more combustible than great chemistry, too true to be written off as magic.

Read the lyrics to "Goin' to Acapulco," and you'll come off thinking that it's a song about a plum-and-rum-peddling seductress. Hear it and realize that's it's nothing less than a shining example of the power of music.

74. "High Water (for Charley Patton)" (from *"Love and Theft,"* 2001)

There are times when a song and the evaluation or interpretation of it can be affected by factors beyond the control of the songwriter. Dylan has had this happen to him many times throughout his career. For just one of many examples, consider the way his lines about the president standing naked from "It's Alright, Ma (I'm Only Bleeding)" were tied to the Watergate scandal when the song was performed live in 1974.

In the surreal days following September 11, 2001, many newspapers and magazines in the United States ran articles detailing certain instances in movies, television, music, and literature that seemed to either capture the emotion of that awful day or eerily presage the events of it. One of these pop-culture coincidences that many of these articles cited was "High Water (for Charlie Patton)," specifically the lines "Nothin' standing there / High water everywhere."

Given Dylan's reputation as an accurate and insightful surveyor of the cultural landscape, and given the fact that *"Love and Theft,"* the album containing the song, was released on 9/11, it was tempting in those heady days to consider Bob more prophet than poet.

Of course, that's nonsense; he's just a man who writes songs and performs them. Yet you can't blame anyone if they assigned such mystical powers to him around that time. After seeing the enormity of human suffering on display that day, nothing made sense anymore anyway, so why not Dylan as singer/songwriter/seer?

"High Water (for Charley Patton)" is, needless to say, not about 9/11 or any specific events leading up to it. The song from which it borrows its title, "High Water Everywhere" was about the flood of Louisiana in 1927 (which also inspired Randy Newman's sublime "Louisiana 1927"). "High Water Everywhere" was written and performed by Charley Patton, hence Dylan's name-checking of the Delta bluesman in the title. (Dylan also gives another bluesman, Big Joe Turner, a role in the song; he heads to Kansas City only to find a wasteland. Bertha Mason, also included in the song, is a character from *Jane Eyre*. She was locked in an attic in the novel, so you could say she had the blues too.)

Even with the similarities, Dylan's song isn't really about a flood either, at least not a literal one. There is, however, a metaphorical disaster brewing. "High Water (for Charley Patton)" touches on a powerful and awful force that's been growing for a long time and has now arrived with unstoppable force behind it.

Dylan has a long line of songs like this one, which leave none too subtle hints about encroaching danger. In his religious period, he presented them as dire warnings to sinners; consider "Slow Train" as one fine example.

As time passed, he became more resigned to such unfortunate events. "Everything Is Broken" off *Oh Mercy* rattles off a laundry list of the world's fractures that the songwriter doesn't even pretend can be healed, while "It's All Good" from *Together Through Life* sarcastically uses the title refrain to harp on the fact that there's nothing out there very good at all.

This widespread calamity in "High Water (for Charley Patton)" manifests itself in many ways. It comes physically in the scenes of destruction Dylan portrays, such as the "coffins droppin' in the streets like balloons made of lead." It appears in intangible ways as well, such as the harmful ignorance displayed by the angry mob ready to lynch Charles Darwin for his outlier views.

The damage is also evident on a personal level, what with relationships in the song crumbling under pressure. It's everywhere indeed, which is why, when the narrator asks to be saved from this metaphorical catastrophe, no help is forthcoming: "'Don't reach out for me,' she said / 'Can't you see I'm drownin' too?'"

The narrator finds contrasting ways to deal with it all. In one verse he comes on like a charismatic scoundrel, plying women with boasts and uncouth come-ons. Later on, he takes on the guise of an unsympathetic preacher railing against perdition. Through it all, his quoting from old blues songs suggests that this malaise is not by any means a new threat. By contrast, it's actually been revving up for quite a while, only now reaching full fruition.

Given a furious, bluegrass arrangement on *"Love and Theft"* led by Larry Campbell's relentless banjo, "High Water (for Charley Patton)" is a massive piece of work. So massive that, coupled with the turbulent timing of the song's release, it deceived even rational people into thinking that its creator had second sight.

73. "'Cross the Green Mountain" (from *The Bootleg Series, Vol. 8: Tell Tale Signs: Rare and Unreleased 1989–2006*, 2008)

There have been dozens of exceptional books written on the history of the Civil War. To single out one particular volume, *Battle Cry of Freedom* by James McPherson, which pretty much tells the story from the seeds of the conflict many years before the war actually began all the way to the final surrender at Appomattox, is a pretty good one-stop overview. The book is essential reading for anyone interested in understanding not only the facts of the story but also the emotions of those involved, from those making the decisions to those in the midst of the fight.

While taking plenty of time to detail every major battle's twists and turns, McPherson also puts the reader right inside the minds of the soldiers by including excerpts of many letters sent by these young men back to loved ones at home. What is immediately striking about these letters is the eloquence of the soldiers, the simple yet poetic way that they described their feelings about being the pawns in this game. The clarity with which they viewed their situation was stunning, and the fact that many of them seemed resigned to a tragic fate in service of their particular side is infinitely haunting.

Listening to "'Cross the Green Mountain," Bob Dylan's own meditation on perhaps the darkest hours of American history, that same haunting feeling is palpable. Dylan is himself a bit of a Civil War buff, as he explained briefly in his autobiography, *Chronicles Volume One*. He also talked in a 2012 interview with *Rolling Stone* about the knowledge that he gleaned about the war not from reading historians, but from reading the reports filed by newspapers at the time.

From those papers, he discovered something far different from what many historians peddle. "There doesn't seem to be anything heroic or honorable about it at all," he said. "It was suicidal. Four years of looting and plunder and murder done the American way."[6]

"'Cross the Green Mountain" only hints at that kind of cynicism, simply because the point of view of the narrator is quite different than Dylan's own personal take. Instead, the song can be read as one of those eloquent letters home from a soldier in the thick of the campaign, much like the ones included in McPherson's book.

Snapshots of the battlefield are mixed with musings on destiny and observations of brothers-in-arms. We know it's the Civil War being described because the song came on the soundtrack to a Civil War movie, *Gods and Generals*, and because of a quick reference to Alabama. Without those clues, Dylan's moving tale could be interpreted as a dissection of war in general.

The soldier frames the whole story as "a monstrous dream," but this is just the defense mechanism that he uses to keep from accepting that these horrible things are actually happening all around him. He sees comrades fall, he watches a captain killed by his own men, and he tries to understand how abstract concepts like glory, pride, honor, and virtue fit together to form this tapestry of carnage and death.

Rendered as it is at a stately pace, the music dripping with pathos, "'Cross the Green Mountain" might as well be a funeral procession, since this war is the last setting many of these boys will know. Dylan never stoops to sentimental tricks to get the emotion flowing; it emanates naturally from the scenes he depicts, harrowing scenes of falling soldiers cast with a beatific glow. The song calls to mind Terrence Malick's *The Thin Red Line* in this regard, with the juxtaposition between Earth's natural beauty and the abomination of men killing other men highlighting how unnatural war really is.

In the end, the "letter to Mother," containing the cruel twist that the person in the letter is "already dead," seems to reveal the narrator's fate to us. Then again, maybe he was dead, in a sense, the moment he stepped on the battlefield. As he is "lifted away" at song's end, it yields the impression that he told this entire tale as his soul was leaving his body. "'Cross the Green Mountain" is notable not just as a Civil War rendering but as an insightful take on all wars because it depicts these wars from the perspective that matters most: The mind and heart of a soldier who bravely meets his end without ever understanding why he has to do so.

72. "Shooting Star" (from *Oh Mercy*, 1989)

Books upon books have been written in an attempt to describe the songs of Bob Dylan, this humble volume included, and yet, at best, these can offer only educated guesses at the songwriter's true intent and meaning.

Perhaps that's one the reasons that fans are so fond of his excellent autobiography, *Chronicles Volume One*. As unconventional as the book might have been in Bob's cherry picking of certain parts of his life to describe while leaving out large chunks of his history (which may come in the sequels if they ever arrive), it provided lucid insight into what he felt about certain songs, specifically the ones from *Oh Mercy*. He goes into great detail in the book about the recording sessions and his writing process for the songs included on that 1989 album.

Thus, some of the answers can be obtained right from the horse's mouth. Here is Bob's description of "Shooting Star," courtesy of *Chronicles Volume One*: "It was frigid and burning, yearning—lonely and apart. Many hundreds of miles of pain went into it."[7] Maybe Dylan missed his calling as a rock critic, because it's difficult to describe the closing track off *Oh Mercy* much better than that.

Dylan's relationship with producer Daniel Lanois, who was at the helm for *Oh Mercy*, is an important part of his later career and its development. The collaboration was the first time he ever recorded with a producer who might be described as an auteur in his own right. Lanois came in with definite ideas on how things should be done, and that caused friction with Bob, who was used to a much more catch-as-catch-can style of recording, especially in the '80s.

The uneasy compromise between the two men led to the best Dylan album of the '80s as the decade came to a close, but Bob went back to the old, less-structured ways for *Under the Red Sky* in 1990, and the results were uninspired. (Not one of the songs from that album made this list, and it's unlikely that omission will cause great controversy among Dylan fans.)

The two men would reunite for *Time Out of Mind* for excellent results again in '97, but it's telling that Dylan has self-produced all of his albums since then. The good news is that the albums since *Time Out of Mind* have been just as good if not better than the Lanois albums, so maybe Bob learned a thing or two from the producer's style, omitted the stuff that got on his nerves, and found a formula that worked for him.

To sum up Bob's general complaint with Lanois, as can be ascertained from the book and various interviews, it's that the producer could be heavy-handed at times, and that's a valid criticism at times—not in the case of "Shooting Star," though. Lanois eases off the throttle on the song, providing some shimmering atmospherics yet allowing Dylan's sweet melody and dejected vocal to do most of the work. The only time an instrument steps to the fore is when Bob comes in at song's end with the harmonica and blows away a whole album's worth of heartache.

Everything in the song stems from the titular spectral phenomenon, which sparks the narrator's memories. He first thinks of the one who got away, how the qualities that entranced him were the very ones that led to her departure. Following that, he puts himself in the reflective spotlight, remembering how he came up short of her expectations, still unable to pinpoint exactly why that was.

After a middle eight diversion allowing Dylan to flash some showier lyric spinning that throws some religious imagery into the mix as a diversion, the last verse of "Shooting Star" is back to dreamy introspection. The star is gone as soon as it appeared, and there is the undeniable feeling that the narrator did all of this ruminating in the fraction of a second in which the star burned its solitary path through the atmosphere. Lonely and apart indeed.

Maybe Bob Dylan as artist and Daniel Lanois as producer butted heads from time to time, but considering their combustible relationship led to pristine beauties like this song, it all seems worth it. Many Dylan songs have so many nooks and crannies that you can get something new from them with every listen. "Shooting Star" is wonderful in part because it never seems to change, inevitably projecting the sweet sadness of a near-miss love.

71. "Angelina" (from *The Bootleg Series, Vol. 1–3: Rare & Unreleased 1961–1991*, 1991)

Hyena, concertina, subpoena: you just have to be impressed with how many rhymes that Bob Dylan comes up for "Angelina" in this fabulous *Shot of Love* outtake. One wonders how far he might have delved into the rhyming dictionary had he decided to include a few more verses. Maybe something about eating farina or possibly a verse describing the game-calling attributes of St. Louis Cardinals' catcher Yadier Molina, perhaps? The possibilities aren't endless, but they are amusing.

Of course, there's a good reason that Dylan chose the name, probably the same reason he chose it for another classic outtake, 1964's "Farewell, Angelina." The obvious religious connotations attached to the name immediately add layers of depth to these songs. In the case of "Angelina," which was recorded at the tail end of Bob's so-called born-again period, the choice of the name is even more telling.

Yet "Angelina" isn't nearly as cut-and-dried pious as some of the songs recorded during that time. As opposed to a pretty straightforward attack on non-believers like "Property of Jesus," which also came from the *Shot of Love* sessions, the song manages to leave a lot of wiggle room for those who might wish to see it through a secular filter.

In many ways, the song resembles something that might have come from the pen of Dylan contemporary Leonard Cohen, a master at commingling spiritual desires with the desires of the flesh. It even sounds a little like a late-period Cohen recording, with its unassuming musical backing and female backing vocalists at the forefront.

"Angelina" is a song to which you can slow dance as long as you don't pay too much attention to those confounding lyrics, lest you lose your step. After all, it's hard to find romance in, for example, a verse about a snake-eyed dude's affinity for a goddess that's half hyena/half Hooters waitress. Yet romance, albeit the kind that takes place in the bizarre world of Dylan's boundless imagination, is ultimately what is in the song's heart.

The question becomes then what kind of romance is he talking about. Is Angelina an actual human being, someone to whom the narrator is attracted but can't seem to bring into his heart in the way he would like? It's likely deeper than that, with the overtones of spiritual angst suggesting that the narrator is trying to fall in love again with his faith, even as he is continuously pulled away by his own weakness and pushed away by the reticence of the titular character, who makes the prospect of him being saved too difficult a prospect for him to consider: "I tried my best to love you but I cannot play this game."

You can find the song's emotional core in the handful of straightforward lines that the narrator sings to Angelina. His frustration at their inability to connect, despite all of the travails that they have apparently overcome, is evident in these flashes of clarity. These travails are represented by the strange cast of characters that populate the song, the monkeys and giants and four-faced angels, heavy with symbolism yet ultimately diverting the focus of the narrator from his love interest.

Dylan stands alone in his ability to take these strange lyrical flights of fancy that keep listeners on their toes, only to come back in for a noirish line like "If you can read my mind, why must I speak?" that hits right in the heart bone. All of the surrealistic folderol sets up the emotional shots like a prizefighter throwing a series of jabs before tossing in a haymaker.

In the final verses, it sounds as if the façades are all crumbling and this world of imagery and symbols is crashing down all around our hero. and heroine. All that leaves is a man singing his heart out to a girl he clearly loves and wants to embrace, if only she'd allow him to do so. He is left hanging in the balance at song's end, his ability to connect with this mystical female an uncertainty even at the fade-out.

The song's power doesn't really depend on whether or not Angelina is a simple girl or a representative of something much deeper. It's the struggle of the narrator that ultimately hits home, something to which anybody can relate. "Angelina" has all the Dylan cleverness you might expect up its sleeve, but it's the heart on that sleeve that is most affecting of all.

70. "I Want You" (from *Blonde on Blonde*, 1966)

There are a lot of different ways for a person to make plain the affection they have for another. There are roundabout ways that use all of the diversions as a means of creating a path to the ultimate declaration of ardor. Contrasting that, there is the direct method, which is generally more effective, dispensing with all the trivialities and getting right to the point.

The brilliance of "I Want You" is that it manages to cram both of these approaches and a whole lot more into its three minutes or so of existence. It's why it's one of the consummate Bob Dylan radio songs, proof that he could do what all of his chart-topping contemporaries could without sacrificing his uniqueness.

"I Want You" reached number twenty on the U.S. charts, which is saying something for a song with such a high degree of difficulty. After all, it's a tough balancing act that Dylan attempts throughout, one which could have unraveled at any time and brought the song crashing from its heights. The playfulness of the lyrics manages to keep the mood light, but at any point it could have gone overboard and overwhelmed the essential drive of the song, that is, the narrator's unwavering desire for the object of the affection.

Dylan pulls this off so nimbly that a number twenty chart spot actually doesn't do it justice; it feels like a number one. It's impossible to tell why some songs hit home with mass audiences more than others, but perhaps "I Want You" was released about a year too soon to make its maximum potential impact.

With its trebly guitars, chiming organ hook, and sprightly melody, the song has a certain Day-Glo quality that would have made it a perfect fit for the Summer of Love in 1967. Instead, it was released on *Blonde on Blonde* in '66. By '67, in typical Dylan fashion, he was going completely against the psychedelic grain with the earthy parables of *John Wesley Harding* and then the throwback brilliance of *The Basement Tapes*.

No matter when the song was released, it can't be denied that this is Dylan at his most lovable, coming on as a charming scamp with good intentions in his heart and an impressive vocabulary at his disposal. There is polysyllabic wordplay and ingenious poetic techniques at every turn, yet it's all playful enough not to come off as being too intimidating.

In the first verse, for example, a whole band full of musical instruments is animated by the songwriter in an attempt to dissuade the narrator from his romantic pursuits. No dice, because, as he movingly sings, "But it's not that way / I wasn't born to lose you." All the fancy rhyming aside, the heartfelt touches like those last lines are what are ultimately going to get him across and win the girl.

Dylan brings in other distractions for the narrator to face, but his single-minded pursuit of the girl he's directly addressing cannot be checked. The others that this girl encounters will fall short, he implies, such as the sleeping saviors on the street. Sound familiar? Bruce Springsteen from "Thunder Road": "Waste your summer prayin' in vain / For a savior to rise from these streets."

The narrator is also honest enough to admit that there are others vying for his attention, such as the daughters who shun him for his attitude and the chambermaid who attends to his every need but can't bring him what he truly wants.

In the final verse, Dylan comes up with a neat bit of inspiration in his performance when he sings the last lines haltingly as if he's improvising them, trying to come up with excuses for his behavior: "Because he took you for a ride / And because time was on his side." It's a ploy right up there with Roger Daltrey stuttering the lyrics to "My Generation."

It's interesting that "I Want You" is a song that is considered to be one of Dylan's most accessible, considering that he nimbly spits out lyrics about guilty undertakers and drunken politicians. Those words may be impressive, but, much like the extraneous characters in the song, they're really nothing more than a fun diversion. What counts the most is the instantly catchy tune and that oh-so-direct refrain.

He wants her, he wants her, he wants her so bad. You can't say it any better than that.

69. "I'll Remember You" (from *Empire Burlesque*, 1985)

There can be only one. If there's nothing else that the *Highlander* movie series has taught us, it should be that. That statement takes on a much more heartfelt meaning on "I'll Remember You," an achingly sweet ballad from *Empire Burlesque*. This song is about that one and only one person that is valued by another above all others.

Many people have the ability to dole out equal amounts of love when it comes to family members or maybe even friends, but that's less likely to be possible when it comes to romantic relationships. It's highly unlikely for a person to say something like, "Well, yeah, I miss Tina and Trina about exactly the same after all these years." It just doesn't happen; one usually comes to loom a little bit larger than the rest over time.

If you're lucky enough to end up with your first choice, you can still vicariously feel the deep well of emotion flowing through this song. A recurring theme in Dylan's work is this idea of the one that got away, who towers above all others in his protagonists' hearts and minds. "I'll Remember You" is the purest distillation of that feeling.

The song doesn't try to disguise its intent with an overly ornate tapestry of lyrics, not that there's anything wrong with that approach, especially when it's Bob who's doing the sewing. Yet sometimes you just need the straight skinny when it comes to a lonely heart, and this song delivers.

Empire Burlesque is a bit of a polarizing album in the Dylan catalog. Many diehard fans cringe at the '80s production and mixing techniques, intimating that Bob was trying to grasp at the popular sounds of the era in an effort to stay relevant. As a result, those folks tend to dismiss the songs included because of those controversial characteristics.

That criticism is certainly valid for some of the up-tempo numbers on the disc, which sound like they were produced to accompany a *Miami Vice* chase scene. Yet songs like "Emotionally Yours," "Never Gonna Be the Same Again," and especially "I'll Remember You" have a sneaky impact; simple though they be in terms of lyrics, Dylan delivers them with everything he has, and his effort wins the day on those songs over any production missteps. If *Nashville Skyline* is Bob's country record, *Empire Burlesque* is undoubtedly his soul album.

On "I'll Remember You," Dylan's emotive vocal is tempered nicely by the backup work of singer Madelyn Quebec. Yes, the production is a bit heavy and obvious in its effort to garner an emotional response from the listener, but this song works in part because it's just a bit over-the-top. The emotions of the lyrics are so deeply felt by the narrator that a restrained performance would have felt like a letdown.

The bridge might be the song's most powerful moment. That's when the narrator asks his long-lost love for some kind of validation that she understands how deeply he felt for her when they were together, feelings that he still can't quite shake: "Didn't I, didn't I try to love you? / Didn't I, didn't I try to care?" His desperation at this moment is touching, coming as it does on the heels of his more measured declarations of affection in the verses.

. While their union is not destined to last in terms of them living happily ever after, they are forever linked in the narrator's memory, and that has to be enough. His iconoclastic tendencies probably made him a bit of a bear to live with anyway. It's probably a good bet that Bob didn't have to use his imagination too much to conjure up the lines that reflect those tendencies.

Dylan clearly has an affinity for this song, performing it live much more often than songs that are more closely identified with him. Maybe he understands that it hits people directly, a perfect contrast to the ones that make you work a bit harder. Or maybe he just occasionally needs to sing the song to somebody on that cosmic radio by which separated lovers are eternally connected.

Bob's old buddy John Lennon once famously sang in a Beatles classic, "In my life I'll love you more." "I'll Remember You" piggybacks on that same sentiment in touching fashion. It's a song that only works if the listener believes it, and Dylan's gut-wrenching performance removes any doubt that this guy will love her more than all the rest.

68. "Gates of Eden" (from *Bringing It All Back Home*, 1965)

In the criminally underrated, faux rock biopic *Walk Hard*, Dewey Cox, as played by John C. Reilly, goes through a period in which he is influenced by Bob Dylan, although Dewey would argue that Bob was influenced by him. He performs a song with some of the most hilariously nonsensical lyrics you'll ever hear ("Stuffed cabbage is the darling of the laundromat," for just one bizarre example).

That song is a goof on the clichéd view of Dylan as someone whose songs are impossible to understand. A parody generally exaggerates some sort of inherent truth, and there are many people who do feel that Bob is beyond comprehension. For those people, "Gates of Eden" is probably difficult to tell apart from the movie's caricature-like approximation of it.

After all, with "utopian hermit monks," "the motorcycle black madonna / two-wheeled gypsy queen," and the "gray flannel dwarf" among the motley crew assembled for this song, you can sort of excuse the nonbelievers for scratching their heads. (Come to think of it, Cox's "apothecary diplomat" would have fit right in.)

As a result, "Gates of Eden" is a good litmus test that will separate those who will willingly follow Dylan down any lyrical path no matter how dense and knotty, and those who will throw up their hands and say it's just not worth it. Not that there's anything wrong with either approach; each must go on their own way accordingly, as the man once said.

Bringing It All Back Home is often described as being Dylan's first electric album, but that only tells part of the story. The album's second side is actually all acoustic, albeit a far cry from the acoustic material that Bob's albums contained in previous years.

The four songs on that second side essentially obliterated everything that had come before it, not just from Dylan but from all of his rock and folk contemporaries, in terms of lyrical complexity and depth. "Mr. Tambourine Man," "Gates of Eden," "It's Alright, Ma (I'm Only Bleeding)," and "It's All Over Now, Baby Blue" required fans to listen actively to get the full, mesmerizing effect. This wasn't music as background noise; it demanded attention.

Out of these, "Gates of Eden" might require the most energy to wrangle it into coherence. The song is unquestionably a challenge, a gauntlet thrown down by Bob to see who is brave enough to pick it up. Those who do go for it will probably lose their way more than a few times. Yet the journey remains fascinating even when the destination is uncertain.

It's probably best for those who are a little bit daunted by such a complex song to not worry if the endless references, thick symbolism, and countless other lyrical curve balls seem impossible to follow all at once. It's better to just let the strange strings of words entrance, allowing the foreboding tone of Dylan's voice to insinuate the meaning that might not be so easily gained from the lyrics.

If a meaning is what you need to have, your best bet is to listen to the final lines of each stanza, which detail what belongs in Eden and what is kept out. None of the bizarre cast of players parading through the verses will make it in, or at least they'll have to put aside their inherent strangeness to get there. Dylan's version of paradise doesn't have room for such eccentricity.

As always with Dylan though, there's more than one way to look at things. Maybe this insane world of shoeless hunters and anthropomorphic lampposts is the real paradise, a place where everybody goes for broke and humanity is revealed in all its beautiful and brutal lunacy. Eden sounds a little too good to be true anyway.

The final verse seems to bring into question whether it's really possible to find truth or meaning anywhere, since the surrealist imagery that populates the narrator's real world is seemingly inseparable from the dreams of his lover. It seems to be one final assertion that believing in anything on either side of the gates is just a prelude to a letdown.

"Gates of Eden" invites practically as many interpretations as there are words to the song, and all of them are likely to be right and wrong at once, which fits right in with the cynical vision that Bob projects here. Its ditches of meaning are practically bottomless. Those who dig deep might not reveal any answers, but they just might reveal their level of Dylan fandom along the way.

67. "To Ramona" (from *Another Side of Bob Dylan*, 1964)

Joan Baez seemed to confirm in her book *And a Voice to Sing With: A Memoir* what many Dylan analysts had long suspected: That she was the inspiration for "To Ramona," one of Bob's most lovely and deeply felt slow songs. She said Dylan would often call her "Ramona" during their time together, going so far as to call her that name in letters to her, hence the song's title.[8]

That bit of knowledge might be illuminating to some who need to pinpoint the specifics of Dylan's songwriting process, but it doesn't really define "To Ramona" in any way. Maybe Bob's original intent was to gently chide Baez for staying unfailingly loyal to a folk movement that he was leaving behind, but the song he created easily bounds over that limited meaning and becomes something much more universal and relevant.

In that way, it is different from his more nakedly autobiographical songs like "Ballad in Plain D" and "Day of the Locusts," which gain most of their impact from their direct relation to events in Dylan's life. As a matter of fact, the view that the song is a dig at Baez actually suggests a somewhat nastier tone than the one that "To Ramona" actually evokes. Instead of recrimination or rancor, the song projects compassion and concern, if maybe a little condescension.

Dylan manages to offer both the heartfelt emotion of a love song and the detached observational qualities of a character sketch within "To Ramona," one of several songs on *Another Side of Bob Dylan* that showed off a more personal side to his songwriting. The nobility of the protest songs gave way on that album to the messier circumstances of love affairs, sacrificing earnestness and good intentions for emotional truth.

The narrator here is playing armchair psychologist to a young girl who is behaving to fulfill the expectations of others rather than doing what is best for her, a situation that is causing her great amounts of pain. It's important to realize, however, that the narrator might not be the most reliable in this situation, since he's got the ulterior motive of intense desire for Ramona. Consider that he wishes to kiss her "cracked country lips." Still, he ultimately wants what's best for her, even as he hopes that what's best for her involves him.

This is a girl who seems to be overly sensitive, and that's something that the narrator knows will get her hurt in a world full of characters prepared to prey on such vulnerable souls. He tries to convince her to look opposite the hurt and suffering sometimes ("There's no use in tryin' / To deal with the dyin'"). Moreover, he tries to get her to realize that one of her main problems is the company she's keeping.

These "fixtures and forces and friends" deceive her constantly, creating "A world that just don't exist." "It's all just a dream babe," he sings, "A vacuum, a scheme, babe." Their "worthless foam from the mouth" is her true enemy, not any perceived weakness inside of her.

These parts of the song certainly feel like Dylan venting against hypocritical folks, or folkies as the case may be, that he has actually encountered along the way, which would play into the whole Baez-as-Ramona angle. Yet the narrator's disdain for these people is ultimately not the point here since he's not the one in turmoil. Their effect on Ramona is what he really wants to mitigate, and his purity of intent transcends any real-life references.

The final verse is the saddest of them all because the narrator knows his words are futile. He tells her to "Do what you think you should do" and then makes a gesture of melancholy solidarity: "And someday maybe / Who knows, baby / I'll come and be cryin' to you."

Considering the hints Dylan leaves here, it can probably be surmised that this girl is suffering from depression. Back in 1964, depression was just something you got over, and it was less likely to be treated as the illness we now know it is. When the narrator says, "For deep in my heart / I know there is no help I can bring," it's an admission that not even the most persuasive and well-meant words can dry some eyes. "To Ramona" is far more empathetic than critical, which is why its connection to Joan Baez need only be as strong as the listener wishes to make it.

66. "Caribbean Wind" (from *Biograph*, 1985)

Dylan has lamented that he let this song get away from him a bit, saying that he wrote and re-wrote it so many times that his original inspiration, which was a song about, in his words, "living with somebody for all the wrong reasons," got lost in the shuffle. That confusion can be heard in the fact that the lyrics as sung on the version released on *Biograph* diverge wildly from other versions that can be found with a cursory search of the internet.

This is yet another song with a bit of a tortured history from the period when Dylan was in a kind of songwriting limbo between the proselytizing of the religious albums of the late '70s and the slick studio recordings of the '80s. In the case of "Caribbean Wind," it was one of the first attempts at laying down material in 1981 for the album that would become *Shot of Love*, although it wouldn't make the cut.

Many fans and critics choose to look at the transformation in Dylan's material at this point as a reflection of changes that were going on in his own personal life in terms of his beliefs and the things that were important to him. While certain aspects of that viewpoint may be true, and it's truly impossible to say thanks to Bob's understandable reluctance to let the public into such personal matters, it overlooks the possibility that he was simply going through another shift in terms of musical direction.

After all, nobody speculated in the late '60s that his switch to country music for *Nashville Skyline* was based on some drastic lifestyle change;

it was simply a matter of Dylan's peripatetic muse pushing him toward a different sound, a pattern that has repeated itself over and over during his career. As such, both the switch toward religious material and the eventual dalliance away from it can be seen in a similar light.

The songs found on *Slow Train* and *Saved* were, relative to other Dylan material, very focused in their approach and their message; you can't listen to a song like "Are You Ready" and miss its clarion call to be saved. What those songs didn't offer up were the curve balls and changeups that had been so long a part of Bob's repertoire of musical pitches.

Those albums didn't have the kind of epic ambition that fans had come to expect either, and one could speculate that Dylan's predilection for long, unwieldy narratives was simply eating at him during this time. As a result, wild and woolly sagas like "Caribbean Wind" began to spill out.

The fact that the song veers more than a little off course is what makes it special. There are Dylan songs in which he purposely tosses in some diversions to eventually steer us back to the main point, and there are those like this one, where the diversions become the attraction. Dylan once said that each line from "A Hard Rain's A-Gonna Fall" could be turned into its own song. In similar fashion, each bend in the road on "Caribbean Wind" could go on forever and never get dull.

Dylan's lines, scattershot as they may be, are filled with urgency and vigor throughout, bringing these characters to life in all their flawed glory. He's helped by a great performance from the *Shot of Love* band, playing up the drama of the lyrics beautifully.

The fact that the song's many different stories don't always cohere plays up the main theme, which is confusion. The narrator seems to be at a place in his life where he doesn't know where to turn, with all of these various people and events influencing him in ways that he can't even fully comprehend.

The one constant is that Caribbean wind. Normally, a Caribbean wind has the connotation of a nice, warm breeze. Yet in Dylan's song, it's anything but innocuous, "bringing everything that's near to me nearer to the fire." It seems, throughout the song, that the narrator is trying everything he can to stop this fate from befalling him, even as he loses his way sometimes. We, as listeners, are all the while fascinated by his adventures in the colliding worlds of faith and flesh.

No, "Caribbean Wind" might not blow us straight from Point A to Point B. Yet it's the stops at Point G, Q, and Z that make it such a thrilling journey.

65. "I Shall Be Released" (from *The Bootleg Series, Vol. 1–3: Rare & Unreleased 1961–1991*, 1991)

When it comes to Bob Dylan songs chosen to be performed at funerals, "I Shall Be Released" is probably the one selected most often, although "Every Grain of Sand" gives it a legitimate run for its money. You can't go wrong with either one, although the notion of life being a prison from which someone who just passed away has escaped probably is easier to grasp for mourners than the more complex ideas of faith and doubt espoused in "Every Grain of Sand."

If it is chosen to be a funeral song, the bereaved have to sift through several competing versions of "I Shall Be Released." The notion of a song being written, recorded, and released in that order has always been a quaint one to Bob, and even some of his very best tracks, like this moving plaint, have taken a roundabout journey to the public's ears.

Dylan wrote the song during the Big Pink sessions in 1967 and recorded a version with The Band that was not included on *The Basement Tapes* album released in 1975. Perhaps that's because by that time, The Band had released their own seminal version of the song to close out their wonderful 1968 debut album, *Music from Big Pink*. As for Bob, he took a more casual crack at the song to help fill out his *Greatest Hits Volume II* package in 1971.

Eventually, the version recorded with The Band in Big Pink made it onto the first *Bootleg Series* collection in 1991. And that's before all of the different live takes are considered, most notably the all-star version that closed out *The Last Waltz*, the 1976 San Francisco concert that served as The Band's swan song.

When a song is this great, it can withstand as many renderings of it as possible. This ranking is based on the tender take in '67, which wins out over the *Greatest Hits* version because its sonority is more suited to the tone of the song. The '71 version, tossed off by Dylan and Happy Traum, is OK, but it's so jaunty that it feels like the narrator doesn't care whether he is released or not.

In that original take back in '67, Richard Manuel adds ethereal high harmonies in the chorus, which really play into the song's hymnal qualities. Indeed, someone who was completely unaware of the song might confuse it for a spiritual along the lines of "Amazing Grace." Writing the song, Dylan clearly channeled something powerful, something that transcends any specific religious belief yet is undeniably spiritual.

Manuel's assistance aside, it's Dylan who does the bulk of the singing and gives a poignant yet understated reading of the material. And what wondrous material it is. It's easy to get lost sometimes in the gospel-like refrain and miss the more prickly parts of the lyrics. Consider that the narrator, trapped in a metaphorical prison, shoots down the wisdom he has been offered that might put his suffering in perspective and hints at revenge: "So I remember ev'ry face / Of ev'ry man who put me here."

Notice also how the final verse takes into consideration those who might not be as fortunate as the narrator to get free of the surly bonds. In that way, the song harkens back to "Chimes of Freedom," Bob's 1964 paean to all those who yearn for deliverance from bondage, be it literal or figurative.

Eventually, the protagonist's resiliency and faith win out over these dark thoughts: "Yet I swear I see my reflection / Some place so high above this wall." That leads directly into that refrain for the ages: "Any day now, any day now / I shall be released." No matter who sings it, no matter what the context, it's hard to hear those lines and not receive some sort of comfort from the unwavering certainty of the lyrics.

For all of the myriad cover versions of Dylan material that exist, it is rare to find any that truly outdo Bob's own performances. As great as *The Bootleg Series* version is, however, "I Shall Be Released" truly belongs to Manuel and his spine-chilling vocal of the song on The Band's version; the loneliness of it is as heartbreaking as it is reassuring. Dylan's words and Manuel's voice: That's a combination that can't ever be topped, reverent enough to send the dead on their way, inspiring enough to uplift those left behind.

64. "Rambling, Gambling Willie" (from *The Bootleg Series, Vol. 1–3: Rare & Unreleased 1961–1991*, 1991)

Dylan absconded with the melody of "Brennan on the Moor," a traditional Irish ballad he had heard from the Clancy Brothers early on in his songwriting career, to write "Rambling, Gambling Willie," a much more lovable outlaw tale. His composition leaves the song that inspired it behind in terms of personality, humor, and heart.

In an example of history coming full circle, the Clancy Brothers eventually did their own version of "Rambling, Gambling Willie," adding traditional instruments and their inimitable harmonies to make it sound like it was passed down through the ages, when in actuality it was written by a twenty-one-year-old kid seemingly expending hardly any effort at all.

"Rambling, Gambling Willie" also serves a historical purpose when evaluating Dylan's career in that it is the first of his major works that did not make it onto a studio album. The song apparently received great consideration for an appearance on Bob's 1963 breakthrough album, *The Freewheelin' Bob Dylan*, but came up short when the final song list was decided. As such, it became the first of a long line of classics that existed only through bootlegs and unauthorized recordings until Dylan finally began officially releasing them, starting with *Biograph* in 1985 and picking up steam with the first edition of *The Bootleg Series* in '91.

It is also one of the first instances of Bob's fascination with outlaws. In later years, he would explore the darker side of the archetype, delving into territory that not only shed light on those characters but also revealed profound truths about the reckless, destructive impulses that dwell within us all. In this earlier attempt, even though it ends on a tragic note, Dylan treads lightly in his portrait of a character akin to the Paul Bunyan of gambling.

Willie doesn't gamble to amass personal fortune. Instead, like a Robin Hood of card sharks, he redistributes his wealth to those less fortunate. Dylan understands that the audience needs to be partially on Willie's side for the song to work properly. Otherwise, Willie's death at the song's end wouldn't be as affecting as it ultimately is, evoking not only sadness but also outrage.

The songwriter is also aware that his character isn't a saint, swindling men out of their money as he does. Having Willie live this kind of life without any sort of comeuppance wouldn't have seemed right either. Bob toes the fine line of admiring Willie without endorsing him.

Willie's flaws humanize him even as his skills make him a legend. Even with his "heart of gold," his demise is an unsurprising one, practically inevitable. Like all legendary characters, he has to have a bit of the immortal about him as well, which Bob acknowledges, giving him just the right epitaph with the line, "Wherever you're a-gamblin' now, nobody knows."

It's interesting to look at this song through a twenty-first-century lens. Poker is now considered a sport and a profession by which many young men and women make a legal living. Although the fervor for Texas Hold'em has waned somewhat in the last few years, the way it has transformed playing cards from a backroom endeavor to big business is stunning, providing quite the contrast to the world Dylan conjured.

It's hard to imagine Willie O'Conley sitting at the table with pitch-black Aviators on and a baseball cap with a logo of some online poker site on it. Dylan makes it clear that, with this guy, it's not earning money that excites him. It's the thrill he gets from outwitting an entire room full of players who are staked much higher than he is.

Bob clearly knew his history as well. As any fan of *Deadwood* could tell you, the "aces backed with eights" that Willie is holding when he is shot is the same "dead man's hand" that Wild Bill Hickok held when he was gunned down from behind. Hickok is in the Poker Hall of Fame; Dylan's fictional character deserves a place himself.

No one can say for sure which of Willie's twenty-seven wives will get the right to use the boat and town that he won in his exploits. What can be stated without a doubt is that "Rambling, Gambling Willie" isn't only the first example of Dylan's ability to transform any folk song and make it gloriously his own, it's also one of the best.

63. "When the Deal Goes Down" (from *Modern Times*, 2006)

If there were a separate countdown for the most romantic Dylan songs ever, "When the Deal Goes Down" would be Top 10, maybe even Top 5. It's impossible to listen to this chestnut off *Modern Times* and not think long and hard about the one you love or, if it sadly applies, pine for the one you loved and lost.

Much credit goes to Fred Ahlert, who wrote the music for "Where the Blue of the Night (Meets the Gold of the Day"), a 1930s Bing Crosby song that clearly influenced Bob's music here. The similarities come mainly in the way the lines are phrased and the tempo; the melodies of the two songs are relatively close cousins as well, although Dylan's quirky delivery takes severe angles that Der Bingle's mellifluous tone never did.

Bob then handed it over to his crack *Modern Times* ensemble so that they could caress it with the gentle touch of a lover. Donnie Herron's steel guitar speaks with lyrical eloquence as George Receli's waltz beat nudges everyone along. Dylan finds what's left of his old crooning voice to squeeze out every last bit of emotion he can muster from that partially borrowed tune.

As is often the case, though, the song would not be what it is if Bob simply changed a note or two from an old standard. If it is so easy to do, why aren't others jumping on the same bandwagon and hijacking old melodies with similar success? The addition of his unique sensibility to the lyrics and the way in which they are presented provides the song with its essence.

It's typical for Dylan to save a spot on his albums for a straightforward love ballad, the meaning of which anyone could grasp without having to wade through a thick stew of heady lyrics. These are songs that highlight his craftsmanship more than his genius, reminders of how well he understands the intricacies of what makes certain songs connect with people while others never do.

It's an underrated part of his skill set, yet one that delights whenever he shows it on songs like "I'll Remember You," "Make You Feel My Love," or even way back to "Tomorrow Is a Long Time." "When the Deal Goes Down" falls proudly in that line, accessible on first listen yet imbued with enough personality and skill to let the listener know that it's not a songwriting hack playing paint-the-numbers. It's Bob Dylan expressing real emotion by means of a familiar idiom.

In the song, he assumes the role of a world-weary guy who has enjoyed some good times, struggled through some bad ones, and might otherwise be ready to call it a day if it weren't for the fact that he stumbled into a love too deep to fathom. As a way of showing his gratitude, he is ready to profess devotion and loyalty that knows no limits or conditions.

He makes it clear that he doesn't have all the answers ("We live and we die / We know not why"). Regrets are also a big part of his autumn years ("I laugh and I cry and I'm haunted by / Things I never meant or wished to say"). If he has learned anything, it's that most of the things that you think will make you happy will only let you down: "I heard a deafening noise, I've felt transient joys / I know that they're not what they seem."

Yet all of these things pale next to this person to whom he gives his undying allegiance and support. The past doesn't matter, and all of his misdeeds are forgiven, as long as he keeps one simple promise: "I'll be with you when the deal goes down."

So, to paraphrase Jerry Seinfeld a bit, just what is "the deal"? It's whatever daunting situation his beloved will face in her life that she would otherwise have had to endure alone if they were not together. When you think of it that way and speculate on the severity of those possible situations, the promise isn't really simple at all. It's the most solemn commitment a person can make. And yet, the right person will inspire someone to make that promise in a heartbeat.

What it boils down to is that the well-being of the other person simply becomes more important than one's own. That's what's at the heart of "When the Deal Goes Down," and Dylan knows it's the same intangible that's at the heart of the greatest romances.

62. "Ballad of a Thin Man" (from *Highway 61 Revisited*, 1965)

Perhaps no musician has ever had a more complicated relationship with the press than Bob Dylan. No one has ever gone through the age-old cycle of being built up and then being torn back down again more than he has.

While he has come to a point in his career where most critics treat his releases with reverence, many of those same critics or others of their ilk were around at the low points to throw their daggers. They've done it with many others, of course, only Dylan kept confounding the narrative by coming back stronger than ever.

At no point was the press ever more obsessed with Bob than in the mid-'60s, a point when he was releasing incendiary music and touring almost non-stop, reinventing what a rock star could be both in terms of the profundity of his songs and his unwillingness to play the fame game as he was expected to do. As a result, "Ballad of a Thin Man," released in 1965, is generally assumed to be a swipe at clueless reporters writing about things that they can't possibly comprehend. Dylan himself has confirmed in interviews over the years that the press was indeed the inspiration for his vitriol in the song.

Yet Dylan has always been able to transcend even his own inspirations and intentions through the sheer force of his talent. "Ballad of a Thin Man" is one of his most thorough takedowns ever, but Bob makes sure not to narrow the scope of his attack in the lyrics. Songs are always more effective if they can have a broad relevance beyond the world of the songwriter. You don't need to know the minutiae of Dylan's history to appreciate "Thin Man"; you just need to have a healthy appetite for eloquent bile and a fondness for the way that the English language can be manipulated in such a way to destroy the defenses of even the most secure individual.

Many will get hung up on looking for clues to the true identity of Mr. Jones, Dylan's target in the song. If you can dispose with the notion that Mr. Jones is anyone in particular, "Ballad of a Thin Man" opens up to become something much more vast. Indeed, Bob's deft slings and arrows are accurate enough to take down practically a whole society of poseurs and pretenders.

It's pretty clear that the first line ("You walk into the room with your pencil in your hand") is a dig at the press and their habit of reprinting misconceptions as fact. Yet the song works as a diatribe against anyone who thinks that he's in when he's out. (Note that the masculine pronoun is in play only because the song names "Mr. Jones," and the title refers to a "Thin Man"; just a little imagination on the part of the listener can turn the song into an equal-opportunity accuser.)

By prancing with sharp spikes on his feet all over the insecurity of his enemies, Dylan leaves these people no alternative but to accept that they are the true outcasts, showing them what a surreally awful place that can be, how "impossible" it truly feels. Note how he cleverly intersperses more respectable scenes with scenes out of some Fellini carnival, geeks and sword-swallowers and midgets disorienting Mr. Jones to no end. By the end of the song, the tables have turned and it's Mr. Jones who is completely out of place: "There ought to be a law against you comin' around."

No amount of conversations with pillars of society or charity tax write-offs can prevent Jones from the realization that he is indeed "all alone." Those sinister piano chords, played by Bob, just keep pounding it into his brain to make sure that he gets the picture, even as he hopelessly struggles to keep up with the conversations going on around him that sound like gibberish. There are many outstanding live versions of the song that have surfaced on various Dylan recordings, but it's hard to match the deadpan relentlessness of the original on *Highway 61 Revisited*.

"Ballad of a Thin Man" is unsparing in its aggressiveness and unforgiving in its assault. Mr. Jones is denied by the songwriter any light at the end of his lonely tunnel. For those listeners who can't point to the press as their main antagonists, they can substitute their own personal thin men and vicariously pick them apart by piggybacking on Dylan's lusciously lacerating lyrics. They're powerful enough to take anybody down.

61. "I'm Not There" (from *I'm Not There: Original Soundtrack*, 2007)

Occasionally confusing but mostly revelatory, *I'm Not There*, director Todd Haynes's attempt to sum up the essence of Bob Dylan on celluloid in 2007, received lots of critical plaudits and made a little bit of money. As great as the movie is, its place in history seems to be mainly as an artifact for Dylan fans to pull apart and dissect. Non-fans pretty much have no point of entry for the movie and shrug it off.

If nothing else, though, the film provided a great service to music fans by yielding an official release of "I'm Not There," a rough recording made by Dylan and The Band at Big Pink in '67 but never finished or officially released. The movie's soundtrack album, otherwise made up of artists covering Bob's classics, concludes with the song.

There are two extremes often taken by those considering "I'm Not There." Some buy into it as some kind of microcosm of Dylan's career, how he was and will always remain elusive to us even as we desperately try to understand him. Others take the divergent path and say that it's just a work-in-progress song with unfinished lyrics that was built up by the obsessives into something that it was never meant to be.

If you take the middle ground, you come to something that's still pretty special but in a more reasonable way. The recording, unfinished and fragmentary, is still undeniably haunting. And that would be the case even if you could somehow strip the mythology away and, as a result, didn't know who the singer and the backing musicians were.

Since the players were Bob Dylan and The Band, all kinds of baggage got attached to "I'm Not There," baggage that only multiplied exponentially for all the years that it went unreleased. Now it's out there for everyone to experience, and it exceeds both the expectation and speculation.

You can argue that Dylan was making up the lyrics as he went along, and maybe he was. Even if that's the case, what he comes up with on the spot is revelatory, like a great improvisational actor. The Joycean stream-of-consciousness definitely plays havoc with the syntax and makes the song hard to follow, as does Bob's slurring. Yet, like a drunken man with moments of clarity, the narrator comes up with words and phrases that stop you short with their evocative power and the depth of the emotion behind them.

For example, how lonely must it be for a girl to be "forsaken by her fate"? And what does it say about the nature of this guy when he says, "I'm released on the heights but I'll dream about the door"? It seems to say something about his innate restlessness and the way that it causes happiness to elude him even when it's in his grasp.

What it all adds up to is a character who is unable to stay with this girl or allow her to leave, keeping her in a nether region of uncertainty and anguish. Added to that, this guy is fully aware of what he is doing, yet he is unable to stop himself, and that causes him sadness on an unprecedented scale.

Of course, you can glean a lot of this insight simply by listening to Dylan's voice, half-awake in the verses yet rising in the refrain to reveal the heavy strain upon him as he attempts to "carry on the grind." The Band are the unemotional bystanders here, Rick Danko strolling just a step behind Bob on bass to prop him up if he falls, Garth Hudson coolly floating up above on organ to bathe the whole tale in an ironic glow.

It all rises to that matter-of-fact yet harrowing admission: "I wish I was there to help her but I'm not there, I'm gone." The elemental power of that line leads you to believe that anyone could have written it, but that's not the case. It could have only been that time, that place, those guys, a cosmic convergence creating a unique musical moment, one that shines through all the seeming casualness of the recording and transcends its history and mystery.

In other words, all of the stuff surrounding the song is trivia. "I'm Not There" is not trivial in any way. It's inscrutable in a way that anyone who has ever had a heart beating inside their chest can understand.

60. "Mississippi" (from "Love and Theft," 2001)

Considering how many times he has come back in his own career, it's a lark to hear Dylan sing, "You can always come back, but you can't come back all the way." He has defied the hard-earned truth of that line time and time again, and stunning songs like "Mississippi" are the reason why.

The song is one of the centerpieces of *"Love and Theft,"* Dylan's 2001 album that looms large in his timeline as not just one of the best of his career, but also one of the most crucial. In retrospect, 1997's *Time Out of Mind* can be identified as the beginning of Bob's late-career renaissance, the momentum of which still hasn't slowed, but, at the time, it was just a great album for a guy who had been in a dry spell for quite some time.

Consider the similar case of *Oh Mercy* in 1989, which, like *Time Out of Mind*, was produced by Daniel Lanois and also came on the heels of a long fallow period in Dylan's career. Its quality seemed to herald a rejuvenation in his recording fortunes, but that didn't quite occur when the lackluster *Under the Red Sky* followed it up.

"Love and Theft" proved that *Time Out of Mind* was no fluke and that no regression was forthcoming. In fact, it is the finest of the post-1997 albums from top to bottom (although *Tempest* is real close). "Mississippi" is a big part of why it's so successful, perfectly summing the album's tone of sober reflection balanced with feisty spirit.

Not that it was easy to bring the song to life. One of common misconceptions about Dylan, perpetrated in part by his own comments from time to time, is that he doesn't take his studio recordings too seriously, using the original versions as placeholders so he can explore the songs in concert. By contrast, he sometimes fidgets so much in an attempt to get the right recording that he loses the gist of what he was after in the first place.

That unfortunate fate almost befell "Mississippi." Dylan and Daniel Lanois battled with the song during the *Time Out of Mind* sessions; the results that show up on the *Tell Tale Signs* disc are fine in their way, but they don't carry the kind of heft that such a deep song deserves.

Bob's own production of the song on *"Love and Theft"* prove that his instincts were right to set this one in a stately, mid-tempo setting and let the wisdom and heart in the lyrics work their magic. No matter how many different ways he might try to reinvent it in subsequent performances, there is no doubting that this version is the definitive one. (That also takes into account Sheryl Crow's version, which actually predates Dylan's own take by a few years but is too jaunty by half.)

The narrator of "Mississippi" finds himself in a tough spot, feeling the effects of passing time all while trying to reconcile with a former flame. He speaks frankly to her ("Your days are numbered, so are mine"); he knows that the two of them have lived long enough that pie-in-the-sky romantic platitudes won't cut it. Yet he also knows that the way back also involves admitting that they each have things for which to atone: "So many things that we never will undo / I know you're sorry, I'm sorry too."

Even as uncertainty and confusion pile up in his addled brain, he finds solace in the fact that he's made it this far, and he knows he didn't make it alone ("I've got nothin' but affection for all those who've sailed with me"). He also understands, even at this stage in the game, that there is always the chance for new beginnings, inviting his intended to come along with him for the ride, with a devilish twinkle in his eye as he sings, "Things should start to get interesting right about now."

What makes "Mississippi" such an achievement is that this character cycles through all of these emotions, and yet it feels like a natural progression. Even as this guy shows a great bit of maturity in the way he perceives his past, his fire is still burning strong for the future.

That sounds like a pretty good summation of Dylan's own journey. He may have stayed in his own personal Mississippi "a day too long," but it wasn't so long that he couldn't recover.

59. "I Don't Believe You (She Acts Like We Never Have Met)" (from *The Bootleg Series, Vol. 4: Bob Dylan Live 1966, The "Royal Albert Hall" Concert*)

Astute readers who know Dylan's discography will note that the album information given above does not represent the original release of "I Don't Believe You (She Acts Like We Never Have Met)." The song was first included on 1964's *Another Side of Bob Dylan*. While that original acoustic version is excellent (it probably would have warranted a spot somewhere just outside the Top 100 of this list), it's the version performed at Free Trade Hall in Manchester, England, and captured on the *Live 1966* edition of *The Bootleg Series* that is the one for the ages.

There are few recordings any more mesmerizing than the so-called Royal Albert Hall performance (so named because it was misidentified for years by bootleggers.) The concert took place on May 17, 1966, just a week or so before the end of a world tour that saw Dylan grow increasingly frustrated by both the aggressiveness of the press and the animosity of audiences unhappy with his switch to electric rock.

Dylan came out and performed an acoustic set full of mind-blowing newer songs like "Mr. Tambourine Man," "Visions of Johanna," and "Desolation Row." The audience was silent throughout before bursting into applause at the end of each song. It's interesting that they didn't catcall throughout these tracks, since, in many ways, these songs were far more removed from Bob's older material in terms of content than the electric songs were in terms of form.

When he brings his backing band on stage, which consisted of then-Hawks and future Band members Robbie Robertson, Rick Danko, Richard Manuel, and Garth Hudson along with Mickey Jones on drums (Levon Helm had departed the tour because he couldn't handle the booing), the audience immediately starts to grow restless. By the time Dylan and friends jump into a raucous, unkempt version of "Tell Me Momma," the live-wire, confrontational energy between band and audience is audible.

This was the famous show where a fan yelled out "Judas!" at Dylan, prompting him to respond, "I don't believe you! You're a liar!" After exhorting the band to "Play (bleeping) loud," they all tear into a venomous version of "Like a Rolling Stone." In many ways, that moment is the culmination of that part of Bob's career because his infamous motorcycle accident would occur just a few months later to cut short the tour and herald a period of lying low for rock's most incendiary star.

Dylan's electric period has gained such mythic status that it's hard to separate the facts from the embellishments surrounding how it all sounded live. Besides being of such historical importance, *Live 1966* is integral because it provides the best evidence of that live sound. And, truth be told, the results are a bit of a mixed bag.

Indeed, the style that he was creating was revolutionary and would pave the way for rock artists to find magic in the music's rougher edges. And the intensity of the music performed by Dylan and his pals that night is undeniable. Yet it was also ragged at times, downright sloppy in others.

"I Don't Believe You" is the one song on that disc where the potential of his electric experiment is fully realized. The performance is tighter than any of the others on the disc by a good margin, each of the performers clear in the mix and right on target. Robertson's licks are precise, the rhythm section of Jones and Danko boom through the proceedings but never get out of whack, and Hudson's brief organ solo is thrillingly colorful. Dylan's wild harmonica squalls somehow fit in perfectly.

With that setting in place, "I Don't Believe You" is transformed from a guy's frustrated but futile complaint about a fickle lover, as it was in its original version, into a glorious catharsis. As Dylan punctuates each line with a wild wail ("She left me here facing the WAAALLLLL"), the musicians build up to a fever pitch before releasing the tension, until the next line ratchets it up all over again.

It's understandable why Dylan couldn't continue on that incendiary musical path much longer. That music was so volatile that it would have been difficult to sustain. The performance of "I Don't Believe You" from *Live 1966* dances on that explosive line so deftly that it stands as one of the rare live performances in Bob's catalog to outdo the original so powerfully that, for one of the few times in his career, the song's lyrics and their meaning are practically irrelevant.

58. "Million Dollar Bash" (from *The Basement Tapes*, 1975)

It is fascinating to trace the way the relationship between Bob Dylan and the five gentlemen who comprised The Band developed. It's also fun to try to figure out just who was influencing whom during the course of that relationship.

Most people give Dylan the credit for helping The Band get a record deal and thereby gain the attention of the listening public. They shared the same manager (Albert Grossman), and the rock press was already aware of the group's association with Bob when it came time for them to record on their own. That may have raised expectations higher that what might be expected for a typical new group, but that was an uptown problem to have since it also guaranteed much attention would be paid to their music.

By contrast, it is also generally assumed that The Band's rootsy influence rubbed off on Dylan when they spent time recording together at the house known as Big Pink in upstate New York in the late '60s, sessions that would be immortalized by *The Great White Wonder* bootleg and eventually by the official release of *The Basement Tapes* in 1975.

Yet the idea of Dylan sort of sitting back and letting his Canadian buddies work their country-living magic on him during this time is a bit of romantic oversimplification. In fact, Bob's songwriting efforts at the time so effortlessly fell in line with the way that The Band would eventually play on their own albums, it could be argued that he helped nudge their sound toward the sublime formula they developed.

Indeed, "Million Dollar Bash" is a song that has a distinct Band feel, even though it is completely Dylan's creation. Robbie Robertson was clearly listening closely (even though, ironically, he doesn't play on the track), as many of his own lighthearted songs on early Band albums have similar collections of oddball characters with oddball names doing oddball things. In other words, Silly Nelly and Turtle, two attendees of the Bash, might as well be related to Crazy Chester from "The Weight" or Ragtime Willie from "Rockin' Chair."

Lunacy doesn't begin to describe what's going on at the "Million Dollar Bash." It's easy when listening to picture The Band sitting out on the back porch at Big Pink playing this swaying little tune (assuming they could get the piano and organ out there) and Dylan singing in a hammock with a pipe in his mouth (although there would have to have been something stronger than tobacco in that pipe to inspire those lyrics).

It's come one, come all to this party. Considering the ragged bunch that parade their way through Dylan's lyrics, the title "Million Dollar Bash" certainly seems to be ironic. These yokels couldn't even dream of that kind of moolah, which may be why some of them seem to be up to no good.

It is exhilarating to hear Dylan manipulate the language like a daft sculptor might manipulate clay. Listen to his description of Turtle: "With his cheeks in a chunk / And his cheese in the cash." It may not make any sense, but it's a load of fun to hear.

Dylan's narrator is as down on his luck as the rest of them, what with the fact that "his stones won't take." Whatever the heck that means, it sounds pretty bad. He's literally beating himself up over his problems ("I punched myself in the face with my fist)," but he can overlook his trials knowing that the Bash is coming up. That joy can be heard in the "Ooh-wee" chorus, as fellow Bashers Rick Danko and Richard Manuel harmonize with Bob as only they can.

The Basement Tapes is generally considered a relaxed, good-timey album. That may be an accurate description of the recording process, but the music itself often got into some heavier stuff. "Million Dollar Bash," however, certainly lives up to that carefree reputation, unforgettably describing the kind of party filled with shady deeds and unsavory characters that you still wouldn't want to miss for the world.

Maybe The Band did show Dylan how to slow down and relax a little, but Dylan seems to have returned the favor by giving them an example of how loosening up can still provide inspired musical results. Either way, it's a give-and-take that altered musical history in unforgettable fashion.

57. "Thunder on the Mountain" (from *Modern Times*, 2006)

As a statement of purpose to start off an album, it's hard to beat "Thunder on the Mountain." "Like a Rolling Stone" set the standard for all such Dylan table-setters way back on *Highway 61 Revisited*, but this song that kicks off *Modern Times* has the same kind of momentum behind it, even if its content is a bit more amiable. It even has the great little instrumental tune-up at the beginning of the song, a perfect way to clear the air before the wonders within the album ensue.

It's always a bit misleading to quote Bob's song lyrics in the same way that you might quote something he said in an interview. Throughout this book, you'll see words like "the narrator" or "the protagonist" when describing the person singing the song, which is a somewhat more accurate way to do it instead of ascribing all of the thoughts and actions and emotions of the song to Dylan himself. With "Thunder on the Mountain," however, it seems pretty safe to say that the man writing the song and his doppelganger within it are practically inseparable.

You can, if you like, think of the song as Dylan's version of a battle rap, his dare to all other songwriters to step across the line and throw down with their own best lyrics, risking that they might end up in the dust with tire tracks on their backs for their trouble. The only difference between "Thunder on the Mountain" and such bragging songs is that Bob lets some of his idiosyncrasies and vulnerabilities into the picture, creating an honest self-portrait in the process.

To forcefully get his point across, he needed just the right gang on his side, some "tough sons of bitches" recruited from "the orphanages." That gang turns out to be the *Modern Times* band, who blow through the Chuck Berry framework of the song and instill it with a confident swagger that perfectly fits Dylan's purpose.

That purpose: To give listeners an idea of where he stood right at that moment back in 2006. It sounded like a thrilling place to be. The opening lines set a scene that's part ominous, part intriguing: "Thunder on the mountain, fires on the moon / There's a ruckus in the alley and the sun will be here soon." This guy isn't shrinking away from any of it, preferring instead to look for opportunity in the midst of the tumult.

He's more than a little randy; R&B songstress Alicia Keys finds that out early on when he expresses his desire for her with no reservations whatsoever about what others might think. He's itching to get into trouble ("I'd like to try something but I'm so far from town"). His targets are those who come down on the wrong side of the eternal battle: "Shame on your greed, shame on your wicked schemes / I'll say this, I don't give a damn about your dreams."

Bob is unapologetic throughout ("I've already confessed, no need to confess again"). Yet for all of his brio, there's still something deep going on beneath the tough exterior: "Feel like my soul is beginning to expand / Look into my heart and you will sort of understand." Dylan often comes off as unapproachable or unknowable in interviews and the like, but moments like that revealing couplet humanize him immensely.

Modern Times felt like a victory lap for Dylan when it was released in 2006. After *"Love and Theft"* followed up *Time Out of Mind* and proved that it was no fluke, there wasn't any more trepidation on the part of his fan base, only anticipation at what he would do next. The resulting album found him and his band operating at such confident levels that it felt like they could get across just about anything, from blues to ballads, from sentimental to sinister.

"Thunder on the Mountain" has a little of all of that in its DNA. It is also a song that can get you fired up listening to it, giving you the impetus to go out and start something yourself. Play it loud on the car stereo, and sing lines like, "I've sucked the milk out of a thousand cows" at the top of your lungs. See if you don't feel like a world-beater, ready to take on approaching twisters and anything else that comes your way.

In other words, Kanye, Jay-Z, and the rest ain't got nothin' on MC Dylan.

56. "If You See Her, Say Hello" (from *Blood on the Tracks*, 1975)

It is somewhat of a miracle that *Blood on the Tracks* turned out as well as it did. Even though the songs are impeccable, the album was a hybrid of two distinct recording styles, and, as such, could have come off sounding disjointed. That these two styles ended up complementing each other brilliantly was either a stroke of luck or an example of Bob Dylan's second sight.

Dylan recorded a full album's worth of material with very spare instrumentation, mostly acoustic guitar and bass with a smattering of organ, in September 1974. The album was just about to come out when Bob, visiting his family in Minnesota for Christmas, decided to re-record several songs with musicians assembled by his brother David. Just a few weeks later, the album, containing an even split of songs from the two sessions, was released.

How Dylan chose between the competing versions is hard to say, just as it is impossible to figure why he felt the New York recordings weren't good enough. The evidence of those New York takes that has been released on *Biograph* and *The Bootleg Series* reveals incredibly intense and intimate versions of songs that were later fleshed out by the fuller band sound that filled out half the finished album.

The discussion of whether or not he made the right choices is more of a fun exercise than an important one, since any opinion besides Bob's is ultimately moot. The album is the album, and no amount of speculation will change that. What's Dylan's last-minute switcheroo proved is that he has better instincts in the recording studio than most people think.

As an example, "If You See Her, Say Hello" sounds pretty sublime no matter what version you take. The New York version has a charming simplicity to it even as it plays up the desolation of Dylan's protagonist. The Minnesota version is a tad more ornate, with guitars that sound like they were left over from the *Pat Garrett & Billy the Kid* soundtrack adding a hint of Tex-Mex to the proceedings, rendering the melancholy more dramatic.

Listening to them one against the other, it's impossible to give either much of an advantage. If Dylan had chosen the New York take, however, it just might have tipped the balance of the album too far in one direction. Maybe the album would have come off a bit more self-pitying and defeated in the finished product. *Blood on the Tracks* is nothing if not well-rounded in the emotional circuit that it runs, and the differing recording styles play a large part in that.

No matter what version you prefer, the important thing is that both sets of musicians beautifully play up the hurt in the lyrics. Dylan portrays one of the most awkward scenes in the post-breakup world, that is, when a person runs into a mutual friend of an ex. Only the coolest customers can come out of this situation with their pride and dignity intact; most people try to act casual but end up inadvertently revealing way too much about the woe they are experiencing.

The lyrics can be read in part as typical small talk that's actually coming out of the character's mouth, yet there also seems to be an inner monologue running in which his true feelings are betrayed. Consider the last verse. "If she's passin' back this way I'm not that hard to find / Tell her she can look me up if she's got the time," is what he says, and it sounds as if he is handling things well. By contrast, "Sundown, yellow moon, I replay the past / I know every scene by heart, they all went by so fast," reflects what's going through his head and what's reverberating in his heart, and it's a much more painful revelation.

Dylan gets every nuance of this situation just right, probably because he was living through it. Even with all the hurt he is clearly feeling, there is still undeniable tenderness in his genuine concern for the girl and her well-being. Again, it goes back to that balance that typifies both the song and the album that contained it.

. Bob made the right decision concerning the recording of "If You See Her, Say Hello," but he could have done a punk-rock version of it and the emotions wouldn't have been altered. It's a song that shows how hard it is to let go of a former love when the reminders are everywhere. Even as Dylan's narrator takes the high road, it still leads him directly to Lonesome Town.

55. "Masters of War" (from *The Freewheelin' Bob Dylan*, 1963)

One of the great things about Bob Dylan as a songwriter is that he has a knack for subtlety and nuance, two things that lesser songwriters tend to overlook in their own efforts. "Masters of War," by contrast, has little tolerance for subtlety, nuance, or anything that can be construed as being committed less than 100 percent to its argument.

A person only needs to look at the final verse of the song, which just might be the most searing set of lines in Dylan's whole catalog (and that says a lot considering he's written songs like "Idiot Wind" and "Positively 4th Street," among many others). In that verse, the narrator wishes that the targets of his anger, those who profit from wars and thus are incentivized to push national leaders toward those wars, would die. He goes one step further though, promising to stand above their graves to ensure that they won't be rising to do their damage anymore.

That's a pretty harsh sentiment, one that clearly surprised Dylan when he stepped back and looked at the song from a distance. As he stated in the liner notes to *The Freewheelin' Bob Dylan*, which contained the song, "I've never really written anything like that before. I don't sing songs that hope people will die, but I couldn't help it in this one. The song is sort of a striking out, a reaction to the last straw, a feeling of 'what can you do?'"9

Such bluntness and stridency are often the hallmark of well-intentioned yet poorly-executed protest songs. Many of Dylan's critics have harped on just this point when denigrating "Masters of War." They consider it to be below the standards of the man who wrote other protest material with more of a tempered approach.

Those critics miss out on the fact that there's a place for songs like this, songs that throw haymakers instead of jabs, as long as they're done well. "Masters of War" is expert work by a young guy who knew exactly what he was doing. Dylan was clearly capable of subtlety; you could hear that on other songs on *The Freewheelin' Bob Dylan*. This song had to be abrasive and harsh to get the required attention.

That first line is a fierce challenge: "Come you masters of war." With that insistent guitar strumming alongside the vocal, the intent can't be any clearer. This is a you're-wrong/I'm-right situation posited by Dylan, and this song will not allow what it considers its enemy to stand. So the songwriter stacks the deck against that enemy, using every heavy-handed trick in the book to accomplish this.

He suggests that innocent children will be jeopardized. He calls the warmongers cowards. He even goes so far as to align with Jesus Christ, the ultimate personification of peace. Even if all these points are reasonable ones to be made against these war profiteers, they are also designed to manipulate the audience to the narrator's side of the story, leaving no room for any opposing opinion to see the light of day.

Many people mishear the exact gist of Dylan's protest, even as Bob has been pretty clear in saying that "Masters of War" was never meant as a pacifist or anti-war song; it instead was meant to deride the so-called "military-industrial complex," as it was labeled by President Dwight D. Eisenhower, by which wars are become just another type of investment. Yet Dylan has never been naïve, and he had to know that lots of listeners would only hear "War is bad" when they heard "Masters of War."

Ultimately, that isn't really of major concern. If he got folks riled up against the targets of his bile, what does it really matter what his methods were or if the message got muddled a bit in the translation? It was a protest song, and it got people protesting. Mission accomplished.

"Masters of War" can't hold a candle, in terms of technique, to many songs ranked below it on this list. Yet there are few recordings in existence that can match the unbridled power of this song, which is saying something considering that it was just a man, a guitar, and his talent wielded with all the subtlety of a hammer to the head. Considering the nefarious methods of the people he was documenting in the song, that roughneck approach was the only way Dylan could make it a fair fight.

54. "Highlands" (from *Time Out of Mind*, 1997)

One of the reasons fans knew Dylan was back on top of his game on *Time Out of Mind* was the inclusion of "Highlands" as the closing song. After all, one of the things that had been missing in his work in the largely fallow period of the late '80s and early '90s was that attention-grabbing, epic final song that so many of his classic albums contained, something along the lines of "It's All Over Now, Baby Blue" or "Sad-Eyed Lady of the Lowlands" to leave listeners wanting more.

At sixteen minutes, "Highlands" is certainly epic, although it doesn't grab your attention so much as wear it down. And, even at that imposing length, it is so profoundly fascinating that one doesn't ever want it to end.

"Highlands" is one of those barometer songs that separate true Dylan believers from casual fans. Much like an episode of *Seinfeld*, it is a song about nothing in that very little actually happens to the narrator within it. His seemingly trivial dalliances, when taken as a whole, end up presenting a touching portrait of a guy longing for a home that seems to be only available to him in his mind. He implies that he'll only really arrive there when he finally shuffles off the mortal coil that seems to be choking the life out of him.

The Scottish poet Robert Burns wrote "My Heart's in the Highlands," an ode to his home country's charms that "Highlands" quotes as the refrain. There is no existential malaise creeping through the poem as there is through Dylan's narrative. Yet that elemental desire to escape to a place of comfort and familiarity is shared by Robbie and Bobby.

Such a place is the last chance of respite for Dylan's narrator, a guy who is barely connected even to himself, let alone to other people. Daniel Lanois's pea-soup production and the repetition of the same musical figure for so long make the song feel like the movie *Groundhog Day* as directed by David Lynch. It's a fitting accompaniment to the tale of a guy who seems to be wandering forever without ever getting anywhere.

"Feel like I'm drifting / From scene to scene," he sings, and it's an accurate description of the narrative. There is no purpose in his travels, no rhyme or reason to his activities. His inner life, as rendered in his idyllic descriptions of the Highlands, is far more vivid than his random interactions in the hazy physical world.

This theater of the mundanely bizarre (or maybe it's the bizarrely mundane) plays out in his meeting with a subtly hostile Boston waitress who talks in circles, at least those parts that he can hear. (Maybe the bad hearing is from all those years listening too loudly to Neil Young.) Their conversation, all sly insinuations and befuddled misunderstanding, highlights the narrator's inability to communicate, which is why he spends most of the song "Talking to myself in a monologue."

And so, he wanders on, alternating between telling ruminations on his sorry state and daydreams of his happy place. In the midst of his waking reverie, the image of some well-intentioned pest asking this guy if he's registered to vote is priceless.

The sly humor is just a way for him to cover up the great isolation he feels in a world he no longer understands. Heck, maybe he never understood it. Whatever the case, the disoriented spells he suffers last longer and longer as the years pass.

Through it all, though, he can cling tight to the Highlands, a place to which he retreats more often with every passing day to escape the subtle horrors of his daily life. At least he leaves us with a glimmer of hope at song's end: "But I'm already there in my mind / And that's good enough for now."

The story goes that someone asked Dylan, after he and his band had recorded this behemoth of a song, for a shorter version, and he replied, "That was the short version."[10] True Dylan fans want to hear that long version, wherever it may be. After all, "Highlands" is an epic that can stand proudly right alongside not just his great album closers, but also among all Bob's super-long songs that seem to fly by in an instant. Besides, even the long version can't possibly be long enough to accurately represent the drear of this guy's existence.

53. "Girl from the North Country" (from *The Freewheelin' Bob Dylan*, 1963)

Even though he hasn't done it for a long, long time, the enduring image of Bob Dylan that rattles around the minds of most of his fans is that of him on stage alone with an acoustic guitar and harmonica. The reality is that it's been quite some time since Dylan has appeared in that fashion. In recent years, he has always been accompanied by a full band, and he doesn't really play the guitar on stage anymore, choosing instead the keyboards or grand piano. (The harmonica, thankfully, is still in his arsenal.)

That has also been the case when it comes to Dylan's recording career. His last solo acoustic performances, save for a stray song here or there, came on the first side of *Bringing It All Back Home* all the way back in 1965. That iconic image that exists of Bob is mostly drawn from recordings from long ago, old video clips, or memory.

There is a reason that the troubadour image of Dylan persists with such stubbornness to this day. It's because of how impactful songs like "Girl from the North Country" are. Bob gave a tender performance of the song, which borrows its melody and lyrical motif from the folk classic "Scarborough Fair," back in 1963 on *The Freewheelin' Bob Dylan*. There was absolutely no filter when he performed in this manner, which is why, most likely, that certain people miss it so much.

By adding instruments, the songs become, in a strange way, less and less about Bob Dylan. In the full band songs, he often comes across more like a really effective messenger of the information in the songs. Maybe that slight barrier is part of what appeals to him about that style, or maybe he just prefers the effect of a crack group of musicians bringing his words and music to vivid life.

There are advantages to both styles, and it's hard to argue against Bob's turn to electric music back in the '60s, considering how revelatory the music that came out of that period, and the stuff that he has recorded ever since really, turned out to be. Yet there is no way to replace the intimacy of an acoustic, solo performance.

As an example, consider "Girl from the North Country." It's much harder to separate Dylan from the character that he's playing in the song than it is for a song like, say, "Just Like a Woman." Maybe they're both autobiographical, maybe they're not; that isn't as important as much as how the accompaniment affects the way those songs are heard.

When people hear "Girl from the North Country" in its original, solo acoustic form, it's more likely they'll subconsciously associate Bob with the character in the song who needs to ask about this girl. They'll think that he was the guy who likes the girl's hair hanging long. They'll assume that it's his dark nights and bright days that are haunted by thoughts of her.

Compare that to the version on *Nashville Skyline*. As fun as that Johnny Cash duet is, it doesn't hit home in the same way emotionally. They're just two guys playing their roles and playing off each other.

Bob gave a great rendering of the song at his Thirtieth Anniversary Concert back in 1992, a frenzied, breathless take that turned the narrator's quest to find out information about the girl much more desperate. Because it was an acoustic performance, it allowed the audience to connect this version of Dylan with that 1963 version and speculate what the passing of time has done to his motivation regarding this absent female. It's unlikely that such a connection would have been made had he sung that night with a backing band.

It's always enlightening to get as close to Dylan as possible, especially on the heartbreaking songs. It sounds like every chord change, every variation in inflection, and every harmonica note is a direct reflection of what's happening in his heart and soul.

Is that all just perception? Of course it is. Yet that perception becomes reality when one listens to the song. And when that song is one as simple and powerful as "Girl from the North Country," the effect is overwhelming. It may not be the real Dylan inside the song, but a listener can easily believe it is. It's also why every Bob Dylan fan, in their heart of hearts, hopes that there's one more acoustic guitar, harmonica, and vocal album waiting somewhere down the road.

52. "Sign on the Window" (from *New Morning*, 1971)

It's interesting how good domestic life sounds after you've had your heart broken one too many times by the flavor of the month. That seems to be the lesson that can be taken away from "Sign on the Window," one of the most successful experiments on Bob Dylan's quirkiest album ever.

Coming on the heels of *Self Portrait*, an album that couldn't have been received any worse had Dylan spent two hours belching into a microphone, anything would have seemed like a comeback. *New Morning* was the 1971 album that automatically sounded good by comparison, but the relief that fans and critics felt when they heard something resembling a coherent album somewhat distracted listeners from the fact that Bob had delivered one of the quirkiest discs of his career.

Maybe he sensed that he was going to get a break on this one, thus feeling emboldened enough to try new things. As a result, weird, wild tracks like the beatnik-jazz lark "If Dogs Run Free" and the playful ballad "Winterlude" sit boldly alongside a blow-by-blow account of Dylan's receiving an honorary degree from Princeton ("Day of the Locusts") and a gospel song about angel statues watching a city street ("Three Angels").

In that context, a song about a spurned lover dreaming of a bucolic existence in Utah seems almost normal. The most well-known songs from *New Morning* these days are "If Not for You," thanks to its inclusion on George Harrison's *All Things Must Pass*, and "The Man in Me," thanks to its inclusion in *The Big Lebowski*. "Sign on the Window" is the album's finest song by a pretty good margin, the one where the LP's musical wanderlust pays the greatest dividends.

Many Dylan fans hear "Sign on the Window" as the man's longing for the simple life, mostly based on the touching last verse about fishing in Utah with a new wife and a brood of children. That interpretation overlooks the first two verses and the bridge, which set the song up firmly in Bob's canon of love-gone-wrong songs.

Whatever interpretation you take, one thing that is for sure is that this underrated gem features some lovely music. Dylan's piano playing is the highlight throughout, and the short instrumental break featuring Al Kooper's organ, achieving a pipe-like effect, is awful nice. Throw in the fact that the forlorn melody hits all the right emotional notes, and you've got a song that needn't have uttered a word to capture attention. Kooper apparently wanted to add strings to the whole affair, but Bob left the song as is, and you can't blame his decision one bit.

Dylan's narrator spends the first verse relating all of the indications flashing in front of him that his current relationship may not be in the best shape, signs that alternately say "Lonely," "No Company Allowed,"

"Y' Don't Own Me," and "Three's a Crowd." Short of a sign saying "Beat It, Pal," it can't get much more obvious than that.

The second verse follows with the reason for all these message-bearing signs. It seems his ex has moved on with a new guy and high-tailed it to the West Coast, leaving him in their wake. Dylan compares the girl's fitful nature to the moon, only the moon might be easier for him to understand or predict.

In the bridge, ominous precipitation fills his surroundings, even as the sweet musical interlude seems to act as a rainbow, at the end of which the narrator begins to realize what's important to him. All of these experiences lead up to his overwhelming urge to start a family.

The other way to look at this song is that, this being Dylan, the three verses are all different stories and not related to one another. Still, the linear reading of the storyline is the most affecting. His daydreaming for the family life seems less like an attainable goal than a pleasant diversion used to avoid harsh reality. He might as well be dreaming about settling down with Snow White and the Seven Dwarfs for how realistic his hopes are.

The fact that Dylan had kids of his own by the time the song was released might lead one to the more sentimental reading. Yet what makes "Sign on the Window" such an emotional grabber and one of the most unheralded songs in Bob's career is the sad possibility that the narrator's ideal domestic life may be nothing more than a pipe dream.

51. "Where Are You Tonight? (Journey through Dark Heat)" (from Street Legal, 1978)

One of the main reasons that critics piled on Bob Dylan for his 1978 album *Street Legal* was that they felt that his songs were a poor fit for the type of radio-ready, slick studio sound that he was attempting to cultivate. These critics were obviously comparing Dylan to what he had done before, when comparing him to other songwriters in the rock and roll arena might have been more instructive.

When a song like "Where Are You Tonight? (Journey through Dark Heat)" is analyzed in terms of the other rock songs being released circa 1978, there is really no comparison. Nobody else was putting such fascinatingly unwieldy narratives into the typical verse-verse-chorus structure of rock songs at that point. What Dylan was doing, as usual, was pretty novel, and it's not surprising that it caught people off guard.

Dylan has written seemingly a million of these wild and woolly questing tales, especially in his later, post-born-again period. They are often non-linear narratives, with characters seemingly appearing out of nowhere and then just as quickly receding into the darkness, while the narrator makes his weary way on his journey toward redemption or ruin, whichever he might encounter first.

Most other Dylan songs that follow that template are musically very minimal, usually just a blues or ballad motif repeated over and over for the entire course of the song, something along the lines of "Can't Escape from You" or "Standing in the Doorway." Yet "Where Are You Tonight" is a dynamic musical track in a modern format. The tight rhyme scheme invites listeners to sing along, and the soulful beat even might cause a few of them to bob their heads or even dance a bit to the travails of Bob's protagonist.

There is no doubt that the lyrics are fantastic, but they carry only half the weight on the track. Dylan's emotive vocal and the way the lyrics build into punchy little crescendos at the end of each line, with the backing vocalists coming in for added impact, also deserve the credit, as does Billy Cross's stinging guitar licks, which drive home the emotion. With all of these other positive forces in place, the shaggy-dog tale that Bob tells here becomes even more captivating than it otherwise might have been.

The music also adds just the right bit of after-hours allure to the tale. Never has a subtitle ("Journey through Dark Heat") been more accurate, because Dylan's narrator spends most of the song in the dark and in heat, literally and figuratively in both cases. His nocturnal sojourn leads him to some pretty shady alleys and some even shadier realizations about what his life has become. Knowing that his only salvation is his former love and that she is now out of his reach, "drifting like a satellite," he enters the night in dogged pursuit only to be constantly thrown off course.

The first lines of the song sound like they could have come from one of the story songs off *Desire*, so cinematic is it in setting the scene: "There's a long-distance train rolling through the rain / Tears on the letter that I write." Into this shadow world the narrator wanders, a world so much like Hades that one wonders when he'll tip the ferry-man.

It's a world of sensory overload, full of strippers and brawls and crying babies and escaped demons. It's almost too much to take: "The truth was obscure, too profound and too pure / To live it you had to explode." Yet he presses on, enduring some memorable encounters along the way: "She could feel my despair as I climbed up her hair / And discovered her invisible self."

That he endures all of these distractions surprises him, but it's an empty victory, as he sings in the closing lines, "I can't believe it, I can't believe I'm alive / But without you it doesn't seem right." We leave the narrator suspended in his journey, eternally searching and never find-ing. Yet, for the listener, the journey through dark heat is both exhilar-ating and cathartic.

"Where Are You Tonight? (Journey through Dark Heat)" finds Dy-lan invigorated by the conventions of the rock and soul idioms the song inhabits rather than being constrained by them. It proved he could play the same game as everybody else, even if he was still in a slightly different league.

50. "When the Ship Comes In" (from *The Times They Are A-Changin'*, 1964)

It's never a good idea to get on the bad side of a great songwriter. They'll always have the bully pulpit, they'll always get the last word, and they'll use that word to eviscerate you.

Some hotel clerk allegedly denied Bob Dylan a hotel room back in 1963 based on his unkempt appearance, and only Joan Baez's vouching for him got him in the door. Dylan spent his time in that hotel room writing "When the Ship Comes In," a song about the vengeance that will surely be visited upon those "foes" who aren't on the right side of the cultural divide.

"When the Ship Comes In" is just one more piece of evidence why *The Times They Are A-Changin'* is on the very short list of albums in contention to be considered the very best in Bob's catalog. As thrilling a breakthrough as *The Freewheelin' Bob Dylan* was just a year before, *Times*, released at the start of 1964, left it behind in terms of ambition, consistency, craftsmanship, and depth.

It's a very sober album; none of the comic songs or talkin' blues that made it onto *The Freewheelin' Bob Dylan* made the cut. It would be the last of Dylan's overt protest albums, so it's almost like he had to include a treatise on every injustice within sight before he stepped away from it all. Indeed, "When the Ship Comes In" envisions a time when the good guys win and songs like "The Lonesome Death of Hattie Carroll" or "Only a Pawn in Their Game" wouldn't even be relevant.

In addition to the hotel incident, Bob was inspired by his exposure to Bertolt Brecht and Kurt Weill's *The Threepenny Opera*, in particular the song "Pirate Jenny." Jenny works doing menial tasks at an inn and imagines revenge visited upon the snobbish guests who treat her like garbage. This revenge is initiated by a ship known as the Black Freighter. When it comes ashore, the crew, at Jenny's behest, kills every last one of her tormentors in unmerciful fashion.

Dylan spoke in *Chronicles Volume One* about how eye-opening it was to hear Brecht's, the lyricist of the duo, unforgiving yet truthful depictions of humanity, and he mentioned "Pirate Jenny" in specific. "This piece left you flat on your back and it demanded to be taken seriously. It lingered. Woody had never written a song like that," he wrote. "It wasn't a protest or topical song and there was no love for people in it."[11]

It's notable that Bob wasn't ready to commit to such an unsparing view in his own work. "When the Ship Comes In" doesn't go in for such blatant brutality, instead preferring to paint its narrative as the inevitable and just outcome of an eternal struggle. Still, his willingness to be influenced by more than just folk, country, and blues played a big role in his development as a songwriter and helps to explain why *The Times They Are A-Changin'* was so stunningly accomplished despite being the work of a twenty-two-year-old.

Dylan actually conceals the conflict in the song until the very end, spending the first several verses detailing every triumphant aspect of the ship's arrival, which is why "When the Ship Comes In" feels uplifting and not bitter. In anticipation of this momentous occasion, not only do fish and seagulls ease the way, but the sun and rocks and sand play their part as well. It's as if the whole universe is lining up to assure that this ship's destiny be fulfilled.

In the final verse, Dylan finally gets around to mentioning the ship's purpose: The eradication of its enemies, which, based on the glowing terms with which the ship is described, would seem to be the enemies of all that is good and decent. These poor souls will be caught unaware when the vessel disembarks and brings its justice down upon them, leaving them in the same figurative boat as some of the Bible's greatest scourges.

Dylan leaves the identity of these enemies unnamed, thereby rendering "When the Ship Comes In" a pretty malleable anthem. Whenever the leaders of a cause want to rail against the opposition, the song works real well. That's kind of amazing considering its extremely specific origins.

In "Pirate Jenny," the title character sings, "You'll never guess to who you're talkin'." That hotel clerk who insulted Bob Dylan can probably relate to that sentiment, but at least he inspired an amazing song.

49. "Dark Eyes" (from *Empire Burlesque*, 1985)

It was a last-minute addition to *Empire Burlesque*, when Dylan and producer Arthur Baker decided that the album was lacking something that would cut through all of the other, heavily produced material. By placing it at the end of the sequence, Bob was saddling it with some heavy expectations, considering the great closing songs that loom so large in his legend.

He must have known he had something great in "Dark Eyes," something mysterious and alluring, yet somehow painfully lonely. Dylan stated in *Chronicles* that the song was inspired by encountering a prostitute who "had a beautifulness, but not for this kind of world."[12] That statement implies another world to which few have access. It's also the world where Bob is the poet laureate for eternity.

Many critical assessments of *Empire Burlesque* peg "Dark Eyes" as the one song worthy of standing amongst Dylan's classics throughout the years. While it is the finest song on the album, there are several other outstanding tracks to be found on the disc that are often unfairly downgraded because of the '80s-style production.

Taking a closer look at the album, "Tight Connection to My Heart (Has Anybody Seen My Love)" and "I'll Remember You" are good enough to be included on this countdown, while "Emotionally Yours" and "Clean Cut Kid" are excellent songs as well. Yes, there is a lot of *au courant*-for-'85 production on those songs, but it doesn't detract in any way from their quality. (If you're looking for songs on the album where the production was indeed a hindrance, look to "When the Night Comes Falling from the Sky" and "Trust Yourself.")

By contrast, "Dark Eyes" is a return to Bob solo with acoustic guitar and harmonica for the first time in many years, so it has a certain nostalgic value to which many fans and critics can't help but gravitate. The ironic thing is that Dylan chose to use his simplest musical backdrop to deliver the most complex set of lyrics on the entire album.

Dylan's narrator has his feet in two worlds in the song, antagonistic entities that would both like to claim him as their own. The world he prefers is the one "Where life and death are memorized," an interesting phrase that seems to connote empathy that's practically burdensome. He can hear the echoes of this chosen destination in the drum beat of the dead, but his feet remain stubbornly in the terrestrial world with its passionless denizens.

That group includes the people in the first verse whose snobbery is somehow evident just from the way Dylan calls them "gentlemen." These are the same people whose first impulse is to fend for themselves and rationalize it away, but Bob is on to their game: "They tell me revenge is sweet and from where they stand, I'm sure it is."

Yet the narrator's chosen world is not a utopia, more like an Island of Misfit Souls. Their price for entry into this outcast enclave is alienation from the blissfully ignorant masses all around them. The narrator portrays that isolation chillingly in the song's closing line: "A million faces at my feet but all I see are dark eyes."

What Dylan has created here is both a sweeping overview of the cold, insensitive world and a character study of a certain kind of temperament that resists the conformity that such a world demands. He suggests that it's not enough just to know the difference between right and wrong, and maybe knowing that difference isn't really the important part of the equation. What's important is that a person needs to have the courage and conviction to stand up against the prevailing tide, even when that means being ostracized or mocked. It's not easy to "slide" away from popular opinion, as the narrator does, when doing so can feel so downright lonely.

Dylan hangs this tale on a lilting melody, making the narrator sound resigned to his strange existence, as if he's learned to stop worrying and live with one foot in both spheres. How all of this sprang from that chance, brief meeting with that prostitute is a question only Bob can answer, but she must have really touched a nerve in him.

In the end, Dylan's choice to render the song in such stark fashion, without the production filters to spin the meaning, seems to make it almost harrowingly personal. "Dark Eyes" ends up revealing far more about its creator than it does about its inspiration.

48. "Pay in Blood" (from Tempest, 2012)

Bob Dylan may have sung once upon a time about feeling "Like a Rolling Stone," but he never sounded so much like the Rolling Stones than on the fierce and fantastic "Pay in Blood" from Tempest. (We're not counting his faithful renditions of "Brown Sugar" from the 2002–2003 leg of the Never-Ending Tour either.) It's a change-of-pace type of song that actually provides the finest moment on an album full of great ones.

Truth be told, it had been a while since Dylan had given his fans anything close to a pure "rock" song before "Pay in Blood" came down the pike. For the most part, his post-*Time Out of Mind* output has been strictly blues based, even the up-tempo songs. On this track, Bob's rhythm section of Tony Garnier on bass and George Receli on drums echo the Stones' Bill Wyman and Charlie Watts circa *Tattoo You*.

The music strikes just the right tone of toughness to back what is one of the most unrelenting assaults in Dylan's career. Bob has never been shy about taking people to task in song likes "Positively 4th Street" or "Idiot Wind," but those songs usually had an undercurrent of hurt running through them to soften the blow.

There are some past songs, from "Masters of War" to "Ain't Talkin'," where Dylan openly wished harm upon his enemies. Yet these songs were so downbeat in tone that the narrators seemed resigned to the revenge they had to take. In "Pay in Blood," Bob's protagonist seems positively gleeful in the role he'll play in his foes' demise, promising over and over again, "I pay in blood, but not my own."

This is not to say that the narrator is walking on sunshine. His very first lines tell of his sorry state: "Well, I'm grinding my life out, steady and sure / Nothing more wretched than what I must endure." Elsewhere, he speaks of the blows he's survived and the poor hand of cards that he's been dealt in his life.

Yet within the rock setting that the song inhabits, these lines don't sound like anything that this guy can't overcome. Indeed, his single-minded sense of purpose ("This is how I spend my days") is ultimately what the listener takes away from the song, along with Dylan's stunning series of insults and threats to whoever has crossed him.

This guy clearly has a pretty cynical view of the state of the world, a view which manifests itself in trenchant couplets like "Another politician pumping out the piss / Another angry beggar blowing you a kiss." If Dylan had chosen to do so, he likely could have continued in that vein and produced one of his damning societal overviews along the lines of "Foot of Pride" or "Everything Is Broken."

Yet this is more of a precision strike than a broad strafing, even as he never gets too specific about just who has wronged him in such a way to inspire his furious invective. Throughout the course of the song, Dylan's narrator threatens to stone his enemy, bind him in chains, and break his head. How would you like to be on the wrong side of this threat: "I got something in my pocket make your eyeballs swim / I got dogs that will tear you limb from limb." This guy is not messing around.

Even as the narrator is willing to go to such violent and nasty lengths to destroy his enemies, he still paints himself as a holy servant. "I'm sworn to uphold the laws of God," he sings. It smacks of Samuel L. Jackson's *Pulp Fiction* character speechifying about being the righteous messenger of God right before he blows some lowlife away.

The easy interpretation of the song is that politicians are the target of Dylan's nastiness here. If they want respect from him, they've got to earn it: "Show me your moral values first." He also sings, "Our nation must be saved and freed," which would seem to suggest that a purge of the powers that be must take place for such liberation to occur.

Yet it's not necessary to limit "Pay in Blood" with that reading of it; it works just as well if not better when the enemy remains a faceless personification of greed, self-interest, and moral turpitude in general. In that way, even the less cynical listeners in the crowd can simply enjoy the cathartic experience of hearing Dylan eviscerate someone in such merciless and masterful fashion, all while rocking out for the first time in ages.

47. "Stuck Inside of Mobile with the Memphis Blues Again" (from *Blonde on Blonde*, 1966)

"Dylan Goes Electric!" is often hailed as one of the singular moments in rock history, but, when placed under closer inspection, the whole thing is a bit deceptive. There is an implication that goes with that headline which suggests that Bob was playing polarizing, abrasive music, but, at least on record, that wasn't really the truth. Very few of the songs from the three-album period between *Bringing It All Back Home* and *Blonde on Blonde*, which contains "Stuck Inside of Mobile with the Memphis Blues Again," are even what might be called "hard rock" today, and those that loosely fit that category aren't exactly assaults on the earlobes.

In his live shows from that era, it was a slightly different story, as Dylan was challenging his audiences nightly to get on board or get out of the way. Even in these shows, however, it wasn't like he was unleashing an hour's worth of feedback on the audience. In fact, the *No Direction Home* documentary features footage of disgruntled fans at his 1966 British concerts complaining that the music was too commercial. These British fans had already been introduced to blues-based rock, so what Dylan was doing seemed to them more of a capitulation than a revolution.

If anything, the alteration in the subject matter and lyrics from his acoustic period to his electric period was far more game-changing. The musical switch was more obvious on first listen, but Dylan's words were leaps and bounds ahead of anything else that was being released at the time.

The way that Dylan opened up the lyrical possibilities was also far more influential than the sound that he and his various mid-'60s band incarnations were creating. Rock and roll had always been electric music; it was what Bob was putting inside of the music that was opening up new avenues to bands and artists everywhere.

"Stuck Inside of Mobile with the Memphis Blues Again" is an excellent example of the fallacy of Dylan's electric period. It is clear as a bell, at least in terms of the music. It's an elegant track, loping about at a mid-tempo pace with great spacing between the instruments so that every one of Dylan's words gets its desired attention. The guitars just prance about, bouncing off Al Kooper's chirping organ, without any force behind them. The music is not the least bit abrasive; it's not even aggressive.

That leaves the lyrics to do the heavy lifting in terms of innovation and evocation, and these words are up to that task. It's a fool's game trying to find any kind of natural progression or linear story here. Dylan often gets mocked for the obscure nature of some of his lyrics, but the bizarre tenor of the words in songs like this have a way of emphasizing the intended emotions far better than a straightforward take might do.

In this case, the narrator gets buffeted about between these goofy characters and absurd situations 'til his activities become almost comforting. This isn't a blues that tears out your heart; it's one that leaves you scratching your head. It's not sorrow that Dylan wants to evoke here; it's haplessness, and he accomplishes this via the surreal tone.

That tone also makes the tangible moments far more impactful. Consider Ruthie's memorable line: "Your debutante just knows what you need / But I know what you want." A moment of sincere human interaction likes that grounds the tale just enough to allow Dylan to go off on further flights of fancy.

The narrator's anguish is presented in such weird, wild fashion that it's impossible to take him too seriously. These problems that he faces aren't really problems so much as they are hassles. His final desire to find out the cost he needs to pay "to get out of / Going through all these things twice" is understandable, but even if he does have to endure this stuff again, it's nothing that's going to kill him. It just might annoy him all over again.

Shakespeare, who makes an appearance in the song, spoke about the "slings and arrows of outrageous fortune." What Dylan's protagonist in "Stuck Inside of Mobile with the Memphis Blues Again" is facing is more like the sticks and stones of ridiculous nonsense. When you consider those goings-on in conjunction with the pleasantly jaunty music, the thing that's truly electric about the song is Dylan's miraculous ability to make the mundane sound so momentous.

46. "Simple Twist of Fate" (from *Blood on the Tracks*, 1975)

"Simple Twist of Fate" is one of the songs from the New York sessions of *Blood on the Tracks* that Bob decided not to do over in the subsequent Minnesota sessions, preferring to keep it in the spare acoustic guitar-and-bass format. He must have intuited that this intimate tale needed to be as spare as possible, if only to play up the limitless loneliness of the tale.

Dylan also seems to have had a couple sets of lyrics for the song. Alert fans will notice that the version of the song found on *The Bootleg Series, Vol. 5: Live 1975* loses the parrot from the original *Blood on the Tracks* take and alters the final verse almost completely. Considering how important that final verse is to the song, it just goes to show how fertile Bob's mind is that the song is deeply moving in both incarnations.

Bob has always sloughed off any perceived autobiographical trappings on *Blood on the Tracks*, claiming instead in *Chronicles* that the album was based on a series of short stories by Anton Chekhov.[13] "Simple Twist of Fate" does indeed come off as literary fiction, at least for the first five verses. In the last, a change of perspective, perhaps the most telling on an album full of such contrasting and contradicting points of view, seems to bring the songwriter into the song whether he wants to be there or not.

Up until that point, the song is notable for the way that Dylan holds back details within the narrative until their eventual reveal changes the story significantly. In the first two verses, there is no indication that this is anything other than two lovers on a date. Maybe their hotel of choice isn't a five-star resort, but the passion seems to be intact.

There are some emotional clues, however, most notably the way this encounter seems to bring up heretofore submerged feelings in the man. His attraction to the woman makes him feel alone; he's a bit confused, and the night's heat bears down on him. All this time, her feelings are not even mentioned, which is understandable once the next few verses unspool.

In the third verse, it is revealed that the woman is suddenly out in the night once again while the man is still back in the shoddy hotel. Despite the man's turbulent emotions and nagging inner monologue, she is completely untouched by the whole affair: "And forgot about a simple twist of fate."

After one of the most woeful harmonica solos in the Dylan canon, the scene reverts to the man in the hotel room and the realization that he is now physically alone, matching the way he felt inside earlier. His hollow denials that he's OK are belied by the creeping emptiness inside him, so he begins a futile search for his paramour.

That's when Dylan finally clues us all in on what he's been holding back about this little affair. The man goes to the docks "where the sailors all come in" to find her, hoping that "maybe she'll pick him out again." That evidence suggests that she was simply looking for a one-night stand or was a prostitute. Either way, it shows just how deluded the man was in his search for some kind of meaningful connection.

The final verse is where Dylan steps out of his omniscient narrator role and addresses the audience in the first person. Again, there are a few ways to read this sudden change. One could infer that he was actually telling a tale about himself the whole time. Remember that he seemed to slip when he said, "I remember well" in the second verse; how could he remember it unless he was the one living it?

Another possible interpretation is that he is comparing this hollow affair with his own blown relationship. Indeed, the last verse seems to suggest a deeper connection ("I still believe she was my twin / But I lost the ring") than the events of the previous five. Maybe it's even a little of both: The one-night dalliance could have been his attempt to numb the memories of the more serious relationship and its demise.

In any case, the most misleading thing about the whole story is probably the title. Blaming it all on fate seems like both the narrator and his protagonist ignoring the role their shortcomings played in their lonely destiny. "Simple Twist of Fate" is part short story in song, part harrowing confessional, but it ultimately captivates no matter how you choose to hear it.

45. "It Ain't Me, Babe" (from *Another Side of Bob Dylan*, 1964)

This is a great example of how, even on a song you love and think you know by heart, Dylan can trick you. Given just a perfunctory listen, "It Ain't Me, Babe" comes off as a guy's admission that he's just no damn good, and, as a result, he is chivalrously stepping away from a girl who holds him in lofty status in her mind.

That interpretation of the song comes in part because of the song's chorus, with Dylan shouting out "No, no, no" not too long after the Beatles had shouted out "Yeah, yeah, yeah" as if to emphasize that there was another point of view to be considered. In the midst of the other deeply personal songs on *Another Side of Bob Dylan,* a song about owning up to one's own weaknesses and frailties seems to be right in keeping with the tenor of the LP.

When the Turtles took the song to the U.S. Top 10 in 1965, they seemed practically gleeful in re-telling Dylan's tale. In their hands, "It Ain't Me, Babe" came off sounding like a guy who knew he was the weak link in the relationship and was completely unapologetic about it. That same year, Johnny and June Carter Cash put out a duet of the song which messed with the context in fascinating ways, taking Bob's measured words and shouting them at each other like two former lovers who were each trying to win the blame game.

Dylan's own version of the song features sad guitar arpeggios, some desperate wheezing on the harmonica, and a woebegone vocal, all of which play into the assumption that the song's narrator is sorry that he can't live up to the girl's expectations. It takes a very close listen to hear the subtle bits of sarcasm and veiled accusations peppered throughout the lyrics, which ultimately reveal that maybe those expectations are unreasonable and it's "Babe" who has a lot of explaining to do.

Dissecting the song in verse-by-verse fashion brings some of these buried aspects to the surface. In the first verse, the guy immediately tells her that she should get out of there, that he's not the one she wants or needs. She needs someone "who's never weak but always strong / To protect you an' defend you whether you are right or wrong."

In the sway of the rhyme and the music, none of that seems unfair to ask. In truth, however, it's a little bit much to expect someone to never have a moment of weakness. And, while two people in love would ideally have each other's backs in any dispute against another, the fact that she even brings up that she needs to be defended even when she's wrong suggests that maybe that occurs a little bit too often.

On to verse two, when the unreasonable nature of her demands starts to become more clear. She wants, "Someone to close his eyes for you, someone to close his heart." The first phrase suggests that he should look the other way when she messes up, while a closed heart doesn't seem conducive to a healthy relationship. She also desires, "Someone who would die for you and more," as if dying for her isn't enough. What more does she want?

That becomes clear in the final verse. She wants someone "To gather flowers constantly / And to come each time you call." The pejorative term for someone who does all of those things is "whipped," and it's understandable why this guy would not want to go down that road. That leads up to the coup de grace: "A lover for your life and nothing more." In other words, his own identity will be subsumed if he stays with her.

After hearing ·all of these things that she needs lined up one after another, it becomes clear why he would seek out the comfort of another ("And anyway I'm not alone"). His heart has hardened like she wanted it, only now it has hardened against the possibility of their reconciliation.

What's ingenious is the way that Dylan pulls this off so covertly, subtly turning what seems like a song of confession into a song of accusation. In the end, "It Ain't Me, Babe" seems to be saying that the girl was the one who really needed to change for the relationship to have worked out. Until she makes those changes, it ain't ever gonna be anybody.

44. "Tweeter and the Monkey Man" (from *Traveling Wilburys Vol. I*, 1988)

Although it's not quite a never-ending tour, Bruce Springsteen has been a steady presence on the road for the past several years, playing his legendary three-to-four shows night after night and showing no sign of letting up in terms of either the quality of his recordings or his enthusiasm for live performing.

With all of those dates to play and hours of show to fill, maybe someday he'll play the Traveling Wilburys' "Tweeter and the Monkey Man." It's part playful homage to the Boss, part wisecracking parody of him. Give some of the credit to Jeff Lynne's production and the Wilburys' great backing vocals, which really play up the drama. Ultimately, it's Bob's cleverness which helps the song transcend all of its references and in-jokes to become not just a good riff on the Boss, but also a truly marvelous Dylan song.

As rock supergroups go, the Wilburys, consisting of George Harrison, Tom Petty, Roy Orbison, Jeff Lynne, and Dylan, are pretty much the gold standard, in terms of the star quality of their members and the quality of their output together. Their debut album in '88 arrived during a short period of time that also produced the smashing successes of Harrison's *Cloud Nine* and Petty's *Full Moon Fever*. All three featured

Lynne's indispensable, rootsy production, so that it seemed practically every song on rock radio around that time had a "Wilbury Twist" to it.

Although the album and its follow-up, 1990's *Volume Three* (wink, wink), were true collaborative efforts, Dylan seems to be the one guy who had leeway to take the lead on the songs he sang, turning the others into his backing group. The copyrights of the three songs on which he sang lead on the first album ("Dirty World," "Congratulations," and "Tweeter and the Monkey Man") were all held by Special Rider Music, Bob's publishing company, indicating that he did the bulk, if not all, of the writing.

Jersey City (Where else?) is the setting for the wacky cast of characters to play out the melodrama of "Tweeter and the Monkey Man." There's the Monkey Man (a first cousin of the Magic Rat from Springsteen's "Jungleland," perhaps) and Tweeter, a pair of hustlers whose moneymaking schemes distract everyone from some interesting secrets. They're joined by Jan, the woman drawn to the Monkey Man's criminal charm, much to the chagrin of her undercover cop husband. It's a love quadrangle that you know is going to go bad in the end; it's just a matter of when and how spectacularly.

Dylan sprinkles in shout-outs to Bruce classics throughout, like "Mansion on the Hill," "Thunder Road," and a few others. There's even a great line that you would swear Bruce penned himself: "In Jersey everything's legal as long as you don't get caught."

Yet he also takes a stock Springsteen set up and makes it much messier with the implication of Tweeter's complicated sexuality ("I knew him long before he ever became a Jersey Girl"). It's as if he's insinuating that, aside from all the film noir touches and thrilling shoot-outs, the real truth about the criminal underworld is far less anthemic than *Born to Run* would have you believe.

The ultimate fate of these two jokers is left up in the air; the last we see of them, "The Monkey Man was on the river bridge using Tweeter as a shield," not exactly the chivalrous actions of Springsteenian blood brothers. The narrator only gives us a hasty epilogue on his way out of town.

Why Dylan felt the need to poke fun at the Boss is hard to say. Bruce had long ceased writing such street operas by the time the Wilburys put this song out. And, from all accounts, the two men are good friends.

In a way, it's an honor, since it puts Springsteen in the same class as John Lennon in terms of artists who were parodied by Bob, pretty good company. (Of course, one-hit wonder Bobbie Gentry, whose "Ode to Billie Joe" was skewered by "Clothes Line Saga" from *The Basement Tapes*, also belongs to that exclusive club.) The song was good-natured in spirit anyway; it's not like he wrote "How Do You Sleep?" at the Boss.

Whatever the reason for its creation, it stands as the best of a small but impressive group of songs Dylan performed as a Wilbury. You don't need to know one iota of the Bruce Springsteen catalog to enjoy "Tweeter and the Monkey Man." If you do though, you'll probably find yourself chuckling in all the right places.

43. "Workingman's Blues #2" (from *Modern Times*, 2006)

If an artist labels something as "#2," chances are it's because there's an original floating around somewhere. Knowing Dylan's affinity for and encyclopedic knowledge of old blues music, it's not surprising that the antecedent for "Workingman's Blues #2" was "Workingman's Blues," an early '30s recording by St. Louis bluesman Charley Jordan.

The similarities between the two songs pretty much end with the theme suggested by the title. Jordan's song is a pretty standard lament for the pitfalls that can befall a working man, which, in his rendering, include the women who rob those working men of the money they've earned for their labor. Dylan's song has the same narrow focus albeit with a broader scope. His lyrical twists and turns eventually lead back to his central point, which is that laborers get the worst of it time and time again.

The music for "Workingman's Blues #2," one of the highlights of 2006's *Modern Times*, is unabashedly lovely. It has a fine melody, and the gorgeous opening instrumental section, where the acoustic guitar plays off the piano (another example of Bob's excellence on the ivories), really sets the stage for what's to come. Drummer George Receli does a great job shifting from the lulling rhythm of the verses into the snare-heavy, marching beat of the refrains. The contrast created there really makes the choruses pop.

Taken together, the musical elements create a moving combination of wonder and melancholy. That's just what the song needs, because there is real tenderness at work here in Bob's tale. In many ways,

"Workingman's Blues #2" is not dissimilar to one of his rambling, no-madic songs, one where the narrator is beset on all sides by ignominies both major and minor. Yet hanging over it all is the specter of the character's unemployment, which has essentially stolen his identity and self-worth, leaving him drifting both literally and figuratively for a sense of purpose.

In the first verse, the narrator contrasts a scene of bucolic beauty ("There's an evenin' haze settlin' over town / Starlight by the edge of the creek") with harsh realities of the working man's marginalization in society. In lesser hands, a line like "The buyin' power of the proletariat's gone down" could have come off as the talking point of a lecture. By placing it in the mouth of this put-upon character, Dylan gets across how macroeconomic factors can combine to wreak havoc on the fortunes of one random individual.

Throughout the song, Dylan cleverly spaces out the harsher aspects of this character's story to keep the song from feeling too much like medicine. This guy keeps getting lost in his memories and entreating his beloved in an effort to find distraction. Every once in a while, however, reality is unavoidable for him. The tangible feeling evoked by the lines "Just sitting here trying to keep the hunger from / Creeping its way into my gut" is powerful stuff.

In the final verse, the narrator delivers his most telling put-down of the entitled people who make decisions affecting his life without ever standing in his shoes: "Some people never worked a day in their life / Don't know what work even means." In the chorus, he imagines a day when he'll need his work boots and shoes once more, before explaining the choice that anyone put in similarly dire straits would have to make: "You can hang back or fight your best on the front lines." The resiliency of the narrator is commendable, yet that alone can't promise him a happy ending.

The album that contains this song may be titled *Modern Times*, but there is an antiquated feeling to many of the recordings on it, both in terms of the music and the language that Dylan uses. Even though the songs may not have sounded like the products of the latest studio tech-nology, they still sounded unmistakably vital. This is in part due to the skill of the musicians, but it's mostly because the concerns raised by Dylan, in typically roundabout fashion, have a habit of reoccurring through time so that they're never really out of date.

As a matter of fact, in the years that have passed since the song was released back in 2006, the plight of the character depicted in the song has become even more relevant and more serious. The sweet musical accompaniment may fool you, as may the diversionary tactics in the lyrics. Make no mistake though: "Workingman's Blues #2" is as much a protest song as "Masters of War."

42. "Black Diamond Bay" (from *Desire*, 1976)

Twist endings most commonly occur within the realm of motion pictures. If it's done well, a shocking climax can raise an otherwise good movie into the ranks of a classic. If executed poorly, it can render everything that happened before it almost incomprehensible. Think of the films of M. Night Shyamalan, and you'll get an idea of both of those extremes.

In the world of popular music, it's a little bit rarer to have twist endings, although they do exist. It's tough to pull off within a song, perhaps because a song gives the writer precious little time to set up the story and nudge the listener's expectations before pulling the rug out.

The Beatles' "Norwegian Wood (This Bird Has Flown)," a song Dylan slyly parodied in "Fourth Time Around," has a great little twist at the end when a romantic interlude ends with an act of arson. Bread's "Diary" ends with a heartbreaking twist when it is revealed that the flowery diary entries that singer David Gates has been reading have not been written about him but rather about his lover's new man.

Those are just a few examples of the precious few good ones out there. Many more twists in songs are ham-fisted and ineffective. "Black Diamond Bay," one of the intricate story songs that populate *Desire*, has a twist so subtle that you might miss it if you're not paying attention. The great thing about the song, one of several on that 1976 Dylan album that clearly bear the influence of co-writer Jacques Levy, is that it's still pretty dazzling even if you do miss the twist.

The denizens of "Black Diamond Bay" all seem to have secrets hanging over them as thick as the island fog. They are clearly connected to each other, but Dylan and Levy don't spell out how. One can guess by their actions: A glance here, a word there. The kicker is that none of these interactions matter because these people are doomed to perish in an oncoming earthquake, although their souls seem to have been damned a long time ago.

Dylan brings natural disaster upon these people slowly. It begins harmlessly enough, when the "moon fades away." Then the storm clouds arrive and the wind sets the trees a-swaying. Once the power goes out and the cranes hustle out of there, it's abundantly clear that there is no hope. Of the main characters, the Greek hangs himself, the woman in the Panama hat sheds a single tear, and the tiny man and the soldier, well, suffice it to say they make the most of their final moments.

For those of you new to the song, this would be the time to say SPOILER ALERT! Just when you're expecting to hear about the aftermath, the scene suddenly shifts, and the narrator speaks of himself in the first person for the first time. It seems he is watching the news and hears Walter Cronkite tell of an earthquake that wiped out an island, leaving nothing but a Panama hat and Greek shoes. The guy can't summon up any type of grief though: "Seems like every time you turn around / There's another hard-luck story that you're gonna hear."

And there's your twist. The closest thing to which it can be compared is the last scene of the '80s TV show *St. Elsewhere*, where it is revealed that the entire series was dreamed up by an autistic boy looking into a snow globe. Yet this twist is also a sly commentary on the way that everyone gets wrapped up in the problems of their own lives and thinks that their suffering is unique, when nothing could be further from the truth.

There are parallels between the song and "Tempest," Dylan's take on the Titanic disaster. In both cases, the song visits people at their ultimate moment of truth, a moment in which true character is revealed. The motives of the players on the stage of "Black Diamond Bay" may be cloudy, but the internal malaise that unites them all is something that not even the earthquake can shake loose. The brief snapshot Dylan provides of the guy in the last verse suggests that he's got the same kind of emptiness dogging him, providing the connection to the doomed island's denizens that he's too blind to see.

That SPOILER ALERT ends now, because it's no spoiler to say that "Black Diamond Bay" is one of the most unheralded classics Dylan, with a big assist from Levy, has ever produced.

41. "Ain't Talkin'" (from *Modern Times*, 2006)

Bob Dylan's fascination with the Western, and the themes encompassed within that distinctly American genre of film, has been a part of his career almost since the beginning, inspiring some of his finest work. All of his previous forays into this world of hard men and the violence that they do come to their thrilling culmination in "Ain't Talkin'," the mammoth closing track off *Modern Times*.

Dylan once got the chance to star in a Western in 1973's *Pat Garrett & Billy the Kid*, playing Alias, an enigmatic ally to Kris Kristofferson's Billy. He wrote the soundtrack to the movie as well, the most memorable product of that being "Knockin' on Heaven's Door," a simple but moving lament of a dying gunfighter that has since become one of his most well-loved songs. The doomed man in the song asks his mom to bury his guns along with him, regretting his violent ways in the final hour.

By the time Dylan got around to writing "Ain't Talkin'," such noble, romantic notions of deathbed regrets are nowhere to be found. His character is merciless, hell-bent on revenge, and not the least bit regretful about any of the damage he's planning to do.

If there is a comparison to a film hero, or, more accurately, anti-hero, to be made, it's with Clint Eastwood's Man-with-No-Name character from his classic '60s spaghetti Westerns. Eastwood's character wreaked havoc on just about everything in his path in those movies, killing a lot of bad men, serving deadly comeuppance to his tormentors in each film's climax, and then splitting town.

A similar kind of man walks through the world of Bob's song. Maybe this guy shows his scars a bit more and meditates on the life he is living more than Clint, a man of few words in his films, ever did. Dylan may have titled the song "Ain't Talkin'," yet his narrator goes rambling on for nine verses and refrains.

Nonetheless, he uses that time to depict a landscape every bit as ruthless as the ones that Clint passed through. If anything, Dylan's character has a bleaker outlook, since he is riding on the road leading to the end of the world. Yet he has clearly made his peace with the necessity of his journey through this hellish place.

The anti-hero in "Ain't Talkin'" is set on his journey by an act of senseless, cowardly violence upon him: "Someone hit me from behind."

That this blow comes as he has his guard down in a peaceful area where one would expect sanctuary only steels his resolve for revenge even more.

Dylan alternates throughout the song between the mundane details of his ride (dry lips, sick mule, blind horse) and contemplation on what it means to have faith in such a harrowing world. He suggests that typical religion is useless in this setting. No altars are to be found here, and "the gardener," a seeming reference to Jesus Christ, "is gone." Unlike in "Knockin' on Heaven's Door," even his mother can't help this guy to eject the evil spirits that dwell within him.

That's not to say, however, that he's without morals. "I practice a faith that's been long-abandoned," he sings, referring to a violent code which his allies, who seem to be nowhere in sight, also uphold. Revenge is the basis of this code, as Dylan spells out mercilessly: "If I catch my enemies ever sleepin' / I'll slaughter 'em where they lie."

.The pain he feels is spelled out vividly in Dylan's descriptions, most memorable of these the "toothache in my heel." Still, since his enemies include not just those specific people who have wronged him but also a greater "they" who cause misery to the world at large, he has a lot of work to do.

The Eastwood comparison is interesting because Clint's ultimate statement on the Western came with *Unforgiven*, which acknowledges the toll such violence takes on a man's soul. Dylan's character in "Ain't Talkin'" wearily accepts that toll as the price of vengeance and makes his deadly choices without reservation.

The last thing one hears on the song is the band's instruments coming together in a heavenly flourish, quite the contrast to the downbeat music that has preceded it. It's a counterintuitive climax, suggesting that the main character has found salvation instead of damnation. That ending somehow befits "Ain't Talkin'," a Western in song where the cowboy rides off into the apocalypse at the end of the film instead of the sunset.

40. "Can You Please Crawl Out Your Window?" (from *Biograph*, 1985)

Accusatory songs were a huge part of Dylan's repertoire in the mid-'60s. Unlike the protest songs, which were directed at causes or people who were representative of those causes, the enemies in the electric songs were obviously people with whom the songwriter had crossed paths and whose actions may have had personal implications on his life. Although their identities always remained well concealed, it was clear from the indignation and passion that burbled up in Bob's voice when he sang them that he was writing what he knew.

Songs like "Like a Rolling Stone" and "Positively 4th Street" could be nasty and unmerciful in the way that they dissected the characters they were addressing, yet they connected with people because Dylan always made it clear that what was driving these tirades was his own disappointment and hurt. He wasn't being nasty just for the heck of it.

On "Can You Please Crawl Out Your Window?" those leavening qualities are harder to spot because of the black humor of the song's lyrics. Maybe that's why the song didn't break out in the same way as those others, but its lack of commercial success doesn't lessen Dylan's achievement here because this is songwriting of the highest degree of difficulty pulled off with no signs of strain.

Dylan tried to find the right tone for the song throughout most of 1965 to no avail. It wasn't until the Hawks (who would become The Band) took a crack at it that it came to life. Against a ticking-clock beat, Garth Hudson's carnival organ swirls, Richard Manuel's honky-tonk piano rolls, and Robbie Robertson's dirty guitar licks come together in bizarrely satisfying ways, while Dylan lobs his lyrics about like hand grenades.

It can be argued that maybe it all turned out a bit too unruly, since U.S. radio turned a deaf ear to the single; it reached only number fifty-eight on the Billboard charts (it did hit the Top 20 in Great Britain). It has lived on just fine in the Dylan legend, however, as one of those rarities that has every bit as much going for it as the evergreens. In the case of "Can You Please Crawl Out Your Window?" the standout qualities on display are its songwriter's excitingly reckless way with the English language, his devilish sense of humor, and the remorseless application of those skills against a pair of hapless targets.

The tale is told by a narrator who castigates a girl reluctant to leave her Svengali-like boyfriend. Whether he wants a one-night stand or something more long lasting isn't made clear, although one gets the feeling that his current poor opinion of the girl would prevent any permanent relationship. Whatever the case, he just wants the girl to make what, in his mind, is the right choice and to jump right out the window into his waiting arms. To accomplish this, he lists all the ways in which this other guy controls her and plays a power trip.

The second verse is just one shining example of Dylan's thrillingly deft manipulation of his vocabulary, which allows him to take down both of the offenders in the song. First he goes after the other guy: "With his businesslike anger and his bloodhounds that kneel / If he needs a third eye he just grows it." All of this dude's affectations of power are used to mask the creeping insecurity inside him.

As a result, this control freak uses the girl to make him feel better about himself: "He just needs you to talk or to hand him his chalk / Or to pick it up after he throws it." Through the bile, one can hear the narrator's ironic admiration for his competition for the girl's affections. Maybe he secretly wishes he had that kind of hold over her as well.

Still, he mocks the way that she feels addicted to this current boyfriend: "How can you say he will haunt you? / You can go back to him any time that you want to." This boiling frustration in the narrator connects the song to Dylan's more serious accusatory tracks (he even quotes "Positively 4th Street" in the song's closing moments to drive the point home). Even in a song so seemingly lighthearted, the core of "Can You Please Crawl Out Your Window?" is filled with deep disappointment for a girl so misguided that she can't even see the window let alone try to escape from it.

39. "Senor (Tales of Yankee Power)" (from *Street Legal*, 1978)

One of the things that Dylan has always been able to do better than just about anybody is to convey the underlying emotions of the characters in his songs even when their motivations are murky and their actions are hard to follow. No song exemplifies that ability better than "Senor (Tales of Yankee Power)," one of those songs that listeners can inherently understand even as they might find it difficult to explain to anybody else.

Street Legal has been vilified unfairly by critics since its release in 1978, but "Senor" usually escapes unscathed from those condemnations. While several other songs from that album are woefully underrated and have made this list, it is fair to say that this song is the finest from that LP.

As a matter of fact, with its mystical trappings and the strange story at its heart, it feels like it easily could have come off Dylan's preceding album, 1976's *Desire*. While it's not wrapped up quite as tightly as some of the intricately designed story songs on *Desire*, it somehow feels more related to those songs than it does to some of the more personal plaints that are found on *Street Legal*.

Dylan himself once gave a rambling monologue in a 1978 concert explaining the song's inspiration. He told an ominous tale about a chance encounter on a train near the Mexican border with an ancient man who was wearing only a blanket and whose eyes were "burning out," in Bob's words. Dylan's typically counterintuitive reaction: "I said, 'Well, this is the man I want to talk to.'"[14]

A tale like that is part of the reason that Dylan can pull off songs like "Senor" with such conviction. He could have fabricated that whole story for the sake of the show, but it doesn't really matter. By maintaining such privacy and living such a mysterious life away from the stage and recording studio, Bob practically encourages listeners to indulge in the fantastic notion that he has lived within the songs he has written, even one as far out there as "Senor."

That old man Dylan claims to have met seems to have inspired the character "Senor," who serves as the narrator's right-hand man and the sounding board for all his questions and concerns. The narrator desperately needs some assistance because he has been knocked down, physically and spiritually. As such, he seeks help from his amigo not only to get up but also to do some damage once he's standing again.

The verses convey the main thrust of the narrative. The two protagonists are in the midst of a ride to an unknown destination ("Lincoln County Road or Armageddon"), a journey that may just be part of an endless circle of hell for the narrator ("Seems like I been down this way before"). They make a pit stop, which is when the narrator starts barraging Senor with questions.

He feels the pressure building up inside him in this dead-end joint and is ready to strike, but he cautiously waits for Senor's approval. At song's end, he seems poised to go ahead with or without his buddy: "Can you tell me what we're waiting for, Senor?"

In the two bridges, the narrator takes time to contemplate the recent past that has brought them to this crossroads. The first bridge suggests that he's searching for a woman, but the second bridge implies generalized chaos, with the narrator naked and prostrate, a ship of fools floating into oblivion, and a gypsy implying that none of this torment can be easily explained away: "Son, this ain't a dream no more, it's the real thing."

The lyrics slowly make their way toward an impending confrontation, and the musical backing captures the creeping dread brilliantly. The sultry solos of saxophonist Steve Douglas and guitarist Billy Cross are pitch-perfect, and the whole recording is exotic but in a quietly unsettling way. *Street Legal* was knocked for its poor sound quality when it came out, but it's hard to find anything wrong with the recording of this song based on current evidence.

The narrator and Senor are abandoned by the songwriter on the precipice of their fate; we listeners get to fill in the blanks. That's as it should be, because what happens to them isn't as important as the inner turmoil that led them to this point. Thanks to Dylan, it's easy to identify with "Senor (Tales of Yankee Power)" without having to walk in such dusty, doomed boots.

38. "Foot of Pride" (from *The Bootleg Series, Vol. 1–3: Rare & Unreleased 1961–1991*, 1991)

There's nothing quite as exciting as when Bob Dylan gets fed up. It seems like he lets the wrongs and misdeeds that he sees all around him build up until the breaking point is reached. That's when he has to regurgitate all the bile accreted inside of him in the most comprehensive fashion possible in songs like "Foot of Pride."

Infidels will always be the great what-if album in the Dylan catalog. The 1983 release included some interesting mid-tempo tracks ("Jokerman," "I and I," and "License to Kill") that are a bit too unreachable to be classics, a few charming but ineffectual ballads ("Sweetheart like You" and "Don't Fall Apart on Me Tonight"), and a couple overdone rockers ("Union Sundown" and "Neighborhood Bully") with social commentary a shade or two too blunt. There isn't anything earthshaking to be found among the eight songs on the LP.

Left on the cutting-room floor: "Blind Willie McTell" and "Foot of Pride," two of the finest songs that Dylan ever wrote. They are both longish songs and would have required pruning some of the other material so that they could take up space on *Infidels*, but they certainly were worth that sacrifice. Bob's choice to leave them off is confounding yet typical of a guy who truly cares not what others might think of his process.

Luckily, the two songs were unearthed once first volumes of *The Bootleg Series* were released in 1991, giving fans a chance to hear what they had missed. When songs like "Foot of Pride," "Blind Willie McTell," and some other great ones were taken into account, the early '80s, long considered a fallow part of Dylan's career, seemed like an awfully productive period after all.

"Foot of Pride" takes its title from the Thirty-Sixth Psalm, and while there are certainly biblical allusions throughout the song and Old Testament overtones to Dylan's promise that vengeance will come upon the song's wrongdoers, it shouldn't be viewed as a strictly religious song. After all, it's not necessarily a religious imperative to expect people to be decent and not prey upon each other. Even though this song presents a world where such nobler intentions are ignored, Dylan sings it exultantly, as if he knows for sure that everybody is going to get exactly what they deserve, both for good and bad, even if it takes the afterlife for that to happen.

Pride is just one of the many transgressions committed in this litany of foul play. Greed is pretty high on the list as well, exhibited by obvious suspects like businessmen as well as seemingly well-meaning institutions like churches and colleges. (Dylan's assault on higher education isn't a new one; he made snide cracks about college all the way back on "Like a Rolling Stone" and spoke about his unease with university muckety-mucks on "Day of the Locusts.") In addition, lack of self-awareness may not technically be a sin, but Bob shows little sympathy for those who fall blindly for the schemes of the wicked.

Yet Dylan keeps this all from seeming like a hectoring assault that you might expect coming from a bellowing preacher on Sunday morning television. He does this by interspersing the gritty tales of the wicked, like ruthless businessman Red and his tempting yet ultimately destructive piece of arm candy named Delilah. These characters practically vibrate with their awful humanity, proving to be just as fascinating as they are toxic.

This is an endlessly quotable song because Dylan breathlessly stuffs each line with clever puns ("But he drinks, and drinks can be fixed") and thought-provoking asides ("They kill babies in the crib and say only the good die young"). Overall, there's so much nonsense that must be endured by the righteous that it can be simply overwhelming: "In these times of compassion when conformity's in fashion / Say one more stupid thing to me before the final nail is driven in."

All of it comes packaged in a chunky blues-rock arrangement, bolstered by ace guitarist Mark Knopfler, which clears the way to allow Dylan to run roughshod over all the hypocrisy. "Foot of Pride," which ends with an unspecified "you" (the entire listening audience, perhaps) in a God-forsaken city wiped out by plague, is an amazing display of lyrical dexterity and unrelenting attitude. As complex as Bob's wordplay might be, the points that he makes about the decline and fall of human decency are the simplest of common sense.

37. "Sara" (from *Desire*, 1976)

This much can be said for absolute sure about Sara Dylan's relationship with Bob Dylan. She married him on November 22, 1965, and their divorced was finalized June 29, 1977. The couple had four children together; she also had a daughter from her first marriage who was adopted by Bob when they married.

That stuff is all on the public record. Everything else about her is secondhand information and speculation from dueling biographers. Despite what have probably been numerous lucrative entreaties to do so, the story of her life with Bob and everything subsequent to that remains untold, at least by Sara herself.

As such, she is regarded with fascination by Dylan fans, in part because of all the amazing songs she inspired. It's not just the songs written while they were married, both the happy and the heartbreaking, but also a lot of songs written after the divorce. Whenever he sings one of his songs about lonely men haunted by a past love, men who ruminate on the one who got away, with eloquent remorse, it's tempting to hear Bob's own longing for Sara in them.

It is true that there is no way to prove any of these later-period songs are for sure about Sara. After all, Bob married again after their divorce, and has likely had several other relationships in the thirty-five years or so since his divorce from Sara, so speculating on the identity of his muses for songs is a guessing game at best.

Yet it's easy to make the jump to that conclusion based on the songs that are without a doubt about Sara, songs that were written during the couple's time together. There is "Sad-Eyed Lady of the Lowlands," a towering tribute from *Blonde on Blonde*. There are the tormented songs of discord found on *Blood on the Tracks*, which, Bob's protestations to the contrary, were most likely a veiled reflection on the marriage's implosion.

And, of course, there is "Sara," the most direct of them all, a song that combines sweet memories, glowing words of tribute, and entreaties from Dylan for forgiveness and reconciliation. The story goes that Sara Dylan was actually present at the recording session for the song and watched from the other side of the glass as Bob delivered one of his most heartfelt performances ever, and the vibes from that moment helped to spark a brief period of détente between the two.

It's understandable why Sara would be moved because the song manages to be brilliant in its execution even as it is brazen in its honesty. Although it usually happened the other way around, this is one song where Dylan followed the lead of John Lennon, who fearlessly let his listeners into his personal life in his music, especially when it came to his relationship with Yoko Ono. With "Sara," Bob let all the walls down, and the results were breathtaking.

The verses are given to the memories of their lives together, back when their children were just babies frolicking on a beach, all the way back to when they married and he wrote "Sad-Eyed Lady of the Lowlands" for her. In the refrains, he sings her praises even as he admits his eternal befuddlement at her nature: "So easy to look at, so hard to define."

Those are the things that likely stuck with listeners when the song was first released in 1976, but the subsequent separation is what brings the song into clearer focus. Dylan frames the song around a family visit to the beach, but when he returns to that scene in the final verse, the beach is deserted. That harrowing image of desolation makes sense in the context of the divorce that would take place just a year after the song's release.

With Scarlet Rivera sighing alongside of him on the violin, Dylan's vocal is vulnerable and wounded, the sound of a man knowing he's used up most of his last chances. "Sara" may have been an ultimately futile gesture, but it is the best glimpse we have of the woman who inspired it.

Come to think of it, it might also be the best glimpse of the guy who wrote it.

Dylan sings in one refrain, "Loving you is the one thing I'll never regret." Bob's buddy Willie Nelson once said that "99 percent of the world's lovers are not with their first choice. That's what makes the jukebox play."[15] All evidence points to Sara being Bob's first choice, and, my, oh my, what a jukebox she has inspired.

36. "Tombstone Blues" (from *Highway 61 Revisited*, 1965)

Dylan's conversion to electric rock is somewhat overstated by rock historians simply because many of the songs included on those three mid-'60s "electric" albums (*Bringing It All Back Home*, *Highway 61 Revisited*, and *Blonde on Blonde*) were mid-tempo numbers and the music, on those particular songs, was anything but raucous; it was often downright elegant. "Tombstone Blues," however, lives up to the rowdy reputation of that period and maybe even exceeds it.

"Tombstone Blues" is one of the defining moments of 1965's *Highway 61 Revisited*, an album that suffers somewhat from middle-child syndrome. *Bringing It All Back Home* gets attention as being the first Dylan album to prominently feature electric instruments in rock music settings. *Blonde on Blonde* gets attention because of its sheer ambition, four LP sides full of Dylan running amok, his super-dynamic, inexhaustible talent practically overflowing from the vinyl.

Highway 61 Revisited doesn't have either the historical import of being the first, like *Bringing It All Back Home*, or the hugeness of *Blonde on Blonde*. Yet it's probably the most cohesive listening experience of the three. "Like a Rolling Stone" stands apart a bit as the massive single that it was intended to be, but the other nine songs segue smoothly from frenzied rockers to yearning mid-tempo tracks to "Desolation Row," which seems to sum up everything that has come before it, not just on the album, but in the entire history of the world.

"Tombstone Blues" is an example of how far Dylan had come with his electric music in such a short time. Musically, it's an unkempt, unwieldy battering ram of a blues song. Mike Bloomfield's guitar fills are all weird angles and jagged edges, meant to jolt the listener to attention. The rapid beat kept by Bobby Gregg leaves little time for contemplation, which means that, while you're still scratching your head over one of Dylan's surreal one-liners, another three have flown right by you.

Comparing the song to, say, "Maggie's Farm," from *Bringing It All Back Home*, reveals just how much more smoothly Dylan was able to fit his complex wordplay into the driving music. "Maggie's Farm," a great song no doubt, doesn't sustain its momentum in quite the same way as "Tombstone Blues," which along with the title track to *Highway 61 Revisited*, represents the apotheosis of the full-throttle attacking style that Bob was courting in the mid-'60s. By the time that *Blonde on Blonde* came around, he had mostly abandoned that style; that album's strongest point was its collection of ballads.

Never has a first line been more on-the-money than the opening salvo of "Tombstone Blues": "The sweet pretty things are in bed now of course." After all, the world that Dylan goes on to describe in the song would crush such innocent creatures. It is a world full of hustlers, liars, and all-out nincompoops, yet it's undeniably a rush to the innocent bystanders in the audience. In other words, it's a fun place to visit, but you wouldn't want to live there.

"Tombstone Blues," chock-full of quotable lines and phrases, is also one of the finest examples of Dylan's technique of taking the names of historical figures and mashing them all up in strange contexts and situations. From biblical characters like the King of the Philistines to historical names like Galileo and Jack the Ripper to pop-culture icons like Cecil B. DeMille, all are fair game to be pulled into the chaos of the song. Not only do these names liven up the song and give listeners a little bit of pause when they appear, they also strengthen Bob's point that the sacred and profane are interchangeable; it's all just a matter of perspective.

Dylan eventually brings everything back down to the Earth with his last verse, when the narrator speaks to a "dear lady" directly and confesses his desire to write her a song that would calm her down, what with her brain burdened by "her useless and pointless knowledge." It's a subtle way of saying that the lessons she learned in history books diverge from what matters most anyway, so why dwell on them? All is phony, as the man once said.

This "melody so plain" does anything but calm its listeners, instead inflaming their brains with these weird notions and bizarre circumstances. Somehow, someway, the glorious anarchy of "Tombstone

Blues" ends up bearing a striking resemblance to the truth, especially when Dylan holds up the mirror to it just so.

35. "Subterranean Homesick Blues" (from *Bringing It All Back Home*, 1965)

In a 2011 interview with *Rolling Stone* magazine, Eminem was asked about his ability to write the intricate rhymes that are such a hallmark of his work. The interviewer tested these lyrical skills by giving the rapper the task of building a set of rhymes about the interview itself. The next day, he performed his newly written set of lines, piling phrase after phrase on top of each other until the incoherent became coherent, showing that not only could his mind rifle through millions of words to create rhymes on the spot, but that he could also form from these rhymes an overarching structure that wouldn't collapse. The most amazing thing: When the reporter asked Eminem how long it took him to come up with all of this, he said, "About two minutes."[16]

This type of stream-of-consciousness rapping is often referred to as "freestyling." Many other rappers have similar skills, but they'd have to be on top of their game to approach the verbal wizardry that Bob Dylan showed off way back when on "Subterranean Homesick Blues." The recklessness of the adjoining rhymes suggests that much of the song was done off the top of Bob's head, simply because consciously trying to accomplish this likely would have sounded forced. Yet the song as a whole comes together in riotous fashion. Most listeners need those cue cards from the famous *Don't Look Back* opening just to be able to follow along; for Bob, it was all there in his melon.

"Subterranean Homesick Blues" is one of those landmark tracks in Dylan's history. It was the opening track and first single from *Bringing It All Back Home*, which meant that it was the first evidence of the transformation to electric blues and rock music he was undergoing circa 1965. Clearly, not everyone knew what to make of such a heady track. Although it was the first Top 40 U.S. hit Bob had recorded, it only reached number thirty-nine, not exactly a runaway smash.

Musically, it's a bit of an uneasy mix between the locomotive rhythm and jagged guitar licks, demonstrating that the new sound that he was cultivating, although it packed a punch, still had some way to go before it was airtight. Lyrically, on the other hand, it is one of those rare sets of words that were groundbreaking in their time and still sound vivid and vital in the present time.

What sets the song apart from Dylan's previous output to that point isn't the rat-a-tat scansion, derived in part from Chuck Berry's "Too Much Monkey Business," or the absurdity of the lyrics, which can be found in some of the comedic talking blues songs on *The Freewheelin' Bob Dylan*. What is truly different is the impassive way in which he delivers his stinging narrative.

In the past, Dylan had fearlessly written about the world's darker side, alternately railing against it or empathizing with those oppressed by it. On "Subterranean Homesick Blues," he doesn't judge it or show any emotion about his dystopian worldview; he just reports it, and in so doing, makes it somehow more harrowing even as he cracks wise. It's why the famous video of the song that begins the documentary *Don't Look Back* is so on-point: He drops his knowledge just as he drops those cue cards, then walks away from it all, leaving the listeners and viewers to decide what to do with it.

In the song, the nonsensical bumps right up against the profound. So feel free to get caught up in the rhyming-dictionary wildness of lines like "Don't wear sandals / Try to avoid scandals." Just don't miss the warnings to "Look out, kid" or else you'll end up busted, broke, and on the day shift for the rest of your life. Learn these lessons well, sons and daughters, or else you're doomed to repeat your mistakes: "God knows when, but you're doin' it again."

This is another song that reads like Dylan's own personal *Bartlett's Quotation* book, but there is sneaky substance beyond the one-liners. That substance can easily get lost amidst the loose-limbed ramble of the music and the mischief of the wordplay, but the sum total of those elements is a not-so-subtle warning to his listeners that they always stay vigilant. As revolutionary as it might have been in form, perhaps the most incendiary quality of "Subterranean Homesick Blues" was its creator's indifference about whether his listeners heed that warning or not.

34. "Sugar Baby" (from *"Love and Theft,"* 2001)

Dylan's knack for picking picture-perfect closing songs for his albums was in full force when he tabbed "Sugar Baby" to finish *"Love and Theft."* What makes it such a clever choice is that it's a complete 180-

degree turn from all that came before it. The rest of the album is at turns feisty, playful, ribald, fierce, and defiant; sometimes, all of those moods are struck in a single song.

Yet "Sugar Baby" is the antithesis to all of that. The song is a rumination in the twilight hours on lost love, lost time, and lost happiness. It's as if everything else on the album was a front, albeit a convincing one. With all of these fabrications stripped away, the narrator's true heart is revealed, once the pieces of it are delicately scraped off the floor.

Dylan produced *"Love and Theft"* himself under the Jack Frost pseudonym, but he owes a debt to Daniel Lanois's trademark style on "Sugar Baby." The song has that hazy, shimmering echo that Lanois favors, which is highlighted even more by the spare musical backing. The four-note guitar riffs that frame the song have the feel of inevitability after they are repeated so often, a trenchant musical commentary on the narrator's own inescapable destiny.

It also can't be overstated just how effective Dylan's vocal performance is on the song. His phrasing is incredibly unique here. Certain times he'll drag out the opening syllables of a line only to cram in the remaining words in a rush at the end. Other times, he'll reverse that. It's completely intuitive and yet incredibly engaging.

There is also something to be said for the quality of his voice in the song. It's easy to take potshots at the cragginess of Dylan's late-period vocals, but the truth is that he remains an unparalleled interpretive singer even with his limited range. He manages to project whatever the song requires.

In the case of "Sugar Baby," what he projects is a kind of loneliness that only someone who has spent a lot of time on this planet can possibly feel. At times during the song, it seems like he might not even make it through the next line, so weary does he sound. That's completely apropos of the character he's playing.

The aged sound of his voice also plays into the nature of the relationship that he has with the titular girl. The connotation of the title "Sugar Baby" is that this girl may depend on the narrator for financial support, and there are other subtle suggestions in the lyrics that this is a typical May-December relationship, so it makes sense for Dylan to sound so fatigued.

The narrator seems to take turns addressing the titular girl and speaking to the audience at large about his sad tale. After all, it's clear that "Sugar Baby" is long gone, so his admonitions to her are futile. He envies her innocence and hope, even as he warns her of the day those traits will disappear: "One day you'll open up your eyes and you'll see where we are."

In the opening lines, he manages to both display his jaded wisdom and suggest that such wisdom isn't equal recompense for the sorrow that it brings: "I got my back to the sun 'cause the light is too intense / I can see what everybody in the world is up against." That's a pretty heavy burden to bear, as are the ghosts from his past: "Some of these memories you can learn to live with and some of them you can't."

When the narrator pleads to both the wayward girl and his audience to look for heavenly aid before Gabriel horn's blows to signal the end of all things, you get the feeling that he might as well be talking to himself. As for the refrain, some people might hear nastiness in the line, "Sugar Baby, get on down the line, you ain't got no brains, no how." Another point of view is that the line is representative of a selfless act by this guy, using some meanness to ensure that this girl stays out of his lonely orbit.

After all, considering the despair and desolation that is the narrator's lot in life, absence from him is the only way the girl could ever be truly happy. This final act of mercy is also the last shot at redemption for the narrator of "Sugar Baby," just another in Dylan's long line of sublime final acts.

33. "Brownsville Girl" (from *Knocked Out Loaded*, 1986)

The movie starring Gregory Peck that Dylan references in "Brownsville Girl" is *The Gunfighter*, a 1950 Western parable about a gunfighter whose past as the fastest draw comes back to haunt him when he tries to forge a new future. The narrator in the song keeps getting a sense of déjà vu about the movie, imagining that he's the guy in the film that everybody is looking at funny.

When you consider Dylan circa 1986, you can imagine how he would relate to such a story. He was in the midst of a period when critics were having a field day with his recent work, contending that his songwriting pen wasn't the weapon it once was. Yet "Brownsville Girl" showed that, like a rusty marksman, he could still summon his old skill when threatened. The fact that the song was surrounded by mostly mediocre material on *Knocked Out Loaded* only emphasizes this connection even more.

The run of great albums since *Time Out of Mind* might make some people forget the rocky stretch of LPs Dylan had for about two decades after *Desire* in 1976. Some of these albums, like *Street Legal* and *Empire Burlesque*, have held up much better than their reviews at the time would suggest. Others, like the one-two punch, or lack thereof, of *Knocked Out Loaded* in '86 and *Down in the Groove* in '87, are harder to defend.

As a result, songs like "Brownsville Girl," containing eleven ambitious minutes full of astounding imagination, could be seen in two different lights. On the one hand, they were revelatory in that they showed that the master could still reach back and produce something fantastic. On the other hand, they were equally frustrating to fans who wondered how such brilliance could be surrounded by forgettable stuff all around it.

Co-written by playwright/actor Sam Shepard and originally recorded during the *Empire Burlesque* sessions as "New Danville Girl," "Brownsville Girl," with Dylan's exhortations seconded by cooing female backing vocalists, is a meditation on how fate is not a random twist but rather a consequence of certain key decisions made during one's life. Some people, like Henry Porter's wife Ruby, make choices they think are safe yet leave them stranded in an existence in which they drift through life instead of living it. Others, like the narrator, also pay the price for taking a different tack and "going all the way 'til the wheels fall off and burn."

His price is a life of shifting perspectives and alternate realities, where his past and present intertwine to the point where he isn't sure where or who he is most times. As with so many great Dylan wanderers, he's haunted by a past love even as he's with somebody new.

As this pair rides through the Southwest, they miss out on Henry Porter, who may just be the narrator's alter ego. Eventually, he's left with his life of cinema-going and quasi contentment: "You know I feel pretty good but that ain't sayin' much. I could feel a whole lot better / If you were just here to show me how." The emotional content of lines like this means a whole lot more to the song than the convoluted narrative.

That Gregory Peck movie is to this character what Rosebud was to Kane, a reminder of a time when he still could locate his better self, "long before the stars were torn down." At moments when the regret over his mistakes becomes too much, being shot in the back probably seems like a merciful fate.

In 2010, reports from Hollywood surfaced that a movie script based on "Brownsville Girl" was in the early stages of development, with Brad Pitt attached to play Henry Porter. While his previous screenwriting efforts have been spotty at best, it was somehow dismaying to hear that Dylan wasn't the one writing the screenplay. He tells the shambolic, incongruous, moving tale so well in the song, in part because it feels like he has somehow lived the lives of all of the characters, so who better to bring it to the big screen?

And maybe, if the movie gets made, some ambitious songwriter in the future might start a song with "Well, there was this movie I seen one time / It was confusing as hell and it starred Brad Pitt." Let's just say that every Dylan fan still kicking will be having their own déjà vu when they hear it, remembering when their hero was the fastest song-writing gun in the West.

32. "Blowin' in the Wind" (from *The Freewheelin' Bob Dylan*, 1963)

There are some songs on this countdown that are so monumental that it's difficult to approach them with any kind of meaningful perspective. For example, what kind of trenchant analysis can be delivered when discussing something so profound and wise as "Blowin' in the Wind?" It's nothing less than a litany of life's great mysteries, so how can that possibly be elucidated? The whole point of the song is that those mysteries are unanswerable.

The great folly in discussing this song is to write it off as simple. Indeed, the questions that Dylan asks are simple questions, albeit with notoriously elusive answers. Yet he was the first rock-era songwriter to gather them all together in such a coherent form and make such a powerful statement. What is the limit that must be reached before things change: That's essentially what he was asking. And, once that limit is reached, won't it be too late?

The song is also notable because of the role it played in Dylan's career. Before he even got the chance to record his own version of the song and make it the centerpiece of *The Freewheelin' Bob Dylan* in 1963, the song was already a major sensation. Peter, Paul and Mary became the first in a long line of successful interpreters of Bob's music when their version of "Blowin' in the Wind" hit number two on the pop charts in August 1962.

As a result, "Blowin' in the Wind" was the first most of the world had heard of Bob Dylan. It's difficult to think of any other major artist that has lasted a long time in the upper echelons of the music world whose first well-known song turned out to be the song with which they were ultimately identified. Although it can be argued that "Like a Rolling Stone" is Dylan's signature song, that's probably only true for a rock-based audience. "Blowin' in the Wind" has been translated into every possible genre, thereby putting it in front of the most ears. Considering all that, it's fair to say that more people think of "Blowin'" when they think of Bob Dylan than any other song in his repertoire.

In other words, the guy came out fully formed as a legend, even though some people didn't know what race he was. The legend goes that some black artists thought that Dylan had to be black; otherwise, he couldn't have so insightfully detailed their plight. "Blowin' in the Wind" even inspired Sam Cooke to go from singing about Cupid and Saturday night to promising that "A Change Is Gonna Come."

Moreover, the song changed the rules for what a song presented to a wide audience could be about. When Peter, Paul and Mary brought the song to the public, they presented these eternal questions to teenagers in between "Sugar Shack," "Surfin' U.S.A.," and "Blue Velvet," the song's contemporaries on the charts. One can only imagine how heads must have spun.

"Blowin' in the Wind" is so filled with common sense that it boggles the mind that nobody wrote it before. Dylan often talks about himself, as many songwriters do, as a kind of conduit for the ideas that appear in his brain from some unknown origin. That's a modest approach, but it's probably the only one you can take with such a song. How else could someone like Dylan wrap his head around the fact that he had composed a song like this that would touch so many hearts and minds, something that seems less like it was written and more like it was bestowed upon mankind?

It seems almost blasphemous to have this song, one that is often ranked among the greatest of all time when such things are compiled, ranked below thirty-one others in this list. The justification for this is that "Blowin' in the Wind" is a more humble triumph, in its way, than some of Bob's others. The receding nature of Dylan's acoustic rendering of it suggests that there's nothing too momentous about the song, and it's true that it doesn't have the ambition or force behind it that some of the songs that beat it out on the list do possess.

That said, it is endlessly impressive that Bob was just twenty-one when he wrote "Blowin' in the Wind" and yet still possessed the wherewithal to realize, like Socrates, that the only thing he knew for sure is that he didn't have the answers. How could someone so young come to such an important realization?

The answer, my friend . . .

31. "Most of the Time" (from *Oh Mercy*, 1989)

It can be anything that triggers the memory of a failed relationship, from a location where the two ex-lovers once walked past, to an aroma of a certain perfume or favorite dessert, to some old picture found in a drawer of two smiling faces, faces that don't seem to match up with the anguish-wracked ones that finally said goodbye.

Those who have ever had their hearts broken know that there are long periods of blissful forgetfulness interrupted by stabs of memory that can stop a person in their tracks and take their breath away. Those are the moments at the heart of Bob Dylan's wistful portrait of love's epilogue, "Most of the Time."

Many pop songs have used the tactic of denying feelings as a way of showing just how prevalent those feelings really are. The 1975 10cc smash "I'm Not in Love" told the story of a guy who incessantly denies his love for the girl he's addressing even as the evidence piles up to the contrary. John Waite's 1984 number one "Missing You" is built around denial as well, in that his girl is gone and he insists that he's over her when it's clear that nothing could be further from the truth.

Dylan's song is on the same wavelength but takes a more measured approach than the examples mentioned above. The narrator of "Most of the Time" is putting up a brave face about his current turmoil by listing a litany of all the things that he is able to do even in the absence of his love. Notice that the girl is addressed in the third person throughout, an indication that the guy is talking to friends who are likely bombarding him with well-meaning inquiries about his state of mind and heart.

Yet his honesty keeps getting the best of him, which is why he keeps qualifying his statements of strength and fortitude with "most of the time." That suggests that a small portion of his waking hours is spent living out the opposite of all of those statements, meaning that there are times when he is weak, discontented, afraid of his feelings, simply woeful in general.

Daniel Lanois's production work is simply stellar on this gorgeous track off *Oh Mercy*, really seconding the emotions of the lyrics. Every instrument seems to stagger and moan, barely able to carry on, and yet, much like the narrator, they do. Echoey sound effects seem to present every sound as a strange refraction of itself, as if reality has become forever altered by the girl's departure.

Still the narrator carries on his noble quest to get over her. This effort is a partial success, but when it fails, it's a train wreck. Note the way Dylan's phrasing plays this up: "I don't even notice," he sings, but then he pauses before the two-note bomb drops: "She's gone." Later, "Don't even remember" is sung in deadpan fashion, but the emotion of the memory causes his voice to quiver when he completes the thought: "What her lips felt like on mine."

It's a perfectly pitched vocal performance, coming in the service of plainspoken yet incisive lyrics. Subtle hints to the true state of the narrator are everywhere. It's clear that even the so-called good times that this guy is having, when he's not lost in painful remembrance, aren't all that hot. He can "survive," he can "endure," he's "halfway content." Those phrases don't exactly suggest a portrait of happiness. It's like he's muddling through his existence, handling the psychological aspects of his breakup in his stumbling stride while his insides are torn apart.

There are songs that will wallow in a broken relationship with every single line and word, and many of them are done quite well. Roy Orbison, Dylan's bandmate in the Wilburys, pretty much made a career of them. Yet these songs rely on the outsized nature of the emotions to get their point across and can often come off as overdone.

Dylan is too sharp to allow that to happen. His realistic and fearlessly honest take on the situation makes his song so impactful because it is relatable to those who've gone through similar romantic turbulence themselves. "Most of the Time" is one of Bob's all-time heartbreakers not so much for what it says but for what it tries to hold back, an attempt that is unsuccessful in the most moving way possible.

30. "A Hard Rain's A-Gonna Fall" (from *The Freewheelin' Bob Dylan*, 1963)

In the liner notes to *The Freewheelin' Bob Dylan*, the twenty-two-year-old songwriter famously assessed "A Hard Rain's A-Gonna Fall" thusly: "Every line in it is actually the start of a whole song. But when I wrote it, I thought I wouldn't have enough time alive to write all those songs, so I put all I could into this one."[17]

It's a pretty good bet that most Dylan fans would love to have heard what Bob might have produced had he actually taken on that assignment of expanding those lines into full songs. Then again, maybe he has indeed accomplished that destiny, since one could imagine how those lines could easily springboard, if not literally then thematically, into the varied songs that have appeared on this list and all the other worthy ones that were left off it.

The writing of "A Hard Rain's A-Gonna Fall" is often linked to the run-up to the Cuban Missile Crisis in 1962, but Dylan's creation is just too mammoth to be bound by any one historical inspiration. If the song had never existed, and somebody wrote it today, it would sound every bit as timely and relevant.

Dylan, his mind aflame with poetic possibilities far outside the reach of his Woody Guthrie apprenticeship, spouts off torrents of words suggesting startlingly vivid images; when they are all taken together as one statement, it's overwhelming, but in a good way. There is nothing left out; it's all on display so it's impossible to even try to ignore it or look the other way. The truths spelled out here are too vast to avoid.

The narrator is a bystander in the song, passively listening and watching everything in front of him and closely regarding all of the people who cross his path. It is Dylan's subtle way of suggesting that it's best to know all the angles before deciding on any definitive course of action. The education that the narrator receives doesn't come through any school; it's an education borne of experience and clear-eyed observation.

Dylan was wise to frame the song as he did in the pattern of the traditional ballad "Lord Randall," with a mother asking her son about his journeys, playing up the kind of bond that can be so easily broken by the terrors being described. And they are terrors, ghastly images peppered throughout that are relayed without an iota of judgment by Bob's underplayed delivery. The point is that he shouldn't have to shout these things out; they should be evident to any person with a working brain and an open mind.

The last verse is one of the most powerfully evocative in Bob's career. The once-innocent young boy, now privy to all these horrible events and blatant sins, steps from the comfort of his mother's protection into the heart of the tumult. His goal is to illuminate the ignorant on the troubles surrounding them, even if it means his own end: "Then I'll stand on the ocean until I start sinkin'." Only he won't take this chore lightly: "And I'll know my song well before I start singin'."

Looking back at *The Freewheelin' Bob Dylan*, "A Hard Rain's A-Gonna Fall" sticks out as a song that was more ambitious than anything else he was writing at the time. Even the follow-up album, *The Times They Are A-Changin'*, for as brilliant as it was, lacked anything of such scope, preferring to stick to more focused targets and themes. It wasn't until the mid-'60s that these epics would become a regular occurrence.

Still, "A Hard Rain" stands apart from other tapestries like "Gates of Eden" or "Desolation Row" because of the innocent point of view. The narrator is by no means naïve, but he hasn't yet become jaded to the heartbreaks and injustices that he sees all around him. As such, his hurt is palpable. That underlying sense of disappointment is there in those other songs as well, but it is harder to spot, buried as it is under the obfuscating lyrical trickery and hipster sneer that Dylan had affected by the time those later songs were composed.

Dylan simply found new ways to plumb the depths of humanity in those subsequent songs, even as it seemed that he simply said it all with this first one. Even if he never uttered a word after "A Hard Rain's A-Gonna Fall," he would still have fulfilled the promise of that haunting final verse and told us all we needed to know.

29. "Last Thoughts on Woody Guthrie" (from *The Bootleg Series, Vol. 1–3: Rare & Unreleased 1961–1991*, 1991)

It might seem unusual to include what is essentially a poem on a list of songs, but there is justification for having "Last Thoughts on Woody Guthrie" among Dylan's musical oeuvre. First of all, Bob himself put his spoken-word performance of it on the first edition of *The Bootleg Series*. He also includes it among the songs on his BobDylan.com website, the words to the poem available to fans as readily as the lyrics to "Just Like a Woman" or "Man Gave Names to All the Animals."

The better reason, however, is that it's impossible to really take any meaningful look at Dylan's work without acknowledging the debt he owed to Woody Guthrie. Bob's first meaningful recording, "Song to Woody," found on his self-titled 1962 debut album which otherwise consisted almost entirely of cover material, was an earnest tribute and is undoubtedly moving, but it doesn't quite have the stuff to merit inclusion with the more advanced material that comprise this countdown.

By contrast, "Last Thoughts on Woody Guthrie" is a towering attempt by Dylan to sum up Guthrie and what he meant to him. Bob's talent would have eventually led him to some level of renown and would have found its way to audiences, but it's doubtful that he would have developed in quite the same manner without Guthrie's songs as a template for songwriting honesty and fearlessness. That influence cannot be overstated, so it feels just right that it would take an epic such as this to do proper honor to that influence.

Based on the title, a person unaware of the circumstances might think that the poem was written on the occasion of Guthrie's death. On the contrary, the poem was performed in concert by Dylan on April 12, 1963, in New York City, over four full years before Woody passed away in October 1967. He suffered from the genetic disorder known as Huntington's disease for more than a decade before his death, and it's hard to say whether this neurological disorder allowed him to fully comprehend Dylan's mammoth tribute.

So why then is it called "Last Thoughts on Woody Guthrie"? Maybe because Dylan, who visited Guthrie often in the hospital, knew at that point that the disease had pretty much ravaged the Woody Guthrie that the world knew, and so a tribute was both timely and fitting. Or maybe it was because it was time for Dylan himself to move on from the folk song form that Guthrie had mastered and Bob had imitated, expanded, and made his own in the early part of his career. After all, he would soon be writing songs that far outstripped the boundaries that contained his hero's music, so this poem signaled the end of the first of many eras in Bob's peripatetic musical journey.

Either way, the song works just fine not just as a eulogy but as the epitome of everything that Guthrie's music represents. The inherent knowledge that the life you're living in isn't fair; the self-doubt that you'll ever be able to overcome such obstacles; the feeling that there is a better world if you could just somehow identify it and nail it down, but you can't: It all flows out of Dylan's voice in that performance, hurried and fumbling as if there's so much to say and not near enough time to say it.

When someone feels all those feelings at once, it's impossible to articulate it, and "yer eyes get swimmy from the tears in your head." Dylan implies that the usual places to look for answers are dead ends. "Good God almighty / THAT STUFF AIN'T REAL" is the realization that one is bound to reach.

The words ring so true because Dylan clearly felt all these feelings himself and went on a similar journey of self-discovery, which is where Guthrie's music came into the picture. The closing image of the poem, God and Woody Guthrie in the Grand Canyon at sundown, is where the answers lie, according to Bob. You need not actually head out there; all you have to do is listen to the music.

"Last Thoughts on Woody Guthrie" shows exactly where Dylan found his answers. It makes you wonder if Dylan knew back then that his own music would serve the same purpose for so many of his listeners.

28. "It's All Over Now, Baby Blue" (from *Bringing It All Back Home*, 1965)

A whole lot of energy has been expended over the years by people trying to find out the true identity of Baby Blue. Dylanologists have speculated that it could have been a former lover, an estranged friend, a political movement, the folk music crowd, or even Dylan himself. The debate has killed lots of trees and now inhabits many megabytes of computer space.

When the true nature of "It's All Over Now, Baby Blue" is considered, it's a bit perplexing that anyone would care so much about it. After all, whoever or whatever Baby Blue was intended to represent, Dylan doesn't seem all that mad at them. It's understandable that people would want to know the target of the vitriol of "Positively 4th Street" out of morbid curiosity, but this character is coddled by Bob as much as he, or she, or it, is castigated.

Part of the reason the song has inspired so many amateur sleuths is the context in which Dylan wielded it over the years. In the documentary *Don't Look Back*, Donovan, then an up-and-coming Dylan acolyte on the British folk scene, plays a lovely if benign number for a hotel room full of folks, including Bob. Dylan then responds with a tossed-off version of "It's All Over Now, Baby Blue" that seems to imply that he would not be knocked off his perch anytime soon by any upstarts.

On July 25, 1965, Dylan gave his truncated, inflammatory performance at the Newport Folk Festival in Rhode Island. After he bolted the stage following the boos and catcalls of the audience unhappy with the electric music, he was encouraged to come out and at least finish the set. The song he chose to perform was "It's All Over Now, Baby Blue," and the message of that choice couldn't have been any clearer.

Those somewhat antagonistic renderings of the song might have fed into the image of it as a put-down. In truth, it's more a song about transformation, which makes its inclusion as the closing song on *Bringing It All Back Home* the most telling. That was the album in which Dylan began making drastic changes to his image and sound, so the song could be read in that context as a message to his fans to join him in the brave new musical world he was forging.

Indeed, you can imagine that Bob was singing to his audience as a whole in "It's All Over Now, Baby Blue" in much the same manner and tone as he was in, for example, "The Times They Are A-Changin'." The message isn't quite as dire here, but it's similar in nature. Dylan is saying that you shouldn't ever get too caught up in one scene because, like the weather, it will change if you wait awhile.

The choice of the name *Baby Blue* is crucial here as well because it suggests an innocence that can easily cross over into naïveté. All of the signposts in this character's world are being upended, what with the sky folding, the carpet moving, and saints marching right through, bringing chaos to her ordered life. In addition, all of the people on whom she used to have the upper hand (the vagabond, the painter, her ex-lover) are reappearing in her life in a much stronger position than when she left them.

Yet Dylan, singing loud and high above his acoustic guitar and the prancing bass of William E. Lee, implies that all this upheaval doesn't have to be a bad thing. "Leave your stepping stones behind, something calls for you / Forget the dead you've left, they will not follow you," he sings in a couplet worthy of Shakespeare. Even if things are topsy-turvy, it just gives her the chance to start again: "Strike another match, go start anew." The end is just another beginning, a cycle that will repeat itself ad infinitum.

There really isn't any audible bitterness toward Baby Blue, so if there is a real person behind the character, Dylan's affection for her is tangible in the song, albeit measured. After all, the song's lesson could easily be applied to love affairs, which can't be trusted to last.

No matter to whom it was directed, the advice proffered by "It's All Over Now, Baby Blue" was clearly valued by its author. After all, we've lost track of how many new matches Bob has struck over the years, yet he always ends up burning bright.

27. "Ring Them Bells" (from *Oh Mercy*, 1989)

For all the success that he had in his career, there is a polarizing aspect to Bob Dylan that doesn't really apply to some of his other contemporaries in the pantheon of legendary rock artists. It's fair to say that Dylan doesn't have a lot of what might be deemed casual fans, those people who dabble in his music and like certain songs but aren't diehards.

With Dylan, people tend to go all in or they don't go in at all. For those who fall into that latter category, there are multiple reasons why they don't "get" Bob's music. There are those who can't get by the vocals, the old "I can't understand what he's singing" argument, in part perpetrated by a caricature-like approximation of his concert voice used by comics and impersonators from time to time. Still others might feel that his music is a bit of an acquired taste and that his lyrics are too complicated to decode.

These may be legitimate reasons for not liking Dylan, but there is also a good portion of non-fans who are likely turned off by the aloof figure that Bob strikes in public. He doesn't really play the personality game required of celebrities these days, and that kind of attitude often can be interpreted as unfeeling or stoic.

That last view might be the most erroneous of all, because no artist has ever showed as much compassion in his music as Bob Dylan has for the past half century. One shining example of this compassion is "Ring Them Bells," which is moving enough to bring even the most ardent Bob non-believers to their senses.

First of all, the music that accompanies Dylan's lyrics on this *Oh Mercy* classic is unabashedly beautiful, which goes against another popular misconception of Bob as a guy with a lot of words and no tunes. The melody is bittersweet and lovely, brought to life by nothing more than Dylan's piano, producer Daniel Lanois's shimmering guitar, and some atmospheric keyboard effects. The empty spaces in the music allow Bob to really dive into the tune that he composed, and he sings every word as if it were the most important word he's ever sung.

There is a version of the song included on the bonus disc of *The Bootleg Series, Vol. 8: Tell Tale Signs: Rare and Unreleased 1989–2006* that strips everything away but Dylan's piano and vocal, and it's breathtaking. Again, it's the kind of thing that a skeptic of Bob's work needs to hear before passing any further judgment.

There is no weirdness or standoffishness in the words that Dylan chooses here, yet that doesn't mean that "Ring Them Bells" is a simple song. It is actually a profound plea to all those who hear it, calling them to remember that everyone they meet is hurting in some way, even if it's slight, and that all personal interactions should reflect and acknowledge this silent suffering.

This is another song that uses a lot of religious imagery, but that imagery is used to deliver the message, not define it. Dylan isn't looking for anyone to jump on any spiritual bandwagon here; he just wants them to listen, because the bells toll for everyone. "The world's on its side," he sings, which suggests that anyone, no matter how seemingly secure they might be, could get toppled without the proper vigilance. Everyone who walks the Earth is essentially one of the song's lost sheep in one way or another, so the bells are absolutely necessary to guide us home.

The last lines play up the import of this situation: "And the fighting is strong / And they're breaking down the distance between right and wrong." Dylan expressed dissatisfaction with these lines in *Chronicles*, which goes in-depth into the creative process behind the songs on *Oh Mercy*. That concern seems like a case of perfectionism on Bob's part because those lines make sense in a cosmic kind of way. If the barriers he mentions start to break down and the blurred lines tempt people to cross, the consequences are such that turning humanity around at that point and pointing it toward a more benign fate may no longer be an option.

"Ring The Bells" is really a song that's impossible to assail, not only in terms of its presentation but also for the message it conveys. It's a universally beneficial message, which is why it's too bad that those not in the choir of Dylan faithful might miss out on it. ·

26. "She's Your Lover Now" (from *The Bootleg Series, Vol. 1–3: Rare & Unreleased 1961–1991*, 1991)

In the battle for the title of All-Time-Classic, Unreleased-on-a-Studio-Album Dylan Song, "She's Your Lover Now" puts up a vicious fight, even though it comes up a tad short. *Blonde on Blonde* was one of the most ahead-of-its-time albums ever, and yet this song probably was even ahead of *Blonde on Blonde*, if that makes any sense or is even possible.

Just listen to it: It's got a crazy rhyme scheme, with the verses unfurling in all sorts of directions; the perspectives shift on a dime; the arrangement never settles into any one single groove but still manages to bustle forward at a fevered momentum. It's just all over the place, and yet perfectly together. Heck, even the mucked-up ending on *The Bootleg Series* version, with the take terminating prematurely after Dylan screws up his lyrics, makes sense somehow.

The bootleg hunters know there's a solo piano version that has its merits as well, considering it has the last verse, with its hilariously terse dismissal of the other guy ("And you, there's been nothing of you I can recall / I just saw you that one time. You were just there, that's all") intact. It's mesmerizing in a slow-motion way, yet the take on *Bootleg Series* is the one that really captures the hyper energy of the lyrics.

In that version, the Hawks, with Sandy Konikoff filling in on drums for an absent Levon Helm, are in fine alchemic form, instinctively dropping in and out with their instruments to sweeten the deal without ever overdoing it. While there is debate among Dylan experts about who played what on the recording, with Al Kooper and Bobby Gregg also mentioned as possible contributors to the track, it definitely sounds like it's the band that would become The Band doing all the work, especially considering that the swirling, enveloping organ sounds like Garth Hudson's handiwork.

It's a hard song to wrangle into coherent shape, but once you get a grip on the players, it starts to come into sharp focus. "She's Your Lover Now" is basically a love triangle that has been deprived of one of its three points, the narrator, who turns his attention to the remaining two. When speaking to his ex, he questions her about her motives and why things didn't work out, while bemoaning her unreasonable expectations: "Now you stand here expectin' me to remember somethin' you forgot to say."

When he turns to her new lover, the sneer in the vocals becomes ever more audible. Dylan's sarcasm, so famously on display in *Don't Look Back*, is turned on full bore each time the narrator turns to this clown. He implies that the new guy is ineffectual and that he's only getting by because his flattery appeals to her narcissism: "Yes, you, you just sit around and ask for ashtrays, can't you reach? / I see you kiss her on the cheek every time she gives a speech." As each verse rounds to a close, the narrator warns this sycophant that she'll be more than he can handle: "She'll be standin' on the bar soon / With a fish head an' a harpoon" is just one of the more surreal hypothetical situations he mentions to prove his point.

The refrain is brilliant because of how the meaning of it can change. "She's your lover now" can be read as "She's your problem now," in which case the narrator is finally rid of this painful baggage and gets the last laugh. Yet it can also be a stark admission of defeat on his part, acknowledgment that all his complaints about her behavior are just empty bravado and that his chance to win her back has evaporated. If that's the case, none of the scenarios he provides in the song to the new guy are quite as damning as the isolation that he himself is about to feel. Dylan's vocal doesn't skew too far one way or the other, with echoes of elation and dejection both faintly evident. He leaves it to the listener to decide.

It's very difficult to imagine another songwriter even attempting a songwriting high-wire act as nimble as "She's Your Lover Now," let along pulling it off so well. The song really resonates when a relation-ship goes down the tubes. Depending on where you're at in your recov-ery from that breakup, you might hear this song as a sad farewell, a satisfying good riddance, or a cathartic combination of both.

25. "Things Have Changed" (from *The Essential Bob Dylan*, 2000)

Considering all of the awards and honorary titles and the like that have been bestowed upon Bob Dylan over the years, it's no wonder that he never seems all that overwhelmed to receive them. One thinks of his lines from "Is Your Love in Vain?" when considering Dylan's somewhat stoic reaction to these honors: "I have dined with kings, I've been of-fered wings / And I've never been too impressed."

The exception to Bob's seeming indifference to these awards came in 2001 when "Things Have Changed" was named best song at the 2001 Academy Awards. Appearing via satellite to accept the award after per-forming the song, he seemed genuinely shocked and touched to be chosen.

One good guess as to why Dylan seemed so surprisingly affected that night is that his lifelong affinity for motion pictures made this one a little more special than the rest. It's hard to think of another artist who has used the movies more in his songs, whether it's borrowing a line or two from some old flick, which he's done many times, or using cinemat-ic techniques to frame his songs, as in the narratives of *Desire*, or even framing an entire song around a long-forgotten Western ("Brownsville Girl").

The ironic thing about Dylan's fascination with Hollywood is that "Things Have Changed" is a prime illustration of the advantages that a well-written song has over even a solid movie like *Wonder Boys*, the film that featured Bob's Oscar winner. It can be argued that the movie, an amiable, darkly funny tale of a down-on-his-luck English professor well played by Michael Douglas, takes 107 minutes to sum up its tar-geted themes and evoke its desired emotions, a job that Bob's ditty does in a little less than five.

In many ways, it's not a fair fight to compare the two. *Wonder Boys*, for all its offbeat charm, is now just a line on the resume of its makers and actors and doesn't hold much more sway than that in celluloid history. Dylan's song is an evergreen. The film can't be blamed for the way it pales in comparison since it's hard to name too many movies that portray a middle-aged man, in all his various moods and preoccupations, any better than "Things Have Changed."

Riding a chunky acoustic groove, Dylan prowls the nightlife in front of him like an alien surveying a strange planet. This environs is not his home anymore, not that any place could be in his harried condition. The first line spells it out rather frankly: "A worried man with a worried mind." The rest of the song spins off from this statement in surprising ways that still remain consistent to the anguished core.

The narrator's awareness of his harsh surroundings is matched only by his inability to do anything about it. Even the clichés that he spouts drip with menace because you believe that there's no exaggeration involved: "Standing on the gallows with my head in the noose / Any minute now I'm expecting all hell to break loose." Even those things that should bring pleasure, like the woman in his lap, serve to confuse him.

One of the great ironies of middle age is that a person builds up all this wisdom yet is often ill equipped to use it. The narrator has the wherewithal to toss off a passel of memorable one-liners: "Lot of water under the bridge, lot of other stuff too"; "All the truth in the world adds up to one big lie"; "You can't win with a losing hand."

These lines have the kind of snap and heft to rank with any one of Dylan's very best from his '60s and '70s heyday, foreshadowing that he would finger the pulse of the new millennium as well as he would the previous one. Still, the narrator can't do much to get himself out of his rut. That's in large part because he's tentative to the point of paralysis: "I'm not that eager to make a mistake."

That killer refrain ("I used to care but things have changed") may sound like it comes from a man jaded by life's truths. Yet it's more an act of self-preservation from a guy who just wants to wander the world and not get hurt by it anymore.

There is a lot of fascinating stuff at work in "Things Have Changed." In fact, there's so much going on that you'd swear that *Wonder Boys* was inspired by Dylan's song rather than the other way around.

24. "I Threw It All Away" (from *Nashville Skyline*, 1969)

Nashville Skyline was Bob Dylan's full-out foray into country music. He had flirted with the music in the mid-'60s and had recorded his previous two albums in Nashville, the C&W capital of the world, using session players who brought a country · sensibility to Dylan's ever-evolving sound. As a result, the transformation may have seemed sudden to the uninitiated, but Bob really didn't have to change all that much to make the crossover.

It's interesting that the album, which seems like such an outlier in the Dylan catalog, is also one of the most successful he has ever released. To that point in his career, *Nashville Skyline*, released in 1969, was Bob's biggest hit album, hitting number three in the U.S. album charts and number one in the United Kingdom.

While the album might have seemed at the time like an attempt by Dylan to simplify and to court a broader audience, it can also be seen as a challenge to an artist who was considered by most to be the preeminent songwriter in rock music. How would he adjust to the more regimented structure of country music? Could he work under those strictures and still produce classics as memorable as those written by Hank Williams, one of his all-time heroes?

One might have expected Bob to try to subvert the conventions of country music to get his desired effect. By contrast, he embraced them. Dylan answered the challenge of writing pure, affecting country songs time and again on the album, but "I Threw It All Away" stands apart from the rest. It is a triumph every bit as vast as some of his electric rock masterpieces. There's a reason that the "three chords and the truth" ethos has captivated so many fans from all over the world, and Bob taps into it on this heartrending song.

Because of its tighter structure, "I Threw It All Away" is one of the least difficult Dylan songs for other artists to handle. It has the feel of a country standard, so someone wanting to cover it just has to stay out of its way and tap into the emotion. Elvis Costello did a fabulous version on his covers album, *Kojak Variety*. Another to seek out is the take done by Scott Walker, the '60s cult artist and monumental voice of the Walker Brothers. When Walker sings the song, it sounds like the lament of Zeus.

Those two and a few others covers are fine, but none can quite match the plainspoken power of the original. It's barely over two minutes, and yet there are infinite wells of heartbreak to be located within it. What Dylan taps into on "I Threw It All Away" is a double-whammy situation that is unbearable for anyone who must endure it. It occurs when someone not only loses the person they love, which is bad enough, but does so because of their own mistakes and failings. The combination of sadness and guilt creates levels of pain that even a farsighted dentist couldn't match.

This is one of Dylan's most moving melodies, and he also deserves credit for the nifty little acoustic guitar hook that bookends the song. It's a lovely performance by the band, which, on that track, included future country legend Charlie Daniels on guitar. Even though it is no doubt a country track, this song could work in any format, as long as the audience is willing to wallow in the exquisite sadness.

The vocal performance is smooth and understated, perhaps Dylan's best on that one-of-a-kind album, as he lets the regret of the lyrics speak for itself. He sings the words without a trace of irony, knowing that any snark would have sunk the emotion of the song. Bob frames the story as if the narrator is talking to a stranger at a bar, imparting the sad life lesson that he learned the hard way.

Dylan doesn't get into psychological reasoning for why the narrator gives up the one thing in his life that brings him happiness, nor does he specify the nature of his errors. None of that matters anymore for this poor guy since the damage is done. "I Threw It All Away" is rare among Bob's songs in that it stays as neat as possible; no overstuffed lyrical lines or unkempt harmonica solos. Simplicity is the name of the game, all the better to convey the purity of the sorrow on display.

23. "One of Us Must Know (Sooner or Later)" (from *Blonde on Blonde*, 1966)

Once he started to eschew the solo acoustic performances that were the hallmark of his first few albums, it was incumbent upon Bob Dylan to find band members to bring his musical ideas to brimming life. It became clear early on that Bob was never going to stick with one single band for any period of time, preferring to catch lightning in a bottle with ad hoc assemblages of musicians only to let the stopper out of that bottle and start the process all over again the next time around.

Obviously, the success of Dylan's songs has much to do with the writing and Bob's performances, but it's important to note what the instrumentalists brought to the table. Many of these session players have distinguished resumes, but they often dug down for a little something special when they played with Dylan.

For example, piano man Paul Griffin has one of the most impressive lists of credits you're ever going to see. Among many other classic tracks, he played on the the Shirelles' "Will You Still Love Me Tomorrow?" and the Isley Brothers' "Twist and Shout," two seminal '60s hits. That's also Griffin playing the somber chords to capture the feeling of "the day the music died" on Don McLean's "American Pie."

Those recordings certainly loom large in music history, but his performance on "One of Us Must Know (Sooner or Later)" is every bit as monumental. It's Griffin who provides the impetus for one of Dylan's greatest and most dramatic choruses ever, exploding as it does out of the more restrained verses, with the piano clearing the path.

As a matter of fact, every one of the instrumentalists acquits himself well on this recording that ends the first side of *Blonde on Blonde*. Give credit to Bob Johnston, the album's producer, for pulling the disparate parts together, because the band was a hybrid of the Hawks (Robbie Robertson and Rick Danko) and session men (Griffin, Al Kooper, Bobby Gregg). Dylan himself helps matters with a pair of wailing harmonica solos.

He also sings the stuffing out of the song. The phrasing is unique, especially those long drawn out notes that lead to the chorus ("I didn't know that you were sayin' goodbye for goooooooooooooooooooooood"). With such a rock-solid frame in place, Dylan's lyrics needed to just be OK for the song to succeed. They're great though, which is why "One of Us Must Know (Sooner or Later)" holds such a lofty spot on this list.

There's no denying that the narrator comes on like quite the jerk at times, an early example of Dylan's willingness to play an unsympathetic role in one of his songs. In the first verse, he's particularly harsh when he implies that he hurt this girl for the same reason some people climb a mountain: "You just happened to be there, that's all." Yet as the song progresses, it becomes clear that he's taken aback by how much this girl affected him and how her goodbye hurt more than he wished to let on.

The miscommunications and misconceptions begin to take their toll on the relationship. Dylan overstuffs the lines with the narrator's excuses and clarifications, but things still keep getting worse between the pair. Their best intentions go unrealized: "And I told you as you clawed out my eyes / That I never really meant to do you any harm." In trying so hard to make their points, these two people stop listening to each other.

The way that the refrain is phrased is crucial: "Sooner or later, one of us must know." In other words, she'll eventually figure out that, even at his nastiest, he truly loved her, and he'll eventually figure out that she had no choice but to push him away. The great irony, of course, is that the perspective they might someday gain will be futile since the relationship is over and cannot be resuscitated.

It's hard to believe that this song flopped as a single, although the raw, unsweetened view of a relationship's unraveling, sung by Dylan without ·a trace of sentimental gushing, was probably a bit harsh for mass consumption. On *Blonde on Blonde*, among the other acidic ballads, it's a perfect fit. Lyrically, "One of Us Must Know (Sooner or Later)" is a pretty solemn take on the fallout of love interrupted. Musically, thanks to the stellar efforts of Griffin and company, it cries its heart out.

22. "Highway 61 Revisited" (from *Highway 61 Revisited*, 1965)

Bob Dylan's choice of Highway 61 as the titular location for both his landmark 1965 album *Highway 61 Revisited* and the song of the same name is telling. The highway crosses the United States from south to north and its route essentially rolls along with the Mississippi River and runs through both Memphis and New Orleans, so it's no wonder that it's often referred to as the Blues Highway.

While those locations certainly have the historical cachet, the fact that Highway 61 also passed nearby Hibbing, Minnesota, Dylan's boyhood hometown, is another reason that it worked its way into Bob's crazed rendering. The wanderlust that led him to the bigger world outside his humble snowbound burg was likely exacerbated by his proximity to a road that led to the home of a type of·music that meant so much to him.

Yet Dylan saying that this famous road is to be "revisited" is just another way of telling his audience that they'll never look at it quite the same again once he's through with it. The slide-whistle that kicks off the song is an immediate indication that chaos is about to reign, so it's best to hold on tight. The ride is going to be bumpy, but it definitely won't be dull.

It's quite the contradiction to hear emotional guitar stabs of virtuoso electric guitarist Michael Bloomfield, torrents of notes that epitomize the song's link to classic blues, being used in the service of Dylan's surreally comic lyrics. Biblical characters mix with familiar faces from blues songs (Georgia Sam, the roving gambler) and interact on the highway, but they're altered by the songwriter to fit the tumultuous times in which Dylan was writing.

Keep in mind that "Highway 61 Revisited" was written at a time when Bob still mined the Bible for its storytelling value and not as a means of showing that he was saved. Even though the bare bones of the story of God's demand of the supreme sacrifice from Abraham are honored here, Dylan adds a healthy dose of hipster patois and a heaving helping of anarchic attitude.

As a result, Abraham mouths off to God, while God's threat ("The next time you see me comin' you better run") is more potent than portent. Dylan manages to draw parallels that most others wouldn't make by bringing this hallowed tale to Highway 61. It implies that God and Abe, as he is called in casual fashion, are no different than the motley crew that follows them into Dylan's wild tapestry. Clearly nothing is sacred.

Some of these folks in "Highway 61 Revisited" are victims, like Georgia Sam, who is left naked, bleeding, spurned by welfare, and heading to the highway as a last resort so as not to be left alone in his misery. Others, like the Mack the Finger and Louis the King, are looking to do the victimizing, willing to bilk unsuspecting folks with their worthless products.

There is no better indication of the ruthlessness and insanity inherent in Dylan's creation than the roving gambler, who realizes that there is a much bigger score to be made than the nickels and dimes he can collect at a card table. Why not start a war as the biggest possible profit-making scheme of all? Maybe those "Masters of War" that Bob had warned about a few years previous to the recording of this song didn't fall into their graves after all.

Everybody that Dylan depicts in the song exudes danger, tossing off ominous threats and waving guns around like they're an extension of their hands. Yet the anything-goes nature of the music and Dylan's one-liners keep everything from getting exceedingly heavy. As a matter of fact, it's one of the most invigorating recordings in the man's catalog.

"Highway 61 Revisited" fades out with all of these bizarre situations unresolved, Dylan humming and grooving among the searing guitar licks as if he's in ecstasy. When the deal finally does go down, there seem to be two possible outcomes for the travelers on this road: Either they'll strike it rich or they'll end up facedown on the concrete with track marks on their backs. Bob makes it clear that the journey is more important than the result anyway. For a certain type of outcast, Highway 61 is the only place to truly feel alive.

21. "Don't Think Twice, It's All Right" (from *The Freewheelin' Bob Dylan*, 1963)

Bob Dylan famously sang in "My Back Pages," "I was so much older then, I'm younger than that now." That line is generally perceived as self-criticism at his earlier topical material. Dylan was probably being too harsh on his earlier self if knocking those older songs was indeed his intent, but he might have indeed had a point in implying that the protest songs lacked a bit of subtlety and nuance, maybe not compared to other songwriters of the day, but certainly compared with what was to come from Bob.

Yet on *The Freewheelin' Bob Dylan*, the same album that contained much of that topical material, Dylan also wrote a few love songs that were well beyond his years. There is nothing naive about these songs, and Bob's self-awareness is extremely useful in picking apart the bones of relationships that have gone awry.

Pulling off the difficult task of seeming both realistic about a crumbling affair and heartfelt about the anguish the prospect of that breakup causes, "Don't Think Twice, It's All Right" is a love song that is alternately wise like a sage and cracks wise like a kid with hurt feelings. Hidden in the understated vocal, which sounds as if the narrator has had every last bit of emotion drained from him, are some pretty harsh accusations. Yet the song ultimately projects a tone that is more wistful than bitter.

Why did Dylan already have a softer touch on the love songs at this point in his career than he did on the protest material? It could be that he was writing with firsthand perspective on songs like this and "Girl from the North Country," which both could be found on *The Freewheelin' Bob Dylan*. He clearly was inspired by something personal in the composition of these songs.

As a result, bits of humor and self-deprecation sneak into this material, humanizing it a bit more when it's compared to the unwavering earnestness of songs like "Masters of War" and "A Hard Rain's A-Gonna Fall." Neither approach is better or worse, really, as they are both suited to the material they express.

Yet Dylan was on to something with love songs like "Don't Think Twice, It's All Right" in the way that he keeps his closeness to the subject matter in check and allows a cool, detached perspective to override the proceedings. By doing this, when the real emotion does sneak through the façade, like when he finally bids the girl in this song farewell in the final verse, it's a much more powerful effect than if he had spent the whole time moaning and groaning for his lost love. He would return to this technique over and over again in his career, and this song is one of the first and finest examples of it.

The opening lines of each verse read as a litany of all the things the guy no longer feels the girl needs to do, many of which she never did in the first place. Dylan also sets up his punch lines with a timing of a master joke teller, even if his narrator is a sad clown these days, the humor deflecting the rawness of the hurt he clearly feels.

Each line right before the refrain is a particularly harsh jab: "You're the reason I'm trav'lin on"; "We never did too much talkin' anyway"; "I give her my heart but she wanted my soul"; "You just kinda wasted my precious time." Imagine those lines howled instead of crooned, and you'd swear they were part of "Idiot Wind." Nonetheless, the narrator undercuts their severity with the gentle refrain. Maybe he means to ease the mind of the girl by telling her not to think twice, or maybe some sarcasm is seeping out. What cannot be debated is that the love story is over, and all his measured musings and masking techniques won't change that fact.

When you consider all the evidence, "Don't Think Twice, It's All Right" is partly an evenhanded assessment of a love that just wasn't meant to be, the sagacious reflections of an old soul. The other part of it emanates from the hurt feelings of a twenty-one-year-old guy, Dylan's age at the time he wrote the song, who can't understand any of it. It all adds up to a moving mixture of insight and emotion, and that's a potent combination at any age.

20. "The Ballad of Frankie Lee and Judas Priest" (from *John Wesley Harding*, 1967)

It's somehow apt that a song that features a pretty detailed narrative and a conclusion in which he even tells us the moral is one which might be one of the most perplexing songs Bob Dylan has ever released. "The Ballad of Frankie Lee and Judas Priest" is one where you don't need to understand a thing about it to enjoy it, yet it also provides a tantalizing search for meaning for those who wish to go after it.

What can't be denied is that the song is the most instantly enjoyable track on Dylan's most mysterious album, 1967's *John Wesley Harding*. The surface catchiness of the song, coupled with Dylan's breezy word-play, far outweighs anything else on that hushed, moody collection.

The splashiness of the track is balanced out by the depth of the story Dylan creates; in fact, it's got just as many, or more, layers as the dense allegories that are found elsewhere on *John Wesley Harding*. Considering where Bob was in his career, mellowing out after a wild three or four years of constant touring and recording, it's easy to spot the inspiration for this story about temptation, excess, and the ultimate result of it all.

Yet there are enough contradictory forces at play in the lyrics to make such a simple dissection problematic. Dylan dodges and feigns throughout the song, seemingly dangling the song's answers right in front of his listeners only to yank them away when they gets too close.

Compare it to "Lily, Rosemary and the Jack of Hearts," another mammoth story song, to see what Dylan is really up to here. On "Lily," he leaves out big chunks of the narrative and yet the blanks get filled in the more you listen to it. With "The Ballad of Frankie Lee and Judas Priest," every action is laid right out in front of the listener, but the motivations and inner workings of the characters are hard to pin down.

"Lily" leaves you asking "Who?" and "What?" questions that can eventually be answered by uncovering the song's clues. This song leaves you asking "Why?" and repeated listens only seem to reveal more possible answers without ever producing a definitive one.

There's a fine line that Dylan expertly walks here. There's no doubt that the song keeps us guessing as to why these two characters make the choices they do. Yet if it were impenetrable, it wouldn't hold the same allure. It gives us enough hints to allow us to forge our own interpretations. In that way, the song serves as a kind of moral Rorschach test.

For example, which character deserves the sympathies of the listener? Frankie Lee is a gambler, and he clearly has some serious impulse control issues which ultimately lead to his demise. Yet he also seems genuinely concerned for his friend Judas Priest when he hears that he's "stranded in a house."

Judas, on the other hand, offers money to his pal when he needs it and seems to have the wisdom his friend lacks. Yet he also seems to condescend to Frankie Lee at times, and worst of all, he does nothing to stop him from his untimely end, perhaps even leading him right to it. And then there's the name Judas, which immediately gives us pause about whether he can be trusted.

Little conundrums like this are all over the place. Yet it's hard to get too caught up on a single one since Dylan sets this strange parable to a jaunty rhythm which has listeners tapping their feet as much as scratching their heads.

Bob puts the onus on the listener to do the work, because, in the immortal words of the neighbor boy, "Nothing is revealed." Can Dylan's stated moral at the end of the song ("Don't go mistaking paradise for that home across the road") even be trusted? Certainly, it can be tied to the events of the narrative easily enough, but you can also separate it from those events by interpreting things a little differently.

Those mysteries and contradictions may be why "The Ballad of Frankie Lee and Judas Priest" is so captivating. Dylan wants us to stand inside the shoes of the protagonists and ponder what we would do if faced with the same predicaments. Those who choose their own adventure are ultimately responsible for whatever fate they are granted, and that might be the ultimate "moral of this song."

19. "The Times They Are A-Changin'" (from *The Times They Are A-Changin'*, 1964)

"Each time I sing it, I feel like I wrote it the day before."[18]

That's Bob Dylan in a 1978 interview, describing "The Times They Are A-Changin'." It seems that even its writer is at a loss to explain the eerie way in which this song stays relevant. Part of it has to do, obviously, with Bob's skill in writing it, but it really goes beyond that. That quote hints at this mysterious power a little bit, in that it references the song's strange ability to freeze time even as it inexorably moves ahead.

The song was the centerpiece and title track to Bob's 1964 album, a stunning collection of songs well above and beyond anything else that was being produced at that time. While *The Freewheelin' Bob Dylan* had several classic songs, it lacked consistency in terms of both tone and quality. *The Times They Are A-Changin'* got everything right though, and the title track summed up in general all of the specific, weighty themes that he would tackle on the rest of the album.

While Dylan has hinted that the Civil Rights movement was essentially the spearhead for the song, he never mentions a specific cause in the lyrics, thereby keeping things purposefully vague. Not only does that strategy allow any movement to co-opt the song, it also keeps it from ever sounding dated, making it useful to just about any group with any cause at any time in history. "The Times They Are A-Changin'" is also an effective catch-all soundtrack for anyone wanting to summarize turbulent times, and, in truth, pretty much all times are turbulent in their own way.

Moreover, Dylan's careful phrasing, keeping the song forever in the present, never allows the past to muscle in. The title phrase is cleverly set up to reflect constant turmoil and transformation. Was Bob conscious of this as he wrote it? Perhaps, but it's doubtful that even he could have envisioned when he wrote the song what kind of legs it would have.

One other generally overlooked facet of the song that helps to extend its relevance is its inclusiveness. The knee-jerk reaction to "The Times They Are-A-Changin'" is to label it as a young-against-old song, but it's not as simple as that. The way that Bob starts each verse with the word "Come" is important because it hints at a need for dialogue between the disparate groups.

In other words, he's not telling the mothers and fathers and senators and congressmen to get lost. They can be a part of the change the song references if they would just recognize that it's not only necessary, but that it's going to happen one way or another, with or without their cooperation. He wants them to "heed the call," not ignore it. The best-case scenario would be a unifying of all these groups toward a common goal, not the exclusion of those who disagree, which would only perpetrate the same kind of negativity against which the song is railing.

By the time the last verse comes around, there is no more time left for these groups to assemble: "The line is drawn, the curse it is cast." The change is already in progress. Then again, according to the song, it always has been in progress.

The odd thing about these lyrics written all the way back in 1963 (although the song wasn't released until a year later) is that they are still relevant in part because the prophecies they foretell have not completely come to pass. There are still certain groups who are waiting for their time to be first, while others have been enjoying the view in front for a long time. (The fact that the song's handwritten lyrics were purchased for a king's ransom a few years back by a hedge-fund manager could be deemed either ironic or apropos depending upon the level of cynicism of the beholder.)

Yet the song is so powerful, so inevitable, that it is impossible to listen to it without believing that the last verse will finally, completely occur some sweet day when, with Dylan making one more reference to time, "the present now will later be past." When that day arrives, maybe then "The Times They Are A-Changin'" can be put away in the relic drawer and viewed with nostalgia. Until then, at least the song will be around to bring solace and hope to those waiting for their time to come.

18. "Positively 4th Street" (from *Bob Dylan's Greatest Hits*, 1967)

It takes just twelve verses without a single chorus for Bob Dylan to portray focused bitterness to the umpteenth degree in "Positively 4th Street," one of the biggest singles of his career, released in 1965. Like a master surgeon at work, he clinically dissects his target to reveal that there is nothing inside but rancor and pettiness. By broadcasting this

.discovery via the radio airwaves, he ensured that the entire world could know the true nature of his enemy as well as he did.

What little mercy Bob showed with the song comes from the fact that he does not identify the person or persons at whom he levels his screed. Perhaps he had learned somewhat from the lesson of "Ballad in Plain D," a 1964 song about real people who could be easily identified by anyone who knew Dylan's life just a little bit. The songwriter expressed remorse about it afterwards, so, by obfuscating the accused that inspired "4th Street," he could have been taking a precaution against similar regrets.

It's more likely that Dylan realized that the song works better without a specific person in the listeners' minds beforehand, thereby allowing them to vicariously substitute their own targets. In that way, the song stays relevant to the largest number of people. Had he named so-and-so, a la John Lennon's attack on Paul McCartney in "How Do You Sleep?" or, for a modern example, any of Taylor Swift's big hits aimed at her celebrity ex-boyfriends, it might have come off as someone using a bully pulpit to take a cheap shot rather than a catch-all condemnation of jealousy and hypocrisy.

It's natural for Bob's fans to have curiosity about the subject matter, but the unending mystery actually serves the song well in the end. Just ask Carly Simon or Alanis Morrisette, who have gotten great mileage out of the public's fascination with the subject matter of "You're So Vain" and "You Oughta Know," respectively.

The truth, in the case of "Positively 4th Street," probably isn't as salacious as all that anyway since the song is most likely about an amalgam, a character made up of the parts of many people Dylan knew or encountered. That interpretation would jibe with the hypothesis that Bob was pointing his finger at the folk crowd that he felt abandoned him when he started branching out to different styles of music.

Then again, maybe it is about just a single person, and maybe what this person did to Dylan, at least in his estimation, was bad enough to warrant such vitriol. If this is true, the instigator should feel honored, in a strange way, to have inspired possibly the most toxic verbal assault in rock history. Maybe that's why so many people have claimed in various interviews and books over the years that they were the ones who cheesed off Bob. To paraphrase Simon, they think this song is about them.

Considering the fact that Bob put the song out as a single, guaranteeing it a wide audience, he clearly didn't care at all about how it was perceived. Maybe he couldn't have foreseen that such nastiness would ever hit the Top 10 like it did. Putting those lyrics in the context of an arrangement brightened by Al Kooper's chirping organ somehow only made the song sound harsher. So did Bob's deadpan delivery, which ensured that the target knew that this was not just some emotional response to a perceived slight.

In line-by-line, methodical fashion, Dylan eradicates his enemy. He uses this person's own words and actions as the ultimate evidence against him (or her or them) like a prosecuting attorney. The narrator implies, in the course of a relatively short song, that the "you" in the lyrics is two-faced, cowardly, self-hating, mean, deceitful, and spiteful. (But what do you really think about them, Bob?)

As for those famous last few lines, they represent the kind of perfect zinger that everyone wishes they could fire off in the direction of the person that most infuriates them. The narrator posits a scenario where he and his former friend essentially trade places as a way of revelation: "You'd know what a drag it is / To see you."

It's doubtful that Dylan will ever elucidate just who or what could have inspired such an unflattering character sketch, nor should anyone want him to. If he did, "Positively 4th Street" would become an eloquent but limited attack instead of an all-time, all-encompassing put-down.

17. "Just Like a Woman" (from *Blonde on Blonde*, 1966)

Blood on the Tracks is the album usually mentioned as Dylan's ultimate treatise on the perils of romance, but *Blonde on Blonde* can certainly give it a run for its money. Since there were four sides of music to fill, Bob had a lot more room to explore every facet of a relationship. He was also at the absolute peak of his lyrical powers at the time of the album's recording and release in 1966, so the songs that came from that LP are still some of the most comprehensive and moving treatises on the subject matter that rock music has ever produced.

"Just Like a Woman" is the ultimate heartbreaker on the album, a tale of two ships that don't just pass in the night; they hit each other at ramming speed and stagger on to their next destination much the worse for wear. It is the kind of breakup whereby the participants will live and learn from it, but they still might not ever be able to shake its lingering repercussions.

It is important to note that the song is just as much about the spurned narrator as it is about the "Woman" from the title, if only to provide a defense for it against the criticism from some corners that it is sexist. Were the song completely comprised of the narrator listing all the faults of his former lover, this criticism might have more merit, although it would just mean that the narrator is sexist, not that Dylan is. This is a song, not an op-ed piece.

Instead, the narrator is the one who seems to come out on the losing end of the relationship, and any pettiness he shows can be a residual effect of this fact. Besides, it's clear that he admires her even after all that has gone down, realizing that the very things that made him want her in the first place are the things that were fated to drive them apart.

"Just Like a Woman" is just about perfect as a studio recording. The song sort of flutters about at its own elusive pace thanks to Kenny Buttrey's unaggressive snare drums. Like many of Bob's mid-tempo arrangements around this time period, this one gives space for each instrumentalist to fill in gaps without every really forcing themselves into the forefront. What that leads to is an excessively pretty texture to the recording, although it still manages to have enough grit around the edges to keep from being too saccharine. It also means that, when an instrument does come to the fore like Dylan's harmonica solo at the end, the impact is magnified.

The woman/girl in the song is one who has forsaken the innocence that first enthralled the narrator, her ribbons and bows replaced by amphetamines and pearls. He suggests that this has made her just another one of the pack, "just like all the rest," and that her specialness has been dulled by her new maturity.

Her newfound penchant for emotional larceny and deception (she "takes" and "fakes just like a woman") leave him struggling to see how he can coexist with her ("I just can't fit"). Yet he doesn't really begrudge her this evolution; it's just that she has moved on to a different plane, and that leaves him stranded. Hence those painfully evocative first two lines: "Nobody feels any pain / Tonight as I stand inside the rain." It's as if he envies her numbness to the pesky emotions that are paralyzing him.

Despite her newfound, cooler persona, instances of the old fragility still shine through ("She breaks just like a little girl"), and that's clearly the part of her that attracts him the most. Yet he has no choice but to let her go, asking only that, once he makes it to her jaded level sometime in the future, she not throw the past in his face: "Please don't let on that you knew me when / I was hungry and it was your world."

In those crushing last lines, Dylan exposes the futility of the masks that people wear in relationships to prevent themselves from feeling vulnerable. "Just Like a Woman" is a song that doesn't sugarcoat the sharp, invigorating pain of love, yet it insists that it is still preferable to the dull ache of settling for the safer, more mature alternative.

16. "Lily, Rosemary and the Jack of Hearts" (from *Blood on the Tracks*, 1975)

There's an "Aha!" moment that Dylan fans tend to have when listening to "Lily, Rosemary and the Jack of Hearts," the mammoth, Old West-inspired song that somehow fits perfectly with the anguished tales of love and loss on *Blood on the Tracks*. It's that moment when the general gist of the song's story finally emerges. It probably won't happen the first time; it may not even happen the tenth. Yet it inevitably does happen, and it's like a rite of passage for Dylan fandom.

No two interpretations of the song's events are exactly the same. That's the fun part of it. Reasonable minds can argue and debate all day long about who did what to whom and how these people were all related. What can't be denied is that Dylan, in the course of this song, manages to create vivid portraits of three people, their desires and hurts and regrets and fears and joys all laid bare. That's a task that usually warrants a bit more time than the eight-minutes-and-change length of the song.

Those three people are not the title three, because the Jack of Hearts is essentially a plot cipher, the hub around which the other characters (Lily, Rosemary, and Big Jim) revolve. His own motivations and emotions are never privy to us, nor are they privy to the other characters. That's what makes him so effective in his task that fateful night at the cabaret.

Some interpretations have the Jack of Hearts deeply entwined in these people's lives. Maybe from the characters' perspective he is, but it's likely there are other versions of Lily, Rosemary, and Big Jim lurking somewhere in each town to which he travels, just more pawns for him to play. That may not be the most romantic view, but, considering the aftermath he leaves in his wake with two of the three dead and the town in shambles, it's impossible to say that the Jack is a saint, even though he may look like one.

The Jack's charisma is such that he is able to win over these two ladies who are jaded to the rest of the world. Lily is a survivor ("She did whatever she had to do"), using men to get her where she needed to be; the Jack alone appears to have won her heart. Rosemary's connection to the Jack is a bit more difficult to parse, but her ultimate decision to off Big Jim clearly seems to have been inspired by him ("She was with Big Jim but she was leanin' to the Jack of Hearts").

Rosemary is the most fascinating character in the song, a woman whose self-esteem seems to be in constant jeopardy, which explains why she would marry a successful brute like Big Jim. Her conscience still nags at her though, as does the drudgery of her life as a trophy wife. The Jack provides her with her opportunity "to do just one good deed before she dies."

For all of Big Jim's outward display of money and power, his insecurity leads to his demise. One gets the sense that he doesn't really love Lily or Rosemary, but views them as possessions. As such, the Jack's association with them is a threat to his dominance that must be eradicated, but he is ultimately outflanked in the end.

Meanwhile, the Jack's associates use this distraction to make their big score with the bank safe. Dylan brilliantly teases us with this side plot throughout the song. Those first few times through the song, a listener might not be able to imagine why the narrator bothers giving updates about the drilling. The townspeople make that same mistake, at their own peril ("The drillin' in the wall kept up but no one seemed to pay it any mind").

The clues are all there. Big Jim wonders if he's seen the Jack's face on a "picture upon somebody's shelf"; that picture could have belonged to Lily or Rosemary. Rosemary's drinking is to steel her courage, and her "reflection in the knife" is telling because that knife will eventually be the murder weapon. It's a masterful job by Dylan of tying all these seemingly disconnected aspects together into such a complete picture.

Dylan trusts his audience to make the necessary leaps rather than spoon-feeding them the story. "Lily, Rosemary and the Jack of Hearts" is ultimately less about the exact sequence of events than it is about the frailty of human nature as reflected in the tragic fate of these characters. Only the Jack of Hearts escapes unscathed, still out there somewhere planning his next big score.

15. "Red River Shore" (from *The Bootleg Series, Vol. 8: Tell Tale Signs: Rare and Unreleased 1989–2006*, 2008)

There's a certain kind of Dylan song that started popping up around the mid-'80s that could be labeled the Lonely Wanderer song, several of which have already appeared on this countdown. The narrator in these songs is always singing in the first person, telling of his travels while making existential musings on his surroundings, all while pining for a love that he lost sometime far in the past. There are a number of songs that fit this category: "Mississippi," "Can't Escape from You," "Nettie Moore," "This Dream of You," "Cold Irons Bound," "Sugar Baby," and so on.

"Red River Shore," which was recorded for but not included on 1989's *Oh Mercy* before eventually showing up on the *Tell Tale Signs* collection, is the towering standard against which all of those similar songs are measured, if only because Dylan takes things a bit deeper, a bit darker. The melancholy here is so profound that it threatens to completely wipe the narrator off the map, if it hasn't already done so. Bob once sang, on "I Threw It All Away," that "Love is all there is," and this song takes that statement and extrapolates on it to a harrowing degree.

From the very first lines, it's clear that "Red River Shore" is going to be something special. After a spare guitar intro, Dylan sings, "Some of us turn off the lights and we live in the moonlight shooting by / Some of us scare ourselves to death in the dark to be where the angels fly." Those lines recall Robert Frost's "The Road Not Taken" in the way they delineate the relationship of choices and consequences.

The narrator has chosen a path that gave him a single chance with the girl he loved, a chance he squandered away. As a result, his life is balanced precariously between the sweet memories of their time together and the deep pit of sorrow that comes to the fore when those memories fade. It's similar to the balance struck by the *Oh Mercy*-era band behind Dylan, as they buoy the lovely melody with flourishes alternately sweet and sad.

Each line that he sings is fraught with a slew of meanings. When the narrator recalls the first time he sees her, he sings, "One look at her and I knew right away / She should always be with me." His prophecy came true, but not in the way he intended. She is with him always, but only as a reminder of everything that he has lost.

Like a few other Dylan narrators in a similar predicament, this guy is tortured with feelings of isolation and déjà vu, so that lines like "Though nothing looks familiar to me / I know I've stayed here before" make perfect sense. He has no hopes of replacing her, even with the "Pretty maids all in a row lined up / Outside my cabin door." (Groupies?) His only solace is music: "And the hills will give me a song."

In the last two verses, Dylan twists the knife in even deeper. First the narrator admits that he did try to go back and reunite with the girl once, but "Everybody that I talked to had seen us there / Said they didn't know who I was talking about." All kinds of questions come into play upon this revelation. Has this guy lost it? Is the girl dead? Did she even exist?

The last verse goes deeper down the mystical wormhole, as the narrator speaks of a man with the power to bring the dead back to life. He sings, "Sometimes I think nobody ever saw me here at all / Except the girl from the Red River Shore." Now it's the narrator whose existence is being called into question.

The narrator has essentially become an apparition walking the Earth without the presence of the girl to give his existence meaning. He might as well be a ghost for all the impact that he makes. Maybe he died inside while he was still with her, and that's what caused her to leave. That would explain his wanting to be reanimated and the fact that nobody recognizes him in their former home.

It's pretty haunting stuff, but it's done with such elegance and finesse that it gently plucks every heartstring without trampling on them. No one would ever willingly walk in the shoes of the narrator of "Red River Shore." Maybe that's why we value the Lonely Wanderer in Dylan's songs so much. He walks down those dark roads so we won't have to do it ourselves.

14. "Tangled Up in Blue' (from *Blood on the Tracks,* 1975)

People have been writing songs about breakups pretty much since words were put to music, so you would think that it's all pretty much been done before. Yet part of the genius of *Blood on the Tracks* was that it presented a relationship's dissolution in a way that was unlike anything that had ever been heard before. Nothing is simple, everything is confused, and it's hard to tell who's doing what to whom.

The album was revolutionary because its messiness is so realistic and honest to what it feels like when people who truly love each other separate. "Tangled Up in Blue" was the song driving the bus, one of the great kickoff songs in rock history because it both sets the table for everything we're about to hear and encapsulates it all at once.

The song presents a panoramic view of a relationship by reimagining it as a series of disjointed vignettes that still somehow cohere. Dylan's painting lessons are often cited as a big influence on this song's creation, but a painting is still just two dimensions. "Tangled Up in Blue" leaves two dimensions behind about ten words in, and keeps expanding the scope until the world bursts open with that last harmonica solo.

By toying with time frames and perspectives, Dylan gives the listener the same sense of disorientation that these two people must be feeling as they go through this. Bob made the crucial choice to switch from the third person used in the New York version of the song to the first and second ("I" and "you") in the Minnesota version that ended up on the album, which, along with the stepped-up tempo, turned the song from a thoughtful dissection of the situation into an emotional exorcism.

When the song begins, the way that the narrator wonders about the color of his beloved's hair slyly recalls "Girl from the North Country." As the verses pile up, the couple seems to constantly separate and reunite with the scenes all out of order. In that respect, one could view the song as flashes of memories that hit this guy as he rests in bed, memories that quantum leap these characters into different times and places with no regard for any linear narrative.

So the story jackknifes quickly from her parents' problems with him to their splitting up in the span of just two verses. She promises him they'll meet again, and they do, later in the song, in the damnedest places. First she shows up in a topless bar, leading to the unforgettable line, "I must admit I felt a little uneasy when she bent down to tie the laces of my shoe." (How much do you tip for that?) Following that, they're back at home smoking pipes and reading poetry.

The last verse sets him on the path back to her, from which he isn't likely to stray. We know from the previous verses that it was a circuitous journey to this point, and it isn't likely to be smooth from here. He contrasts the sedate lives of the people he has encountered with his own: "But me, I'm still on the road / Headin' for another joint." "Joint" is really the perfect word there; it suggests a place that is shabby, unsophisticated, generally unworthy of her presence.

He follows that up with a line that signifies how even two people meant for each other can get their lines crossed: "We always did feel the same / We just saw it from a different point of view." They are indeed tangled in a web of circumstance, stubbornness, and confusion, and it's thick enough to keep them apart forever.

It's impossible to separate the songs on *Blood on the Tracks* from Dylan's own personal situation at the time, even if the songs aren't purely autobiographical. In that regard, his "Tangled up in Blue" could be a reenacting of the scenes that he lived through while separating from wife Sara, as filtered through his boundless imagination. Most people who've lived through similar heartbreak know that such mind games are a way to keep the raw truth from seeping in.

No matter how you spin it, when you wake up alone on a sunny day, it still stings, and this masterful song doesn't skimp on the pain. Yet pain is just a part of the post-breakup spectrum. There's reflection, rumination, determination, and demoralization, just for a start. "Tangled Up in Blue" gets all of it, shining a bright, unforgiving light on the full range of these conflicting emotions, even as it fogs up all the details.

13. "Visions of Johanna" (from *Blonde on Blonde*, 1966)

Being without the one you love can play funny tricks on you. The narrator in "Visions of Johanna" describes the world around him as if viewed through a fun-house mirror, yet he manages striking clarity with his observations in the midst of this skewed reality. Ultimately, it's of little consolation or consequence to him because Johanna is all that matters.

Dylan's songwriting gifts have never been so brazenly on display as on this staggering effort from *Blonde on Blonde*. It has perhaps a higher degree of difficulty than any of his songs, in that it must make you interested in the narrator's wanderings without ever diverting focus from what's most important: That he misses Johanna. So you kind of get two for the price of one here, with one of Bob's mind-bending mid-'60s tapestries all rolled up into a love song.

Of course, it's the love part that drives the narrator to observe his surroundings in such a state of morose curiosity. Without Johanna, he attempts to dive into this world so it can serve as a distraction. Only it doesn't distract him enough, and that frustration ultimately plays into his descriptions of the sights and sounds, which, for all the spectacular imagery, hold little appeal to him.

Dylan battled with the song for a while before coming up with the delicate feel of the recording. One of the song structure's most fascinating traits is the way that it pauses between each verse for a brief harmonica whine before Kenny Buttrey's drums kick everybody back into action. It's as if the narrator needs to let some bluesy emotion out before composing himself and continuing with his tale.

The somber stage is set with the second line of the first verse, which could be specific to the narrator's situation in his cold room with the country music playing and the night playing tricks on him, or could just as easily sum up all of civilization: "We sit here stranded, though we're all doin' our best to deny it." He then introduces Louise, the most consistent of the narrator's many distractions in the song.

Although he doesn't seem to mind her, he also isn't bowled over by her: "Louise, she's all right, she's just near." Not exactly a ringing endorsement of her charms. Then again, nothing really seems to get this guy too excited. Bemused maybe, but not excited. The all-night girls, the night watchman, the peddler, the countess, the fiddler: They all come and go, and he notes their existence, but he can't muster too much enthusiasm for their various escapades.

He doesn't even find himself too interesting. The third verse about the "little boy lost" might as well be the narrator talking to himself. "He's sure got a lotta gall," he sings, "to be so useless and all." He seems to be weary of his own sorrow, even as it persists.

The verse in the museum is particularly clever, as Dylan uses the art, alternately lovely and grotesque, to highlight just how jaded this guy has become. Mona Lisa is just another girl with the blues in his book, and the supposed everlasting quality of these works of art is nothing that should be envied by the living. It's just more futile distraction.

His jaded tone does allow him to cut through the nonsense and get to the heart of the matter. The peddler's classic complaint ("Name me someone who's not a parasite, and I'll go out and say a prayer for him") sounds as if the narrator is acting as his ventriloquist. The sarcasm and subtle humor keep "Visions of Johanna" relatable and not just a song-writing flight of fancy.

In the last verse, the narrator, his brain on overload, begins piling rhyme on top of rhyme as if he can't stop, a true show-stopping moment for Dylan. Finally, his "conscience explodes," clearing out all of the extraneous debris, leaving him with just a lonely harmonica blowing in the rain and the one inescapable fact in his mad, mad world: "And these visions of Johanna are now all that remain."

The song is striking for how each of Dylan's lines stands out in its own unique way, but those lines never digress from the weary fate of the narrator. "Visions of Johanna" deftly touches on everything, but still boils it all down to one single thing: If the one who matters most is not with you, everything else is ephemera.

12. "Chimes of Freedom" (from *Another Side of Bob Dylan,* 1964)

While some would say that Bob Dylan wrote protest songs on behalf of causes like Civil Rights, anti-war, and justice in his early years as a songwriter, it would be more accurate to say that he wrote songs for people, real people like Hattie Carroll or Medgar Evers, fictional people like John Brown. The causes were attached to them, but the people, and their suffering, came first.

With "Chimes of Freedom," Dylan simply eliminated the middle-man. In other words, there is no single cause that can be pinpointed in the song, although the downtrodden folks who are referenced may have been affected by any one of a number of societal ills. Yet even those who can't point to a single talking point as the reason for their travails need a voice. Dylan imagines a world where they have one, even if it has to come in the form of a *deus ex machina,* like an otherworldly storm that sweeps away the clouds and sheds light on everyone suffering in silence.

"Chimes of Freedom" is essentially two different songs that complement each other to form a coherent whole. In the verses, there are physical descriptions of the fantastic storm that envelops the narrator and his companions, trapping them in a mixture of fear and awe at the "naked wonder" they see and hear. In the run up to the refrain, there is a startlingly comprehensive list of all those who need freeing and can't manage it on their own. In this, you get to hear Dylan's poetic gifts right alongside his innate empathy, and it is an overwhelming combination.

Another Side of Bob Dylan, the 1964 album that contains "Chimes of Freedom," was a move from the political to the personal for Dylan. It makes sense that the song, which is the closest thing to topical material on the LP, wouldn't be a direct hit on a specific subject a la "The Lonesome Death of Hattie Carroll" or "Masters of War." This song envelops anyone who needs it with its boundless goodwill.

The music is a key component of the song's success. Note how the verses don't start on the dominant chord, thus creating a sense of anticipation that is mirrored by the people in the song awaiting the storm. As each line progresses, that anticipation is much like the split second of fear and excitement we endure between the sight of a lightning bolt and the boom of thunder that follows, until the return to the main chord momentarily orients us again.

Those verses are also filled with some of Bob's most vivid writing. The words he chooses are almost uniformly active and forceful, and the alliterative phrases evoke the sounds of a storm. So we get "majestic bells of bolts," "mad mystic hammering," and "hypnotic splattered mist." Even though this is a purely fictional storm, Dylan entrenches it in our mind's eye with stunning skill.

All of that bluster and boom sets us up for the reason the storm is necessary. Dylan's real bravery in writing this song is including members of society who might not be deemed by some circles as worthy of concern. So alongside "nobler" heroes like pacifist soldiers and the gentle and the kind, we are presented with rebels, rakes, prostitutes (albeit mistitled ones), even prisoners. "All down in taken-for granted situations" is his telling way of classifying these outcasts; in other words, anyone who would judge them could easily, in different circumstances, know their lonely plight.

As inclusive as Dylan is throughout the song, it is nothing compared with the breathtaking final verse. He sweeps everyone up in the liberating maelstrom: "For the countless confused, accused, misused, strung-out ones and worse / An' for every hung-up person in the whole wide universe." He harnesses so much power with his wordplay in these lines that it doesn't seem possible that the sweeping changes promised by these chimes have yet to come to pass.

It's safe to say that even if they don't fit into any of the other categories he mentions, just about every member of the audience has been "hung-up" at some point in their lives. By rounding us all up like he does, Dylan is implying that we must never turn away from the other members of our teeming group, no matter how different they may seem. Until those "Chimes of Freedom" tear through the night and light up the sky, we're the only chance we've got.

11. "Boots of Spanish Leather" (from *The Times They Are A-Changin'*, 1964)

Letter writing has become a lost art form, one of the sadder side effects of communication streamlining. While it is hard to argue that the instant gratification of talking to someone the very moment you want to via cell phones, e-mails, text messaging, and the like is a bad thing, the deeper feelings that can be accurately, eloquently, and movingly conveyed in a letter get lost in the high-speed shuffle.

Couples within relationships are the ones most likely in need of the freedom of expression that letter writing permits. Just as a love letter is useful for those who fear that they'll choke on the big words if they have to speak them, so too does a breakup letter help out those who can't bring themselves to end it face-to-face.

Bob Dylan's "Boots of Spanish Leather," a forlorn love ballad drifting amidst the trenchant topical songs on 1963's *The Times They Are A-Changin'*, is a story told through the contents of revealing letters sent between two people who are about to become ex-lovers. The ingenious he said/she said between the guy stuck at home and the girl preparing to sail to Europe details the subtle disintegration of their relationship. Eventually, the letters are only being sent one way, and it's over.

Someone new to it might need a bunch of listens to the song to figure out just who is saying what to whom and when. Luckily, the emotion is clear enough that "Boots of Spanish Leather" can be enjoyed even before the dynamics of the dialogue became clear. The actual structure is set up so that the verses alternate, the girl taking a verse, then the guy, until the last three verses, when it's the narrator alone who has to speak for both the girl and himself. At that point, she's long gone and not coming back, so a one-sided conversation is the only one they can have.

For the first four verses, the repartee seems friendly enough. She tells him that she's headed off on this overseas trip and asks him what he wants from her travels. He sweetly says that he just wants her back with her love for him intact. By contrast, that sad melody, the same one used for "Girl from the North Country," suggests that all may not be well.

In the fifth verse, the girl seems overly concerned about his well-being and pleads with him to take her gift. "I might be gone a long, long time," she says. Could she bring him something "to make your time more easy passin'?" His exasperation begins to show in his response: "How can, how can you ask me again? / It would only bring me sorrow." Cracks are beginning to appear.

In the seventh verse, he gets the letter that he suspected was coming but hoped he could avoid. It says, "I don't know when I'll be comin' back again / It depends on how I'm feelin'." Even an optimist can tell that those words are the beginning of the end for their time as a couple.

The final two verses are his epistolary response. His mind is able to overrule his heart's objections as he sings, "I'm sure your thoughts are not with me / But with the country to where you're goin'." It's a brave, painful admission to make.

One can imagine his pen shaking as he closes out his final letter. He gives her a little small talk about the weather to hide his obvious pain, and then follows it up by asking for "Spanish boots of Spanish leather." That's all she can possibly give him at this point since her return to him, which is what he really wants, is no longer possible.

That ending is a killer, the guy's false bravado hardly hiding his intense anguish. Maybe she left because she wanted to build a new life. Maybe she was building a new life because she wanted to leave. Either way, the finality of it is excruciating.

It's likely that anyone who has had a rough breakup and lived to tell the tale will recognize the hurt feelings in Dylan's bereft vocal. "Boots of Spanish Leather" is no doubt a triumph of clever construction, but the honesty of those feelings is what makes it so affecting.

Those who haven't had a breakup so painful can slip out of that lonely footwear the moment that the song ends. The song's protagonist isn't quite so lucky, forever pining for his love with only a measly pair of boots and a few tear-stained letters to show for his trouble.

10. "Like a Rolling Stone" (from *Highway 61 Revisited*, 1965)

When lists of the greatest songs in rock and roll history are made by music magazines and websites and the like, "Like a Rolling Stone" is often near or at the very top, and rightfully so. In terms of songs that get a lot of airplay on rock radio, it's hard to argue against its superiority, no matter what measuring is used.

The key words there are "rock and roll history." The songs that are ranked higher than it on this list aren't really rock songs; as a matter of fact, very few Dylan songs are "rock songs" or songs that would ever have any chance at being rock radio hits even if they were released as singles. In many ways they go deeper than all that; "Like a Rolling Stone" manages to carry that depth with it into the rock milieu.

As a matter of fact, the hallowed status of "Like a Rolling Stone" in rock circles makes it hardest to judge among Dylan songs. That's because its exalted reputation is far different from the reality of the song, both musically and lyrically. It's the reputation, in many ways, that carries it to those other all-encompassing lists; it's the actual merits of it that put it at number ten of every song that Bob Dylan has ever written and performed, which, considering the man's catalog, is still great.

The musical reputation of the song is as a trailblazer to a new type of unkempt rock and roll that would be all the rage within a few years. Yet a closer listen to the song as it appears as the lead-off track to *Bringing It All Back Home* reveals a production that, while dense and imaginative, isn't all that wild. Al Kooper's organ part is justifiably legendary, Paul Griffin's chugging piano is an underrated element, and Bobby Gregg hits the snare crack heard 'round the world to get things started. But, of all the instruments, only Dylan's harmonica is played with what you could call abandon.

The live versions that would follow with the Hawks, especially the vengeful performance found on the *Live 1966* edition of *The Bootleg Series*, are another story entirely. That music was fierce, uncompromising, and threatened to run right off the rails at any time. The studio version is undeniably great, but its restraint is evident when you listen to it without any preconceived notions clouding your ears.

As for the lyrics, the reputation has always been that "Like a Rolling Stone" is an angry song, and Dylan himself bolstered that reputation a lot through the years in interviews. What you'll find if you parse the lyrics closely, however, is a lot more sympathy than you might expect.

You can read that famous "How does it feel?" refrain a couple ways. You can say that he's sneering at the girl in the song, forcing her to face the reality that her choices have caused. Yet there is compassion in the way Bob sings the refrain, as in "How are you?" or "Are you all right?" He's legitimately curious about whether or not her new life is fulfilling her expectations.

One also has to concede that being "on your own" with "no direction home" isn't always necessarily a bad thing. That idea also alters the meaning of one of the song's most famous lines, "When you got nothin', you got nothin' to lose." It turns the oft-quoted phrase into a synonym for freedom, something Kris Kristofferson understood when he rephrased the line when writing "Me and Bobby McGee."

While Dylan is clearly castigating the scene that has bewitched this girl, what he feels toward the girl is less anger than disappointment. The spectacular terms he uses to describe the company she keeps serve to show how alluring they must seem to an innocent like her. When he sings, "You're invisible now, you got no secrets to conceal," it seems more an invitation to a fresh start, not an admonition that she has reached the end. These are just a few examples showing that anger is not the only emotion that a listener can take away from the song.

Such malleability of meaning is one of the song's many enduring, endearing traits. Yet in terms of quality, Bob had a few other songs roughly on the same level as "Like a Rolling Stone" and even a few slightly above it. Which is why calling it the best rock song of all time and labeling it the tenth best Dylan song need not be contradictory statements.

9. "Tears of Rage" (from *The Basement Tapes*, 1975)

William Shakespeare's *King Lear* is often cited as Dylan's inspiration for "Tears of Rage." Both are sorrowful howls by fathers embittered with disappointment in their daughters. Things don't end quite so mel-

odramatically in Dylan's song; the body count is mercifully low compared to *Lear*. Yet there is the same sense of elemental sadness borne
of the breakdown of the seemingly impenetrable connection between
father and daughter.

In Stephen Greenblatt's insightful book *Will in the World*, which is
part Shakespeare biography and part analysis of his work, the author
posits that a major reason why his later plays were so revolutionary was
the so-called "excision of motive."[19] The actions of the protagonists in
these plays didn't seem to be driven by any motive that was spelled out
in the narrative. This stratagem made these characters much harder to
predict and, in turn, more psychologically realistic.

Lear was one of the characters that Greenblatt mentioned, which
makes you think twice about where your sympathies should lie in "Tears
of Rage." If Dylan is invoking Lear, the narrator's complaints could be
interpreted as the rantings of a senile old man, while the modern-day
Cordelia in the song could be the one that's in the right.

It's probably not as cut-and-dried as that though. In many ways,
"Tears of Rage" is a close cousin to the Beatles "She's Leaving Home,"
with both songs initially recorded in 1967. The Fab Four's song poig-
nantly tries to see both sides of the story in the generational divide, and
Bob was getting at that as well.

The Band, who provide an indelible assist on Dylan's *Basement
Tapes* version of the song, made it a point to open their first album with
their own mournful take on "Tears of Rage," a conscious reaction to the
anti-parents sentiment that was prevalent at the time in much of youth
culture. It was Dylan, of course, who provided the words for The Band
to make that statement, with Richard Manuel providing the music.

Manuel's tune is as integral to the song's power as the lyrics. He
didn't write songs often, but when he did, Manuel's melodies were
always gorgeously sad. What he created for Dylan's story was simple yet
surprisingly impactful. His moaning backing vocals add to the feeling.

The father seems to be speaking for both parents as he opens the
song with a nostalgic bit of the past contrasted with the anguish they
feel in the present. After noting the family's closeness on a long-ago
holiday, he bemoans the present-day flipside: "And now you'd throw us
all aside / And put us on our way." The choice of Independence Day for
the memory's setting is telling, since the girl's quest for personal independence is what is breaking her father's heart.

In the second verse, a happy memory of the family on the beach is measured against the ungrateful behavior the daughter now exhibits. It's quite a turnaround from Dylan, a guy who once wrote about sons and daughters being beyond the command of their parents. Now that this one girl has escaped that command, the songwriter does a 180 and sympathizes with the other side. Yet as much as we want to feel for the father, there are moments when he seems too unreasonable with his demands to warrant sympathy.

In the chorus, the father's self-pity mingles with his genuine desire to get his little girl back. As Manuel and Rick Danko soar high above him like lonely angels, Dylan brings home the painful payoff. "Tears of rage, tears of grief," he sings, highlighting the wave of emotions that runs over the father. His final moving plea: "Come to me now, you know, we're so alone / And life is brief."

As those three voices come together in harmony on that last line, singing it like a hymn, it doesn't matter who's to blame anymore. All that matters are the consequences of this conflict: The possibility that death will precede their reunion. It's a tragic moment that Shakespeare would envy.

"Tears of Rage" isn't an easy song to get your head around because it plops you down in the middle of the dispute and doesn't allow the daughter any rebuttal. It's kind of like the way you're asked to understand how Lear would be so foolish as to turn his back on the one daughter who actually cares for him. Dylan and Shakespeare both seem to be saying that it should be impossible to figure out how something so pure as the love between a father and daughter could ever go so wrong.

8. "Every Grain of Sand" (from *Shot of Love*, 1981)

There are two pretty special versions of this masterpiece of a song from which Dylan enthusiasts can choose. The version of "Every Grain of Sand" that closes out 1981's *Shot of Love* is understated yet powerful; it has an after-hours quietude to it that allows the listener to really contemplate the lyrics, and Bob's harmonica solos are quite fine.

On the first *Bootleg Series* release, there is an equally fine yet vastly different version, recorded as a publishing demo. The simple piano and acoustic guitar accompaniment on this take gives the song a weightless, elusive quality that is well suited to the content. Moreover, Dylan, in a quasi duet with Jennifer Warnes, sings in a high register that makes him strain at times, sounding almost desperate to find the answers to the questions that he poses. That higher voice also shines a brighter light on the achingly lovely melody, one of Bob's best ever.

This take also has the bonus of Bob's dog barking in the background, and it somehow works. After all, the song talks about the divinity to be found in all God's creations, so why not a divine canine? Plus, the dog has expert timing, seemingly seconding Dylan's emotions with his woofing.

In either rendering, "Every Grain of Sand" is Dylan's finest religious song because it emphasizes the best parts of having faith while still admitting the difficulty to maintain it. And even though there are some oblique biblical references, the lack of specificity in the higher power that is invoked makes it perhaps the most inclusive of his spiritual journeys.

The narrator immediately informs us that he reaches some pretty dodgy places in his quest: "In the time of my confession, in the hour of my deepest need." Note that the voice inside him is "dyin'," which would lend some credence to those people who believe that Dylan's own religious fervor was waning at the time he wrote it. That's probably too much of a leap to make with the song, which is a less confident, more realistic depiction of the peaks and valleys of belief in a higher power.

The language is uniformly beautiful throughout the song. Dylan's word choices are exemplary both in terms of their evocative nature and the way they hold tight to the meter, an underrated trait that helps the song become so memorable. Phrases like "fury of the moment" and "morals of decay" just tend to roll off the tongue even as they make you think deep about their meaning.

It's necessary to show the dark side sometimes to emphasize the light. So it is that the narrator draws us in with details of his own internal struggle: "I gaze into the doorway of temptation's angry flame / And every time I pass that way, I always hear my name." Yet the refrains find him gravitating to the simplest gestures as evidence of God's might, a way of saying that you need to find faith where you can, lest despair win out.

The last verse is a tour de force, one of Dylan's finest moments. The narrator details the crossroads he's standing at in a strikingly memorable manner: "In the bitter dance of loneliness fading into space / In the broken mirror of innocence on each forgotten face." Every word seems to contrast the next, putting the narrator in a nether region between grace and damnation.

That's when he makes his most honest admission about his periodic doubts: "I hear the ancient footsteps like the motion of the sea / Sometimes I turn, there's someone there, other times it's only me." He realizes that he is "hanging in the balance," and at that moment, he clings tightly to the trembling leaves, the numbered hairs, the fallen sparrows, because the alternative is too harrowing to consider.

There's a reason that people often choose "Every Grain of Sand" to be played at funerals. A funeral is a time to reflect on the death of a loved one, a time when faith is tested above all. It's comforting at that moment to think of those loved ones having reached a place of peace where they wait for us to arrive, and the song tells you that all you really need to do to believe is take a good look around.

Dylan wants us to believe, especially at the moments when it is most difficult to believe, that heaven is everywhere. It's in every dog that's barking and in "Every Grain of Sand."

7. "The Lonesome Death of Hattie Carroll" (from *The Times They Are A-Changin'*, 1964)

William Zantzinger died back in 2009 at the age of sixty-nine. By all accounts, he was able to overcome any infamy brought about by "The Lonesome Death of Hattie Carroll," living a relatively quiet, upstanding existence in Charles, Maryland, with the notable exception of a prison sentence for continuing to collect rents on properties he no longer owned.

Hattie Carroll, of course, had no opportunity to live out a similarly quiet life past the evening of February 8, 1963, which is when she died. That, apart from anything else, is the main point we're meant to take away from "The Lonesome Death of Hattie Carroll," the crowning achievement in Bob Dylan's quest to render topical material in a way that combines intelligence to sway the mind with emotional impact to touch the heart.

What might have happened had Dylan been able to deliver the song in front of the three-judge panel that gave Zantzinger a six-month sentence for his role in Carroll's death? Bob is so thorough in his destruction of Zantzinger's character and so tender in his presentation of Carroll that it's hard to come away from the song with anything but the harshest verdict possible.

Yes, Dylan fudged the facts a little bit. Chief among the discrepancies between song and truth are that Zantzinger was not convicted of murder but of manslaughter, mainly due to the fact that his blows to Carroll with a toy cane were not deemed to have directly caused her death. Carroll had preexisting medical conditions, which, according to the coroner, were fatally triggered by the stress from the attack.

Yet these details are tangential to Dylan's essential theory: That Zantzinger was operating under a different set of rules than Carroll, and society's acceptance of those rules was what allowed such tragedies to happen. It's why Bob never has to mention that Zantzinger was white and Carroll was black. Sadly, we know that instinctively.

The actual details of the slaying are kept to a minimum by Dylan. Instead, the bulk of the song is concerned only with the contrasting social standing of the two participants in the story. Zantzinger is presented as a social dandy from a connected family with no remorse for his actions, while Carroll is the quiet maid that does her job and doesn't bother anybody, undeserving of her fate ("And she never did nothing to William Zantzinger").

There are very few attorneys that have the prodigious talent with the English language that Dylan possesses, so trying to defend the accused in the face of his verbal assault is not a fair fight. "The Lonesome Death of Hattie Carroll" is an awe-inspiring display of his gifts, as he piles his arguments together with no concern for traditional song structure; he's just going to keep talking 'til there can be no reasonable doubt, pounding the inequality of Hattie being "on a whole other level" into our brains.

As with so many of Dylan's finest songs, he saves his most powerful stuff for last. In the final verse, he uses the first part to describe the way that justice should be, setting his listeners up. Then comes the gut punch as he finishes by re-telling the judge's final verdict for Zantzinger: "And he handed out strongly, for penalty and repentance / William Zantzinger with a six-month sentence." Bob strums the guitar for an extra moment or two after this final line, as if letting this seemingly impossible outcome sink in.

Throughout the song, Dylan's refrains call out to "You who philoso-phize disgrace / And criticize all our fears," asking them to wait before letting their emotions loose. Those words are aimed at people who might be able to rationalize not only the kind of behavior Zantzinger exhibits but also the setting of the song, a world where whites of privi-lege are served by blacks without much choice other than to serve. Bob's last refrain lets these people know his story is done: "Bury the rag deep in your face / For now's the time for your tears."

And, really, who could stop from weeping after hearing that tale as rendered by someone who pushes all our emotional buttons without stooping to manipulative levels? William Zantzinger spent just six months in jail for the death of Hattie Carroll, but thanks to Bob Dylan's "The Lonesome Death of Hattie Carroll," his punishment was the eter-nal disdain of a jury of listeners.

Needless to say, that will never be enough for those who loved Hat-tie Carroll, but it will have to do.

6. "It's Alright, Ma (I'm Only Bleeding)" (from *Bringing It All Back Home*, 1965)

Maybe the great rock debate of the '60s was the Beatles versus the Stones, but there was an equally fascinating dichotomy at play between the music of the Fab Four and that of Bob Dylan. While they were fans of each other and influenced each other's music, the messages they sent were quite different.

The Beatles had an unparalleled ability to project joy into the world, a handy skill to have in the turbulent '60s, and their adherence to their love-conquers-all ethos was as moving in intent as it was naïve in prac-tice. Dylan, on the other hand, was unmatched at delineating all the pitfalls on the road to bliss. Indeed, one could have struck a pretty good balance in life by taking the best parts of the Beatles' unbridled opti-mism and Bob's healthy cynicism.

On "It's Alright, Ma (I'm Only Bleeding)," that cynicism is so healthy it's practically a mutant. Yet the song performs a crucial service for those who are at that point of their lives when they can no longer count on the protective cocoon of childhood. To defeat your enemies, you first have to identify them. This song is a laundry list of all the people and things that will deceive, dissuade, and destroy you if you let them.

Bob never actually uses the phrase "I'm Only Bleeding" in the lyrics, but it's in your subconscious as you listen, letting you know the consequences if you neglect the message being delivered. And if that doesn't make it clear, the first line will: "Darkness at the break of noon," an indication of the topsy-turvy world that we're about to encounter, a world that looks strikingly like our own.

Dylan's growing fascination with odd song structures pays off huge dividends here. This song needed to be merciless and relentless. As a result, Bob's choice to cram as much as he could into the verses, as the guitar chords slowly descend into the abyss, was totally apropos.

The song is framed by Dylan speaking to an unnamed "you" that is clearly meant to represent anyone who happens to be listening to this extended tirade. He spends the first section of "It's Alright, Ma" revealing what awaits those who succumb to the perils he's about to describe. It's an awful state of paralysis and confusion, made no less lonely by the knowledge that everyone else is feeling the same way.

When he sings, "He not busy being born is busy dying" in this context, it's not really a rallying cry. It's a warning that you need to hustle and scrape just to keep from getting completely steamrolled. We soon find out all the ways that this can happen: schools that lobotomize you, jobs that demoralize you, and advertising that brainwashes you. It's a worldview that makes Orwell's vision of the future in 1984 look like Candy Land by comparison.

Many of Dylan's most famous quotes about naked presidents and swearing money come from here, but there are less brazen lines throughout that make just as much of an impact. For example: "It's only people's games that you got to dodge," a line that suggests that all the overarching issues in the world boil down to one person trying to take advantage of the next person instead of trying to help them out. Look out, kid.

In the very last verse, Dylan switches to the first person "I." It's a subtle way of addressing the fact that even he, the so-called spokesman for a generation, was scuffling along with everybody else to make sense of the madness. He defiantly calls out "What else can you show me?"— bruised and battered but still standing, yet vulnerable to the knockout blow that can come at any moment.

The "It's Alright, Ma" refrains are essential to humanizing the song. They show a child trying to reassure his mother, the relationship symbolizing one bastion of unconditional love in the unforgiving world. When he says, "I can make it," it's hard to believe, with all he's told us, that he can. When he says, "It's life, and life only," we know that life is just too much.

In the Beatles classic, "Strawberry Fields Forever," John Lennon sings, "Living is easy with eyes closed / Misunderstanding all you see." In "It's Alright, Ma (I'm Only Bleeding)," Bob Dylan suggests that living is impossible even with your eyes open because there are people out there who will stop at nothing to pull the wool right over them.

Those two views may be contradictory, but, at times in your life and life only, chances are you'll need to heed them both.

5. "Not Dark Yet" (from *Time Out of Mind*, 1997)

The conundrum facing Bob Dylan fans concerning *Time Out of Mind* was that he was making perhaps the greatest artistic comeback of his career with a group of songs all about how it was all over. That was several classic albums and thousands of performances ago, so his own reports of his demise were premature.

Still, it made for good copy back in the day: Dylan releasing an album that dealt frankly with mortality just as he was staring down a life-threatening illness. Never mind the fact that the songs were written before his serious fungal infection in 1997; critics could just write that discrepancy off as Bob's old prophetic gifts turned on himself. "Not Dark Yet" was the theme song for this misguided analysis, many people hearing it as the last gasp of a dying man.

Yet "Not Dark Yet" was never about death, at least not the literal kind. It's about something somehow worse than that, a dousing of the internal spark that fuels contentment, comfort, and happiness. Dylan's narrator in "Not Dark Yet" has essentially reached the end of himself, and, from such an existence, death would be a respite.

There may be no other Bob Dylan song that makes as much of a musical impact as "Not Dark Yet" does. The instrumental breaks in the song are every bit as moving as the lyrics. Credit goes to Dylan's melody, which rises from stoic acceptance to untethered yearning; to the arrangement, which uses the martial drums and funereal pace to amplify the pathos; and to the band, who pulls off the difficult feat of matching their leader in terms of nuance and tenderness. It is a sad song, for sure, but it's somehow triumphantly sad.

"Shadows are falling, and I been here all day": One line in, and Dylan has already pinpointed the stagnation that has enveloped him. "It's too hot to sleep and time is running away." Like everyone and everything else in his life, time is abandoning him. It's evident from these first two lines how even the simplest declarations can convey infinite levels of torment.

The narrator takes a break now and again from detailing his malaise to offer some bits of wisdom: "Behind every beautiful thing there's been some kind of pain." Yet even the beautiful things provide him with no relief; after detailing a touching letter from a woman, he shrugs it off: "I just don't see why I should even care."

One of the benefits that a long life affords is a modicum of clarity about how the world works, so the narrator can at least see through the familiar deceptions: "I've been down on the bottom of a world full of lies." Compared to London and gay Paree, this symbolic location may seem daunting, but it doesn't change his expectations: "I ain't looking for nothing in anyone's eyes."

The narrator pours out the remnants of his heart in the staggering final verse. The first two lines emphasize his sense of immobility: "I was born here and I'll die here against my will / I know it looks like I'm moving, but I'm standing still." On top of that, the tactile world is fading, as are his memories: "Every nerve in my body is so vacant and numb / I can't even remember what it was I came here to get away from." Then, the ultimate proof that grace is not in the offing for this poor soul: "Don't even hear the murmur of a prayer."

The contrast between light and dark, and all that those terms convey, has always been a huge part of Bob's work. You can hear it in the light denied the forlorn lover in "Don't Think Twice, It's Alright" or the light granted the prisoner in "I Shall be Released." By contrast, imagine the "Dark Eyes" staring at Dylan and the "Dark Heat" he must navigate to find his love.

All of those former lines are a part of our Dylan consciousness, so, when we hear him say, "It's not dark yet, but it's getting there," it makes us stop short. And it's not because we think he (the narrator or Dylan) is dying, but because we think that he's hurting, and hurting so bad that recovery seems in doubt.

With that last sad refrain hanging in the air, the indefatigable music marches on, and we imagine the narrator doing so as well, toward the end of himself, now dangerously near. Everybody dies, but Dylan, in "Not Dark Yet," suggests that, if you're not careful, life might just kill the most important parts of you long before.

4. "Idiot Wind" (from *Blood on the Tracks*, 1975)

Although he never would admit that it was, Bob Dylan's *Blood on the Tracks*, released in 1975, was essentially a concept album about the dissolution of a relationship. It has inspired many others of the same ilk, some good, many more bad, but it still towers above the rest in this sub-genre.

"Idiot Wind" epitomizes the album's unflinching honesty, bravely showing every emotion that can possibly be felt. Dylan isn't afraid to be downright nasty or self-pitying in the song, unflattering traits that are nonetheless apropos for someone going through a hard breakup. Yet he's also ready to accept his share of the blame.

The song is mammoth and wordy because Dylan realized that you can pour so much out of yourself in a situation like this and still not be emotionally spent. Yes, there's plenty of bile and venom in the lyrics, but there's also the confusion borne of desperately trying to understand the other person's side of things.

The choice to speed up the tempo and toy with the lyrics in the switch from the New York to Minnesota versions was inspired. The *Bootleg Series* version from the New York sessions is a bit more of a one-note, "How could you do this to me?" kind of thing. By adding the drums and organ to the song as it would appear on *Blood on the Tracks*, "Idiot Wind" became more of a cathartic experience, especially with Dylan intensely singing as if his sanity depended on it, a man on the edge not able or willing to pull back.

The first verse's wild tale of the narrator murdering a man for his wife's inheritance is Dylan's sly commentary on the perils of believing what you read. That story also allows him to toss off the shackles of autobiography so he could attack the heart of the matter from all angles and render the song universally relevant.

And so, the "Idiot Wind" that blows through town confuses people who meet the narrator ("Their minds are filled with big ideas, images and distorted facts"). Worse yet, it infests the brain of his beloved, who starts to doubt him: "I couldn't believe after all these years, you didn't know me any better than that."

It's then that we are first introduced to that fabulously brusque refrain, the narrator calling the woman that he loves an idiot ("It's a wonder that you still know how to breathe"). The harshness is bracing, but name-calling is the kind of thing that people do when they're flailing.

Dylan brilliantly intertwines the deflecting imagery of fortune-tellers and howling beasts with straight-from-the-heart complaints ("I haven't known peace and quiet for so long I can't remember what it's like") and straight-to-the-gut attacks ("You hurt the ones that I love best and cover up the truth with lies / One day you'll be in the ditch flies buzzin' around your eyes / Blood on your saddle"). It's a harrowing roller coaster of emotions.

Yet the narrator's ex isn't the only target; he can see that her deceits are just par for the course when the "Idiot Wind" is everywhere ("From the Grand Coulee Dam to the Capitol"). As the song progresses though, there are fewer and fewer digressions, and the focus is solely on the girl. Every instance of rational rumination ("It was gravity which pulled us down and destiny which broke us apart") is balanced by verbal spitfire ("I can't remember your face anymore, your mouth has changed, your eyes don't look into mine").

Had Dylan continued in that vein, "Idiot Wind" would still have been an exhilarating bit of venting that the other more tempered songs on *Blood on the Tracks* might have balanced. Yet the final lines twist everything around, as the narrator's vitriol transforms on the fly into a sad reflection on the opportunities to get things right missed by both of them: "And it makes me feel so sorry."

To end this monumental rant with an apology of sorts is a brilliant stroke, one that feels true. In the final chorus, the narrator ups the ante on his sudden burst of understanding, changing the wording to "We're idiots, babe." At last they are united again, if only in terms of their stubbornness, their regret, and, in a matter of time, their loneliness.

The breakups that most people have aren't really this epic, but they always feel this epic to those involved. That's what Dylan taps into in "Idiot Wind." Forty years and counting worth of concept albums have tried to sum up a breaking heart in all its "ragin' glory." Bob nails it in a single song.

3. "Desolation Row" (from *Highway 61 Revisited*, 1965)

There is an indefinable thing that happens when instruments and voices cohere to create something that is pleasing to hear. It's not something that can be consciously attained. It's usually just a matter of it occurring by chance after a lot of trial and error.

If there is any Dylan recording that epitomizes this magical mixture of sounds, it's "Desolation Row," the epic closing track from 1965's *Highway 61 Revisited.* The aural chemistry owes much to Charlie McCoy's instinctive touch on acoustic guitar. After the vaguely Tex-Mex intro he conjured, he answered every one of Bob's lyrics with a little fill. These fills vary slightly from line to line, almost like McCoy is adding his own commentary. Even after ten verses, with a couple killer harmonica solos from Bob thrown in for good measure, you still don't want the thing to end.

Dylan fills up this pristine framework with a half-comic, half-tragic cast of characters marooned on a street that resembles nothing else in existence. Yet we recognize the men and women who populate the place, not because of the famous names that Bob hangs on them, but because of the way their foibles and flaws make them endearingly human.

"Desolation Row," its title notwithstanding, isn't a dark, despairing song. Even with mentions of sinister machines and people being rounded up on the streets, these folks aren't doomed. The openhearted music with which Dylan serenades them just couldn't be a death march.

The societal rejects who have founded this odd community are similar to the people that Dylan collects together in "Chimes of Freedom." The songwriter embraces them in all their weirdness and flawed glory. After all, he's right out there with them ("As Lady and I look out tonight on Desolation Row").

Those who attempt to tie too much significance to the famous historical and fictional names that populate the song are likely on the wrong path. After all, Dylan hints in the last verse that he was just messing around with their identities to try to make sense of this crazy avenue: "I had to rearrange their faces and give them all another name."

If anything, he uses those names as a diversion, allowing the associations they suggest to set listeners up for an expected outcome before subverting it. For example, brilliant Einstein is reduced to "reciting the alphabet." Cinderella and Romeo would seem to be set up for a love for the ages, but his flowery speech gets him ostracized, leaving her with one broom and zero princes.

And it goes on. Casanova, synonymous with romantic confidence, comes off as insecure. Ezra Pound and T. S. Eliot exchange moving poetry for fisticuffs. Gallant notions of any kind are frowned upon here, especially Ophelia's Shakespearean die-for-love ethos, which the narrator quickly denigrates: "Her sin is her lifelessness." It's just a front anyway: "Though her eyes are fixed upon Noah's great rainbow / She spends her time peeking into Desolation Row."

Yet Dylan makes it sound romantic. The nautical verse, which includes infamous Roman ruler Nero and the Titanic, glides along mellifluously. "Between the windows of the sea / Where lovely mermaids flow," Bob sings, as if this rough-and-tumble group was all being delivered to salvation.

Even a seemingly ominous line like "After the ambulances go" is sung with sweetness and wonder by Dylan. It's no wonder then that the narrator pulls himself away from watching this rich tapestry to remonstrate with his pen pal: "Don't send me no more letters, no / Not unless you mail them from Desolation Row."

Had Dylan sung with an eyebrow raised in irony, "Desolation Row" would have come off as a broadside against easy targets. He can even abide the fact that they would sell "postcards of the hanging." He's not condoning the behavior of the people that would gawk at such an ugly spectacle; he just seems to be acknowledging that they know not what they do.

"Desolation Row" presents a bevy of contradictions. On the one hand, there are a bunch of naive fools butting up against each other in a world every bit as threatening in its way as the one Dylan portrayed in "It's Alright, Ma (I'm Only Bleeding)." On the other, they are rendered in the most elegant manner possible, bestowing upon them a grace that they haven't earned but still deserve anyway.

It may be the same old dystopia, but it never sounded so inviting. "Desolation Row" might not be much, but it's all these folks have got. Only Dylan could make it sound like the place to be.

2. "Blind Willie McTell" (from *The Bootleg Series, Vol. 1–3: Rare & Unreleased 1961–1991*, 1991)

While it's tempting to pigeonhole Bob Dylan as a folk singer or rock star, the most accurate description of him is as a blues artist. He has always innately understood that the blues are more about emotion than some preordained musical structure, and he is part of the continuum of the blues, a line that runs through every form of music.

In "Blind Willie McTell," Dylan tells us that no can sing the blues like Willie, a Georgia-born performer famous for "Statesboro Blues." As the most fitting form of tribute, Bob gives the blues performance of his career, tracking a tragic pattern of prejudice and fear that runs through time and over distance.

This song exposes this pattern, too often ignored, as something vile and wicked, a source of unimaginable suffering. The dots are all there in front of our faces, but Dylan connects them for us on "Blind Willie McTell," and the picture created leaves no other option but to sing the blues.

On a recording featuring just Dylan on piano and Mark Knopfler on acoustic guitar, it is Bob's piano that leaves the biggest impression. He plays the chords with a unique rhythm, occasionally suspending the song for a moment to maximize the impact when he does pick things up again.

Bob's singing is also marvelous. For the first few verses, he soulfully sticks to the minor-key tune before ratcheting things up in the final moments to a guttural howl. His heartache gets the best of him as the song progresses, his voice finally losing its composure to really drive the emotion home. Many of Dylan's best songs are wordy affairs, but "Blind Willie McTell" is thrilling for the way he juggles so many difficult topics so efficiently, rendering it compact and powerful.

The narrator in the song is seemingly omnipresent and ageless, able to witness and describe all of the events for us. Most take place somewhere in the American South, its history so rich, complicated, and tied to race. Yet the action extends beyond that ("All the way from New Orleans / To Jerusalem"), the continuum traveling not just across a distance of thousands of miles, but across the mists of time.

Although there are brief moments of revelry, like the "charcoal gypsy maidens" dancing joyously, this observer mostly sees pain, like the awful legacy of slavery. This flashes before him in reverse order, the Civil War's denouement appearing first and the slaves arriving last.

In the fourth verse, Southern traditions, some noble, some dubious, are showcased. The refinement and gentility of the well-dressed young couple is undercut by the illegal whiskey they're drinking. We also rocket back in time to see the degradation of prisoners in a chain gang, but when Dylan follows that up with "I can hear them rebels yell," it conjures the battle cry of Confederate soldiers that struck fear into their Northern enemies.

By mixing up the history into a messy stew, Dylan seems to be saying that it's never easy to pinpoint a cause or assign blame for the ever-present anguish. It's easier for him to give a sweeping condemnation of the human race that goes beyond any regional borders: "But power and greed and corruptible seed / Seem to be all that there is." Much of the world's pain really boils down to those lines.

The final section of the song is a brilliant ploy by Dylan to bring the whole song back to the present-day. He sings, "I'm staring out the window / Of the St. James Hotel," intimating that all of the sights and sounds and smells he just related are roiling in the narrator's brain. The connection can be made to the blues song "St. James Infirmary," but you could also place the narrator in St. James, Minnesota, in Bob's home state.

With the refrain, it all comes back to the blues, specifically Blind Willie McTell, who wins the narrator's admiration and provides a useful distraction from the world of woe he has just described. The continuum is evident yet again.

Dylan didn't think "Blind Willie McTell" worthy of inclusion on 1983's *Infidels*, making this his greatest "lost" treasure, finally un-earthed on *The Bootleg Series* in 1991. Maybe he saw the song's revela-tions as self-evident and therefore not that special. You don't need a history book to perceive them; you only need open your eyes.

Maybe nobody can sing the blues like "Blind Willie McTell," but good luck finding anyone in the same class as Dylan when it comes to this brand of timeless music. With this song, he not only sings the blues, he shows why they need to be sung.

1. "Sad-Eyed Lady of the Lowlands" (from *Blonde on Blonde*, 1966)

The cliché "I love you more than words can say" was rendered irrelevant when Bob Dylan recorded "Sad-Eyed Lady of the Lowlands," a song where he captures the enormity of emotion that most of us may feel but don't have the gifts to express. He simply wrote the greatest love song there is, was, and ever will be.

A supremely special song needs an equally sublime recording, and the magic take of "Sad-Eyed Lady of the Lowlands" qualifies. Dylan gave a brief rundown of how the song would go for his band—just a verse and the chorus—and then he told them to follow him. And the band did just that, while waiting for the signal that he would be winding it up with a harmonica solo.

That solo didn't come until five verses had been completed and some ten minutes had passed. The band would rev up each time expecting the big finish, only to come back down again as the never-ending waltz played on. The tension-and-release is magical, as drummer Kenny Buttrey steadily keeps the beat on high hat while the rest of the band comes swooping in with a flourish every time Dylan sings about his "warehouse eyes."

The lyrics themselves are a series of stunning testaments to the wonder and inscrutability of the titular woman. There is such gallantry in Dylan's words, conjuring up a world where this woman is besieged on all sides by men who only want to control her. She resists them all, even though it causes her great suffering.

There are instances where the narrator paints an almost unflattering picture of her. She is described as wearing "basement clothes," having a "hollow face," and coming up a few cards short of a full deck. These are not rose-colored glasses through which the narrator views her, which makes his devotion all the more moving.

Obviously, he wouldn't love her so if she didn't have bewitching qualities as well, and Dylan uses all his poetic gifts in describing these. "With your silhouette as the sunlight dims / Into your eyes where the moonlight swims" is just one example—a simple and beautifully evocative couplet—to evoke deep feeling.

The song manages to transcend the specificity of its inspiration. "Sad-Eyed Lady of the Lowlands," which closed out *Blonde on Blonde* by occupying an entire side of the double album, was essentially a wedding gift to Sara Dylan, yet even the references to her life somehow resonate much wider.

The narrator piles up the praise, both of her beauty ("your saintlike face") and her nature ("your gentleness now that you just can't help but show"). But he also stands in awe of the way she overcomes the hordes of marauders who seek to extinguish her inner light. That's why he keeps asking the "Who among them" questions, because he knows the answer: None of them can carry, bury, persuade, employ, or destroy her.

And so he decides to try his hand where others have failed. He goes to the "lowlands" himself but doesn't force the matter like the rest of the rabble. With only his humble offerings in tow, he leaves it up to her: "Should I leave them by your gate / Or, sad-eyed lady, should I wait?"

It's easy to conjure the mental image of Dylan at this point in the song, standing outside in the wind and rain, blowing his harmonica with impassioned gusto, staring up at her silhouette in the window, awaiting her reply. Dylan fans live romantically through that image, believing him to always be in front of those gates, fighting the honorable fight for the rest of us.

The skeptics or those ignorant of his gifts may fall for the stereotype that Dylan is a rhyme-spewing robot who protested things once upon a time and now just sings his old songs in a craggy voice. His fans hear compassion, empathy, and profound emotion. His mind is truly amazing, but his songs would be hollow and cold without the heart. This song has infinite heart, and then some.

It is Bob's finest combination of lyrics, melody, and performance. It also has historical importance: it was the last song on the last album of his super-dynamic mid-'60s run before his career's trajectory changed.

Yet "Sad-Eyed Lady of the Lowlands" is ultimately my number one because it says "I love you" more completely, more passionately, than any other song I know. Your own significant other might not have a "child of the hoodlum" or any idea what "curfew plugs" are. Still, as the song fades out, you can definitely say: "There. That's how I feel about you."

Thanks to Dylan, they'll understand.

1. Gilbert Cruz, "The 10 Worst Bob Dylan Songs," *Time*, May 23, 2011, accessed December 3, 2012. entertainment.time.com/2011/05/23/10-worst-bob-dylan-songs.

2. Cameron Crowe, Liner Notes to *Biograph*, Bob Dylan, Columbia Records, CD, 1985.

3. Bill Flanagan, "Bob Dylan interviews with Bill Flanagan," *Telegraph*, April 13, 2009, accessed December 3, 2012. http://www.telegraph.co.uk/culture/music/bob-dylan/5148025/Bob-Dylan-interview-with-Bill-Flanagan.html.

4. BobDylan.com, "The Groom's Still Waiting at the Altar by Bob Dylan," accessed December 3, 2012. http://www.bobdylan.com/us/home#us/songs/grooms-still-waiting-altar.

5. Howard Sounes, *Down the Highway: The Life of Bob Dylan* (New York: Grove Press, 2001), 282.

6. Mikal Gilmore, "Bob Dylan Unleashed: A Wild Ride on His New LP and Striking Back at Critics," *Rolling Stone*, September 27, 2012, accessed April 22, 2013. http://www.rollingstone.com/music/news/bob-dylan-unleashed-a-wild-ride-on-his-new-lp-and-striking-back-at-critics-20120927.

7. Bob Dylan, *Chronicles Volume One* (New York: Simon & Schuster, 2004), 214.

8. Joan Baez, *And a Voice to Sing With: A Memoir* (New York: Simon & Schuster, 2009).

9. Nat Henthoff, Liner Notes to *The Freewheelin' Bob Dylan*, Bob Dylan, Columbia Records, LP, 1963.

10. Uncut, "Life with Bob Dylan, 1989–2006," accessed December 3, 2012.

11. Dylan, *Chronicles*, 273–276.

12. Dylan, *Chronicles*, 209–210.

13. Dylan, *Chronicles*, 122.

14. Oliver Trager, *Keys to the Rain: The Definitive Bob Dylan Encyclopedia*, (New York: Billboard Books, 2004), 548.

15. Good Reads, "Willie Nelson Quotes," accessed December 4, 2012. .

16. Josh Eells, "Eminem on the Road Back from Hell," *Rolling Stone*, October 17, 2011, accessed December 4, 2012. http://www.rollingstone.com/music/news/eminem-on-the-road-back-from-hell-20111017.

17. Henthoff, *Freewheelin'*.

18. Trager, *Keys*, 627.

19. Stephen Greenblatt, *Will in the World: How Shakespeare Became Shakespeare* (New York: W. W. Norton & Company, 2004), 323–329.

. . . AND 100 MORE

101. "Tell Me That It Isn't True" (*Nashville Skyline*, 1969).
102. "Can't Escape from You" (*The Bootleg Series, Vol. 8: Tell Tale Signs: Rare and Unreleased 1989–2006*, 2008).
103. "Tomorrow Is a Long Time" (*Bob Dylan's Greatest Hits Volume II*, 1969).
104. "Dignity" (*Bob Dylan's Greatest Hits Volume 3*, 1994).
105. "Nettie Moore" (*Modern Times*, 2006).
106. "Long and Wasted Years" (*Tempest*, 2012).
107. "Absolutely Sweet Marie" (*Blonde on Blonde*, 1966).
108. "Make You Feel My Love" (*Time Out of Mind*, 1997).
109. "License to Kill" (*Infidels*, 1983).
110. "Dirge" (*Planet Waves*, 1974).
111. "If You Belonged to Me" (*Traveling Wilburys Vol. 3*, 1990).
112. "Emotionally Yours" (*Empire Burlesque*, 1985).
113. "Mama, You Been on My Mind" (*The Bootleg Series, Vol. 1–3: Rare & Unreleased 1961–1991*, 1991).
114. "Love Minus Zero/No Limit" (*Bringing It All Back Home*, 1965).
115. "This Wheel's on Fire" (*The Basement Tapes*, 1975).
116. "One More Cup of Coffee (Valley Below)" (*Desire*, 1976).
117. "Song to Woody" (*Bob Dylan*, 1962).
118. "Ballad of Hollis Brown" (*The Times They Are A-Changin'*, 1964).
119. "Huck's Tune" (*The Bootleg Series, Vol. 8: Tell Tale Signs: Rare and Unreleased 1989–2006*, 2008).

120. "Day of the Locusts" (*New Morning*, 1970).
121. "With God on Our Side" (*The Times They Are A-Changin'*, 1964).
122. "Man in the Long Black Coat" (*Oh Mercy*, 1989).
123. "Property of Jesus" (*Shot of Love*, 1981).
124. "Tweedle Dee & Tweedle Dum" (*"Love and Theft,"* 2001).
125. "Pressing On" (*Saved*, 1980).
126. "Changing of the Guards" (*Street Legal*, 1978).
127. "She Belongs to Me" (*Bringing It All Back Home*, 1965).
128. "Dirty World" (*Traveling Wilburys Vol. 1*, 1988).
129. "You're a Big Girl Now" (*Blood on the Tracks*, 1975).
130. "Oh, Sister" (*Desire*, 1976).
131. "Queen Jane Approximately" (*Highway 61 Revisited*, 1965).
132. "Standing in the Doorway" (*Time Out of Mind*, 1997).
133. "Just like Tom Thumb's Blues" (*Highway 61 Revisited*, 1965).
134. "Restless Farewell" (*The Times They Are A-Changin'*, 1964).
135. "Cold Irons Bound" (*Time Out of Mind*, 1997).
136. "Only a Pawn in Their Game" (*The Times They Are A-Changin'*, 1964).
137. "I'll Keep It with Mine" (*The Bootleg Series, Vol. 1–3: Rare & Unreleased 1961–1991*, 1991).
138. "I Pity the Poor Immigrant" (*John Wesley Harding*, 1967).
139. "Oxford Town" (*The Freewheelin' Bob Dylan*, 1963).
140. "Maggie's Farm" (*Bringing It All Back Home*, 1965).
141. "Fourth Time Around" (*Blonde on Blonde*, 1966).
142. "The Man in Me" (*New Morning*, 1970).
143. "Romance in Durango" (*Desire*, 1976).
144. "You Ain't Going Nowhere" (*The Basement Tapes*, 1975).
145. "Clean Cut Kid" (*Empire Burlesque*, 1985).
146. "Political World" (*Oh Mercy*, 1989).
147. "Tell Ol' Bill" (*The Bootleg Series, Vol. 8: Tell Tale Signs: Rare and Unreleased 1989–2006*, 2008).
148. "Odds and Ends" (*The Basement Tapes*, 1975).
149. "Bob Dylan's Dream" (*The Freewheelin' Bob Dylan*, 1963).
150. "Billy 1," "Billy 4," "Billy 7" (*Pat Garrett & Billy the Kid*, 1973).
151. "If You Gotta Go, Go Now (or Else You Got to Stay All Night)." (*The Bootleg Series, Vol. 1–3: Rare & Unreleased 1961–1991*, 1991).

152. "Nothing Was Delivered" (*The Basement Tapes*, 1975).
153. "Gotta Serve Somebody" (*Slow Train Coming*, 1979).
154. "Disease of Conceit" (*Oh Mercy*, 1989).
155. "All I Really Want to Do" (*Another Side of Bob Dylan*, 1964).
156. "All over You" (*The Bootleg Series, Vol. 9: The Witmark Demos: 1962–1964*, 2010).
157. "John Wesley Harding" (*John Wesley Harding*, 1967).
158. "Tryin' to Get to Heaven" (*Time Out of Mind*, 1997).
159. "Shelter from the Storm" (*Blood on the Tracks*, 1975).
160. "Lonesome Day Blues" (*"Love and Theft,"* 2001).
161. "Handy Dandy" (*Under the Red Sky*, 1990).
162. "Lay Down Your Weary Tune" (*Biograph*, 1985).
163. "I Was Young When I Left Home" (*The Bootleg Series, Vol. 7: No Direction Home: The Soundtrack*, 2005).
164. "Wedding Song" (*Planet Waves*, 1974).
165. "Seven Curses" (*The Bootleg Series, Vol. 1–3: Rare & Unreleased 1961–1991*, 1991).
166. "Leopard-Skin Pill-Box Hat" (*Blonde on Blonde*, 1966).
167. "Everything Is Broken" (*Oh Mercy*, 1989).
168. "Tonight I'll Be Staying Here with You" (*Nashville Skyline*, 1969).
169. "Slow Train" (*Slow Train Coming*, 1979).
170. "Meet Me in the Morning" (*Blood on the Tracks*, 1975).
171. "Sweetheart like You" (*Infidels*, 1985).
172. "If Not for You" (*New Morning*, 1970).
173. "Joey" (*Desire*, 1976).
174. "Open the Door, Homer" (*The Basement Tapes*, 1975).
175. "Knockin' on Heaven's Door" (*Pat Garrett & Billy the Kid*, 1973).
176. "Quinn the Eskimo (The Mighty Quinn)" (*Biograph*, 1985).
177. "Precious Angel" (*Slow Train Coming*, 1979).
178. "Summer Days" (*"Love and Theft,"* 2001).
179. "The Levee's Gonna Break" (*Modern Times*, 2006).
180. "Jokerman" (*Infidels*, 1983).
181. "Maybe Someday" (*Knocked Out Loaded*, 1986).
182. "Too Much of Nothing" (*The Basement Tapes*, 1975).
183. "Moonlight" (*"Love and Theft,"* 2001).
184. "Spanish Harlem Incident" (*Another Side of Bob Dylan*, 1964).

185. "When He Returns" (*Slow Train Coming*, 1981).
186. "Dear Landlord" (*John Wesley Harding*, 1967).
187. "Buckets of Rain" (*Blood on the Tracks*, 1975).
188. "Forgetful Heart" (*Together through Life*, 2009).
189. "North Country Blues" (*The Times They Are A-Changin'*, 1964).
190. "Can't Wait" (*Time Out of Mind*, 1997).
191. "Beyond Here Lies Nothin'" (*Together through Life*, 2009).
192. "Lenny Bruce" (*Shot of Love*, 1981).
193. "Born in Time" (*Under the Red Sky*, 1990).
194. "As I Went Out One Morning" (*John Wesley Harding*, 1967).
195. "Winterlude" (*New Morning*, 1970).
196. "Po' Boy" (*"Love and Theft,"* 2001).
197. "Series of Dreams" (*The Bootleg Series, Vol. 1–3: Rare & Unreleased 1961–1991*, 1991).
198. "I and I" (*Infidels*, 1983).
199. "Talkin' John Birch Paranoid Blues" (*The Bootleg Series, Vol. 1–3: Rare & Unreleased 1961–1991*, 1991).
200. "It's All Good" (*Together through Life*, 2009).

BIBLIOGRAPHY

Baez, Joan. *And a Voice to Sing With: A Memoir*. New York: Simon & Schuster, 2009.
Dylan, Bob. *Chronicles Volume One*. New York: Simon & Schuster, 2004.
Greenblatt, Stephen. *Will in the World: How Shakespeare Became Shakespeare*. New York: W. W. Norton & Company, 2004.
McPherson, James. *Battle Cry of Freedom: The Civil War Era (Oxford History of the United States)*. London: Oxford University Press, 2003.
Sounes, Howard. *Down the Highway: The Life of Bob Dylan*. New York: Grove Press, 2001.
Trager, Oliver. *Keys to the Rain: The Definitive Bob Dylan Encyclopedia*. New York: Billboard Books, 2004.

INDEX

ABOUT THE AUTHOR

Jim Beviglia has been writing about music for nearly a decade for websites and publications. He currently writes for the print and online editions of *American Songwriter* magazine, concentrating on features about classic artists and reviews of new albums. Jim also maintains a blog as his alter ego, The Countdown Kid (http://countdownkid. wordpress.com/), where he counts down the best songs of rock and roll's greatest artists. He resides in Old Forge, Pennsylvania, with his girlfriend, Marie, and his daughter, Daniele.